# CANONIZING
# ECONOMIC
# THEORY

# CANONIZING ECONOMIC THEORY

## How Theories and Ideas are Selected in Economics

### Christopher D. Mackie

*M.E. Sharpe*
Armonk, New York
London, England

**Library of Congress Cataloging-in-Publication Data**

Mackie, Christopher D.
Canonizing economic theory : how theories and ideas are selected in economics /
Christopher D. Mackie.
p. cm.
Includes bibliographical references and index.
ISBN 0–7656–0284–9 (hardcover : alk. paper). —
ISBN 0–7656–0285–7 (pbk. : alk. paper)
1. Economics—History. 2. Economics—Research.
I. Title.
HB75.M17    1998    98—9241
330.1—dc21
CIP

Printed in the United States of America

The paper used in this publication meets the minimum requirements of
American National Standard for Information Sciences—
Permanence of Paper for Printed Library Materials,
ANSI Z 39.48-1984.

BM (c)   10   9   8   7   6   5   4   3   2   1
BM (p)   10   9   8   7   6   5   4   3   2   1

# CONTENTS

# CANONIZING
# ECONOMIC
# THEORY

# INTRODUCTION

# Description of the Problem

The traditional role for historians of economic thought has been to summarize, critique, and trace the development of existing theory. History of thought literature provides valuable information pertaining to the authors, chronology, and relative importance of influential works. Far less effort has been exerted toward answering questions about *why* economic theory exists in its current form: Why have economists chosen the theories they have, which now represent the discipline's formal content? What are the criteria that determine the value of a theory, or of research in general, and how have these criteria changed over time? Economic methodologists, drawing from philosophy of science, have certainly commented on theory choice issues, and their ideas will be considered. However, a more complete investigation is shown to be needed.

## Purpose of This Book

The objective of this study is to analyze the nature of research appraisal and theory selection in economics. This necessarily entails inquiry into how economists view their method of studying human behavior and how they establish the validity of the theories they have chosen to use. Additionally, a systematic study into the variables that have historically influenced those choices is required.

Note that the primary emphasis here is not with individual theorists' thought processes, which determine the nature and guide the production of their work. Instead, the concern is with how a work, once written (that is, once it has achieved an objective existence), enters the accepted—and propagated—body of professional literature. John Maynard Keynes's macroeconomic theory can be used to illustrate the distinction: His particular view of the world, shaped by an uncountable combination of influences along with his own unique intellect, somehow motivated him to write *The General*

*Theory.* How theorists formulate ideas is, in itself, an interesting (and complex) issue, and in the case of Keynes, a thoroughly investigated one.

Once *The General Theory* was written, its message was explained, debated, reformulated, graphed, and mathematicized. Obviously, interpretation of the book's content varied from individual to individual. Nonetheless, there was enough favorable appraisal of that content to propel it to a prominent position within economic theory. How the new Keynesian macroeconomic theory emerged is, in itself, also an issue—and quite distinct from the one described previously. It is this second issue with which this study is primarily concerned.

The significance of understanding how a body of literature evolves to represent a discipline's collective theoretic basis extends beyond pure intellectual curiosity. The manner in which scientists, social or otherwise, assess work in their field contributes to how they define relevant problems and develop methods for solving those problems. To illustrate, consider one economist who assumes that currently accepted theory is so because it is the "correct" theory. Imagine another economist who feels that he was taught the same theory simply because it happened to be the only set of explanations available to his instructors. The two economists will almost certainly have different approaches to studying human behavior because, in their assessments, they will assign different levels of validity to conventional intellectual tools. Such assertions are speculative, however, and must be couched in a relevant philosophy of science context, which will be developed in the first chapter.

## What Is a Theory?

The term "theory" has not been used consistently, either in science or the philosophy of science. Textbooks often define a theory as a cluster of interrelated models or a coherent set of axioms that simplify but assert relationships about the real world. Philosophers maintain an interest in defining terms such as model, hypothesis, and theory, but they continue to find a multitude of usages.

Fortunately, this linguistic puzzle can be sidestepped because its solution is not immediately relevant here. Admittedly, the phrase "theory choice" is not used in a fully consistent manner throughout this thesis, and it need not be. Our interest is in uncovering what makes ideas, hypotheses, and theories—work in general—appealing and, in turn, likely to be accepted by a profession's members. Thus, the objective here is to provide a framework for investigating the factors that allow a work to rise to a position of prominence. Identifying the extent to which a new work satisfies some definition of "theory" is not crucial in meeting this objective. At any rate, the context should make clear whether the term "theory" refers to something relatively narrow, such as the empirical Phillip's Curve, or to a full-blown family of hypotheses, such as neoclassical economics.

## The Theory Choice Process

The first task is to briefly describe the mechanics of the path that delivers a theory from its prepublished to its doctrinal form. In subsequent sections, this path is dissected and its components investigated in greater detail.

Initially a theory or idea is conceived of, then expressed in a communicable form. The form that an author employs may, in itself, affect his theory's potential for success. Subsequently, if the work is appealing, other theoreticians begin concerning themselves with it. Later, it may achieve status as doctrine and become the working equipment of practitioners and ordinary instructors. The route to such status generally involves two stages, a prepublication stage and a post-publication stage. Much research has, of course, progressed through the first stage without achieving success in the second. Further, one would expect that the formula for gaining publication may be quite different from that which is required for attaining professional popularity or status as a major work.

The prepublication phase of theory selection can be compared to the typical model of oligopoly used by microeconomists. Certainly a particularly well written, creative, or insightful piece has a better chance of being published than does a dull or poorly written one, just as a quality product has a better chance of selling than a shoddy one, given similar prices and availability. But one may speculate that other factors, which may be called barriers to entry, exist that can alter this competition where publication in the major journals is the reward. A perfectly competitive publication process (which would be based on assessing articles and books according to strict canons of scientific criteria) may be altered by, not market, but discipline-specific factors that include an author's reputation, base institution, political and academic alignment, or even method of presentation. It is, for example, easy to imagine a high-quality paper, written by a relative unknown, being passed over (at least temporarily) in order to publish a work, even a mediocre work, submitted by a dominant figure in the profession.

Given the modern structure of academic disciplines, publication marks the first step for an author who hopes to gain widespread circulation of his ideas. An investigation into the publication process is therefore a necessary part of a detailed study of theory choice. However, since a primary objective here is to explain why economics consists of a particular body of material, the study must go further. Publication is a necessary but not sufficient condition; publication of research, in the form of an article or a book, does not guarantee that it will have a long-run influence on the discipline's content or methods. For example, a context-specific, applied piece may be useful in addressing a current policy issue but may disappear once it has served its purpose. This study must therefore ascertain how certain works, once they are made accessible, become incorporated into the discipline's established canon.

The processes of theory choice during intellectual upheaval must also differ from those associated with stable periods. When the prevailing climate is characterized by relative dissatisfaction with conventional theory, we might expect wider tolerance for alternative methods, theories, and even political views. This type of intellectual environment might induce changes in research priorities, lead to a reassessment of policy objectives, and produce new terminological and conceptual frameworks. For instance, disenchantment with classical wage and employment theory after the Great Depression coincided with the promotion of new empirical and institutional methods, the development of non-market clearing models, and increased abandonment of laissez-faire.[1]

During periods of "normal science" (such as 1950s and 1960s macroeconomics, or possibly current micro-theory), we would expect divergent views to be pushed to the periphery and labeled "radical." Accepted theories may turn apologetic and repetitive as they go from doctrine to dogma. There is also the danger that these theories may become insensitive to the changing world, leaving them inconsistent with their historical, institutional, and social context. And, if a bandwagon effect dominates scientific curiosity, the basic tenets of the discipline may become cushioned from criticism and testing. These stable periods may better be defined in terms of theory *non-choice* rather than theory choice. For this reason, volatile, as compared with complacent, periods provide a more interesting focus from a theory choice perspective.

**Theory Choice—An Illustrative Example**

For years practicing scientists, and certainly economists, expressed little desire to question traditional explanations depicting the procedures of science. A simplified version of the standard philosophy of science view was implicitly accepted: The state of knowledge evolves rationally—new theories are created that provide better answers to the world's questions, and science moves incrementally closer to unveiling truth. Philosophers of science began challenging this 'received view' of science decades ago, and their ideas began trickling down to individual disciplines comparatively recently. Contemporary economic methodologists now offer sharply contrasting accounts of how their discipline works. These accounts will be reviewed in Chapter 2. For now, a frequently studied example—marginal utility theory—provides a preliminary indication of how complex and seldomly acknowledged factors potentially affect the emergence and evolution of a theory.

George Stigler (1973) argues that the profession's reigning standards and sociology influenced the pace and location of the "marginal revolution." Utility theory, he points out, was at hand for at least seventy-five years before it was fully integrated into economics. In addition, it was not a concern over increasing empirical content that led to its acceptance, but a shift in intellectual values.

The example of utility theory choice demonstrates one particular problem with analyzing economic theory according to traditional interpretations of science. The problem is, how can a particular theory be accepted by one group of reputable practitioners long before it is accepted by another one if, in fact, the process is purely rational? In the case at hand, utility theory gained uniform acceptance on the European continent well before it did in England. Stigler attributes the theory's uneven proliferation to the disparate professional climates prevailing in Great Britain and on the Continent.

If we accept Stigler's account of how marginal utility theory became the underlying explanation of value accepted by economists, then it represents a good example of how sociological aspects within a profession are able to influence its course of study. He begins by arguing that the acceptance of a theory by science—especially one such as economics—is a social act and not an individual one. The scientific environment induces the social act—in this case, the acceptance of marginal analysis as "rediscovered" by Léon Walras, William Stanley Jevons, and Karl Menger.

The foundations for modern utility theory were under construction by the turn of the nineteenth century. Jeremy Bentham's version of the theory, elucidated in his *Principles of Morals and Legislation* (1789), was the first use well known to economists. Yet the theory was not deployed successfully until the 1870s, and it was two generations again before it became a part of the orthodoxy (Stigler 1973, p. 305).

It is important that economics emerged as an academic discipline during the ending decades of the 1800s (ibid., p. 310). Activity during the pre-university phase was dominated by "men of affairs" (businessmen), politicians, bureaucrats, and aristocrats. These nonacademicians had little motivation to study problems that were not directly related to contemporary policy-oriented issues. Since the core of economic study moved to the university, however, the profession has been characterized by researchers motivated less by practical business concerns and more by abstract scholarly activities, which include searching for generalities and fundamental knowledge (ibid., p. 311). In some ways the transition was a reversal of the changes that occurred during the shift from scholasticism to mercantilism.

Utility theory addresses very few of the classicalists' concerns—free trade, corn laws, central banking, and population to name a few (ibid., p. 312). Because, in general, marginal analysis contributes material that appeals primarily to the academic mentality, it is not surprising that utility theory was ultimately adopted by economists based at academic institutions. The nature of the subject matter embodied by utility theory prohibits clear demonstration that it is "correct" by any objective measure. It does not increase empirical content of problems concerning pricing and value, and was only accepted after a new academic mentality made it appropriate (Hutchison 1978, p. 303).

Stigler supports his contention by pointing out that prominent economic writers of the time operating outside academic circles typically wrote on business interests and other applied matters. Academic economists, on the other hand, did not separate "themselves entirely from discussions of contemporary problems, but the sovereign importance of policy questions diminished as the science became more exclusively a university profession. . . . Almost every economist who dealt seriously and professionally with utility theory in the period had an academic base" (Stigler 1973, pp. 311, 314). Since this academic base of economists emerged earlier in France than in England, it is natural that utility theory gained proponents more rapidly on the Continent.

The emergence of marginal analysis may or may not be a representative case study of theory choice in economics. The point of the example is merely to illustrate the inadequacy of overly simplistic explanations of science. Also, the discussion above indicates the potential interest of theory choice questions to economists in general, as answers to these questions reveal insights into the nature of their discipline's content. First, however, before such questions can be meaningfully considered, a more general understanding of what theory choice means and of how it has been dealt with by philosophers and historians of science must be established. Thus, the task immediately at hand is to uncover the various treatments (or non-treatments) of theory choice within the philosophy of science, from John Stuart Mill through the positivists, the hypothetico-deductivists, Karl Popper, and up to the "growth of knowledge" literature.

## Chapter Outline

**Chapter 1** familiarizes the reader with philosophy of science issues that are immediately relevant to the book's topic. The key component of this section outlines how the problem of theory choice has been explained by historians and philosophers of science. The discussion traces the philosophy of science literature from before the development of Mill's received view of science up through the modern growth of knowledge approach. The emphasis, however, is on relatively recent works—those of Karl Popper, Thomas Kuhn, and Imre Lakatos—because it is from these philosophers that most contemporary economic methodologists have drawn their views.

**Chapter 2** critiques the body of economists' research, which seeks to extend philosophy of science explanations to their own discipline. Of interest here are works by Terence Hutchison, Mark Blaug, Spiro Latsis, George Stigler, and Vincent Tarascio, which comment directly on theory choice. Others, including Martin Bronfenbrenner, A.W. Coats, Donald Gordon, Joseph Spengler, E. Roy Weintraub, and Alexander Rosenberg, have also applied philosophy of science theory to economics and touch on peripheral issues. Their articles are examined. A major objective in this chapter is to determine how successful these methodological inquiries have been in accounting for what actually leads to the rejection or acceptance of ideas and theories in economics.

In addition, economics is briefly compared to the natural sciences, with which philosophers of science have more generally concerned themselves. Allowances must be made when looking at a social science such as economics because of its historically relative and institution-specific nature.[2] It is therefore important to note how or if methodologists have accounted for the uniqueness of the economics case.

**Chapter 3** summarizes the shortcomings of existing treatments of theory appraisal and selection and, in so doing, demonstrates the need for a more realistic, discipline-specific approach. The argument that research in economics is not judged solely, or even predominantly, on empirical grounds is developed further. The complex and variable nature of the discipline's subject matter is shown to make "extra-scientific" factors figure more prominently in economics than suggested by philosophy of science literature, which is directed primarily at natural science.

The case is made, then, that a wider range of variables potentially influence the theory choice process than is commonly acknowledged. In Hutchison's words, "a methodologist must feel bound to record the impression that what economists actually do and decide (and have done and decided) is not, and has not been, invariably what, according to tenable methodological scientific canons, they ought to have done or decided" (Latsis 1976, p. 182).

**Chapter 4** organizes the theory choice process into two broadly specified stages—prepublication and post-publication—then examines the first. The factors that affect publication decisions (the most important aspect of the first stage) are then systematically analyzed. Here, existing explanations—ranging from traditional positivism to less rationalist growth of knowledge accounts, to those that seek to escape philosophy of science altogether—provide a starting point. The positivist version of scientific activity is based on long-standing canons of science that emphasize objective, rational epistemological advancement. Several of the comparatively recent growth of knowledge accounts consider how sociological aspects of scientific communities, institutional peculiarities, and external factors (such as historical conditions) affect the practice of science; D. McCloskey and Phillip Mirowski, among others, have discussed the workings of economics via totally different, discipline-specific approaches.

The picture that emerges is new and, perhaps, surprising. By the end of Chapter 4 it is possible to organize, categorically, components of the prepublication theory choice process. Analysis of this process uncovers those characteristics that make an idea or theory appealing from its inception. Method of presentation, existence of discipline-specific standards, and professional training are a few of the factors found to affect research appraisal and publication decisions.

In **Chapter 5,** the second stage of the evaluative process is investigated. Since most work that is published is eventually discarded, it is crucial to consider what distinguishes doctrinal literature from the rest. Indeed, after it has been legitimized via publication, a new work must still gain the profession's general attention if it is to become influential.

Certainly, some aspects of selection and appraisal play a role both during and after publication. However, the competition among published work is unique and must be considered independently. This process, whereby the profession chooses which literature is significant, is what provides the impetus behind the evolution of economic theory.

**Chapter 6,** which offers conclusions and assessment, reiterates why traditional philosophy of science and, in turn, current economic methodology fail to adequately explain how theory choice decisions are actually made—a process that is undeniably central to the development of any science. A final defense of the hypothesized multi-variable explanation of theory choice is offered, and to close, an appeal is made that a more complete understanding of actual method, rather than a casual pledge to an idealized methodology, leads to a more realistic assessment of the function and potential of economics.

## Notes

1. Terence W. Hutchison (1978, p. 291) points out that the level of professional dissatisfaction during a particular period could, perhaps, be roughly measured by quantifying the methodological diversity of articles published by leading journals.

2. Kuhn, Lakatos, and Popper each specify that their theories of science do not necessarily apply to social science.

# CHAPTER 1

# Philosophy of Science Background

## Introduction

Traditionally, philosophers of science have occupied themselves with a wide range of profound epistemological questions. They have struggled to reveal *the* scientific method, to describe correct procedures for acquiring knowledge, and to understand the logical structures underlying scientific reasoning. Additionally, philosophy of science has sought to demarcate scientific explanations from those that are "pseudo-scientific" and, perhaps most ambitiously, to determine the extent to which theories can uncover truths about a hidden, objective reality.

Add to the above list historical approaches to the study of science and the scope of inquiry widens further. Historians may wish to reconstruct past epochs of science according to some philosophical program or even by applying methods of sociology or psychology. The diversity of material that philosophers and historians of science study is considerable.

The distinction between historians and philosophers of science is explicitly made because, despite the necessary interaction, their objectives often differ, and failure to acknowledge this point has led to avoidable confusion. This confusion frequently arises due to inherent ambiguities pertaining to prescriptive versus descriptive elements in methodology discussions. The extent to which an investigator intends to describe *actual* scientific practice has, in many cases, been unclear. Because an explanation of how economic theories are actually chosen is an important end to this project, an effort is made to identify whether methodologists are practicing descriptive historicism or prescriptive philosophy.

As science itself has changed through time, so too has the study of scientific activity. Treatment of the theory choice issue in philosophy and history of science discussions has likewise varied. Regardless of the uneven attention that the topic has received, the study of theory choice is undeniably an inherently crucial component of a complete philosophy or history of science discipline. The theory, because of its fundamental role as the primary carrier of scientific ideas, must be understood in order to analyze the logical structure and historical evolution of knowledge. The process whereby one theory is selected over others is, along with idea creation, the central element of scientific development. Studying philosophy of science without including theory choice is like studying history without considering why certain events and individuals were more influential to its course than others.

The task in this first chapter is twofold. First, it is necessary to examine those elements that conventional philosophy of science identifies as the primary criteria for appraising and, subsequently, choosing among competing scientific explanations and methods. The second task entails critiquing this literature and determining which philosophy of science concern (prescription or description) is emphasized. In due course, both the strengths and limitations of various methodological interpretations of science become evident.

## Formulation of the 'Received View' of Science

The primary concern of philosophers seemed to be, for many centuries, to uncover the logical structure of scientific thought. They established the once-dominant view that the development of scientific theory was and is the culmination of a logical, rational process. Mark Blaug paraphrased John Stuart Mill's version of the common wisdom: "Scientific investigations begin in the free and unprejudiced observation of facts, proceed by inductive inference to the formulation of universal laws about these facts, and finally arrive by further induction at statements of still wider generality known as theories; both laws and theories are ultimately checked for their truth content by comparing their empirical consequences with all the observed facts, including those with which they began" (Blaug 1980, p. 4).

Mill's conception of scientific method is rooted in the work of Francis Bacon, which, in turn, ties it to Greek philosophy, particularly Aristotle. The invention of formal logic is generally attributed to Aristotle but was, of course, only one of his many contributions. He investigated the logical structure of science in *Posterior Analytics,* denouncing Plato's idea that common principles underlie all sciences and arguing against the feasibility of a unified method. Aristotle formulated both deductive (moving from self-evident, a priori premises to incontrovertible conclusions) and inductive (deriving generalization from observations) methods of thought. He sought validity of argument through deductive syllogism and soundness of hypothesis through inductive fact-gathering. The lack of general applicability inherent in the deductive geometric approach inspired his search for valid inductive methods. A discernible ambiguity concerning proper method along with an assertive dogmatism exist in Aristotle's writings, however, which prevents clear discourse explaining exactly how scientific questions should be answered.

Francis Bacon, often considered the first modern philosopher of science and a forerunner to the empiricist tradition, was among those who initiated a challenge to Greek ideas. Not unlike Aristotle, Bacon advocated in his *Novum Organum* ([1621] 1960) the basic method of uncovering general laws by amassing huge collections of information. He differed from Aristotle, however, in that he advanced a role for experiment that Aristotle, and the Greeks in general, did not, as they held a certain contempt for such "practical" activities.

Both Aristotle and Bacon were constrained by logical, as well as practical, problems normally attached to the inductive method. A partial list of these problems includes the lack of objectivity in observation, existence of prior theoretical bases determining course of action, and insufficient observation—or lack of data. With Bacon, as with Aristotle, the role for hypothesis and theory remained unspecified.

The idea of an objectively existing knowledge and of certainty with respect to scientific achievement ties Mill to Bacon as it had tied Bacon to Aristotelian geometry. Mill adhered to the central tenets of Comtian positivism, which emphasizes the importance of demarcating scientific thought from theology and metaphysics. All genuine knowledge, he believed, could only be arrived at through scientific method—the systematic collection and correlation of observed facts (Flew 1984, p. 69). Mill deviated only from Auguste Comte's more radical claims. For example, Mill was skeptical about science's ability to establish laws, immune from refutation, based solely on observation. Mill's method stipulates that the purpose of induction should be to reveal causation. He presented a set of canons that were to guide research into cause and effect of phenomena. Unfortunately, Mill's investigations into the timing and proximity of events seldom generated rigorous evidence to properly claim causal connections.

In addition, although Mill's method may present a "valuable schemata for organizing an investigation, [it] could hardly be generalized into the whole of scientific method. And the reason, in short, is that scientists are not exclusively concerned to discover correlations among phenomena, but are at least as interested in the explanations as to why the correlations that can be discovered are the way they are" (Harre 1972, p. 47). Critics of Mill's position also pointed out that the search for facts is necessarily guided by the investigator's prior notions of what it is he is looking for. In other words, a scientist's actions are motivated by some sort of theory—at least a crude one. Prolonged failure of the inductive method to generate conclusive scientific research—and certainly to describe it—strengthened the relative credibility of deductive approaches, whose proponents critiqued Mill's system forcefully and destructively.

Explicit discussion of theory choice, and even theory appraisal, was absent prior to the introduction of hypothetico-deductivism. Implicit in the writings of Mill is the idea that facts either exist or they do not and, accordingly, scientific statements are either true or false. Metaphysical discourse was considered neither true nor false from an acquisition of knowledge perspective; it was viewed as meaningless. Theory choice was a non-issue, not because conflicting ideas in science did not exist, but because the concern was regarding the structure of explanation. No substantive role for hypotheses exists in Mill's philosophy of science. For Mill, and his Comtian positivist contemporaries, proper science necessarily reveals truths. In essence, theory choices are not called for since only one scientific explanation can exist per naturally occurring phenomena. This somewhat unrealistic view of science, which portrayed scientists experimenting in the hope of discovering correlations among phenomena, persisted well into the nineteenth century (ibid., p. 48).

## The Hypothetico-Deductive Method

Mill's conception of science remained dominant until it was eventually replaced by the hypothetico-deductive model, initiated in a preliminary form by William Whewell in the *History* and *The Philosophy of the Inductive Sciences* (1837 and 1840, respectively). The verificationist component of the movement was further inspired by the writings of Ernst Mach and Pierre Duhem as well as the logical positivists of the Vienna Circle, and culminated with Carl Hempel's and Peter Oppenheim's classic "Studies in the Logic of Explanation."

Hypothetico-deductivism can be defined as "the method of creating scientific theory by making an hypothesis (or set of hypotheses) from which results already obtained could have been deduced, and which also entails new experimental predictions that can be verified or refuted" (Flew 1984, p. 158). This idea, that activities of science are motivated from a preconceived idea or hypothesis, was at the core of Whewell's 1840 opus, *The Philosophy of the Inductive Sciences*. In it, he synthesized history of science with philosophy of science, noting that nineteenth-century philosophers of science were placed in an advantageous position because they could observe how science had actually proceeded and were not limited, as had been their predecessors, to commenting on how it ought to work. Whewell analyzed in detail the roles that observation, experimentation, and even "happy guesses" played in the development of scientific knowledge. He concluded that the inductive method could not be used in an isolated fashion and that it did not enjoy universal application. There was, in essence, no logic of induction comparable to that associated with deduction.

Whewell's most fundamental point was to demonstrate the necessary role for hypotheses in the early stages of scientific inquiry. He posited that, historically, even scientists committed to the inductive method employed hypotheses that dictated their empirical work. However, because of the importance of ingenuity, guessing, and "inventive talent," no set rules for developing hypotheses existed. The mind, Whewell wrote, invents these descriptions and explanations to represent real phenomena and guide research. Thus, Whewell abandoned the received view that "truths" could be uncovered through systematic investigation into the laws of nature. Instead, he claimed that scientific advance is developed in the mind of the scientist through his own particular sensory experience.[1]

Whewell, in asserting the importance of hypotheses in science (and even the idea that theory construction must be amenable to testing and, in particular, falsifying) anticipated Popper. And, to the extent that he saw a certain arbitrariness to the whole scientific endeavor, Whewell anticipated aspects of the "growth of knowledge" literature.

### Karl Popper

Karl Popper's work in the philosophy of science extends important elements from Whewell's hypothetico-deductive version of science while it rejects logical positivist aspects propagated by the Vienna Circle, whose members included Rudolf Carnap, Hans Hahn, Friedrich Waismann, Moritz Schlick, and others. The Vienna philosophers did, however, stimulate Popper's concern for demarcation of science. Although Popper was not involved in the immediate activities of the Vienna Circle, the extent to which they influenced the scope of his study makes it worthwhile to briefly examine their philosophy.

The most productive period for the Vienna Circle was during the 1920s and 1930s. They took from Mach, sometimes regarded as the father of logical positivism, the idea that all science has fundamentally the same subject matter—not reality, but a sensory perception of it. Based on this premise, they advocated a unified approach to science.

The dominant feature of the Vienna philosophy is the "verifiability principle." The verifiability principle states that a meaningful, scientific statement must be posited in a manner such that it can be tested and confirmed through observation. This verifiability principle is what distinguishes science from metaphysics, non-science, and nonsense. Mathematical and logical tautologies were also considered acceptable constructs of science. It was felt that science could most successfully be advanced by combining logical rigor and mathematical method to the empirical tradition of Comte, which confines science to the observable. By strictly delimiting the confines of scientific enterprise, logical positivists hoped to guide scientific research toward a productive direction and away from metaphysical and speculative areas.

Their version of positivism proved dogmatic and restrictive, however. The Vienna Circle had trouble excluding the metaphysical without taking with it scientific generalizations and historical evidence. Certain aspects of scientific enterprise did not lend themselves easily to observational verification, and the group fell prey to many of the problems typically associated with inductivism. Attempts were made, notably by Alfred Ayer and Rudolf Carnap, to modify the 'rules of confirmation'. They prescribed what was hoped to be a more flexible method by distinguishing between strong and weak verification based, respectively, on conclusive and provisional evidence. This relaxation of the confirmation criterion (realizing that science could not realistically be confined to that which could actually be verified) did little to quell criticism and, to a degree, anticipated the angle of attack. The Vienna philosophers were influential, however, in drawing attention to the dilemma surrounding the demarcation of science from non-science.

With few exceptions (Kant, Whewell), the pre-Popperian vision of science was distinguished by its inductive method—a method characterized by rational activity that results in careful expansion of human knowledge. This idea, that science can be reduced to purely logical analysis, maintains an underlying faith in the uniformity of nature.

Popper rejected the view that science should and does proceed by inductively deriving laws of nature through empirical confirmation. For Popper, a statement must be falsifiable, rather than verifiable, to be considered scientific. He did not, however, consider all non-scientific questions epistemologically meaningless as did logical positivists. By emphasizing falsification rather than verification as the demarcator of scientific conjecture, Popper believed the pitfalls of inductive logic could be avoided. A frequently cited example illustrates his point: There can never be enough observations of black crows to conclusively prove that all crows are indeed black. However, a single sighting of a non-black crow nullifies the theory.[2] Popper's method of falsification, prescribing science as a process of bold "conjecture and refutation," proved influential and persists today as a vision of the modern scientific method.

Popper offered explicit criteria for appraising the usefulness of theories. Nearly all the criteria related to how readily a conjecture, hypothesis, or theory lends itself to falsification. More readily refutable theories, from a procedural perspective, are considered superior to abstract, less testable ones. On the basis of this criterion, Popper considered bold theories, stated with clarity, superior to cautious, highly stipulated ones. Likewise, general and simpler theories are preferable to specific and complex ones. Science, Popper believed, should continually put itself at risk by encouraging challenges to current conjecture. For Popper, scientific literature embodied that which is falsifiable but not yet falsified.

Popper was skeptical that theories, not couched in clearly falsifiable terms, were scientific. He considered the predictive power of a theory suspect unless the system under investigation was "well isolated, stationary, and recurrent" (Popper 1968, p. 339). Consequently, Popper was critical of Freud's and Marx's theories. Marx's crisis theory of history, for example, contains no explicit time limits and, as such, is structured in a way that has allowed proponents to continually modify and hold on to it. Popper believed that theories relating to human society could not typically qualify as science because of the high variability of their subject matter and due to ever-changing initial conditions (technology, culture, legal system, etc.).[3]

A quick pass at Popper's ideas creates the impression that he is on fairly solid ground. However, deeper investigation shows that the method of falsification also has problems; some are not unlike those associated with inductivism. At the base level, it represents an advance in thinking to reveal that a statement cannot be logically proven through observation yet that it can be disproved through empirical disconfirmation. However, logical falsification turns out to be considerably less problematic than methodological falsification in science. Popper himself realized this as his own philosophy evolved from a stance of naive falsificationism toward what Imre Lakatos later called sophisticated falsificationism (which allows for a more flexible rejection process).

The first difficulty is that Popper's hypothetico-deductive method is still largely inductive. Recall that Popper advocated tentatively accepting properly stated hypotheses that had, by methods of falsification, not yet been refuted. The acceptance of a hypothesis, albeit tentative, is strictly speaking no less dubious than validating a theory through confirmation. And certainly such a method does not produce a conclusive statement in the sense that a mathematical tautology does. Popper acknowledged this and proposed that it was only possible to establish various degrees of "corroboration"—to demonstrate support—for theories. Thus, Popper was in no better a position than were logical positivists to add "truths" to the existing body of scientific knowledge. He was only able to conduct processes of elimination. Rejection of theories, for Popper, is the high point of scientific enterprise because it is what leads to the development of new theories.

A second problem with the falsificationist method concerns the ability of scientists to truly falsify statements and theories. A hypothetical example illustrates the potential problem: Pretend that some scientists are going to test the statement, "All men are mortal." Now suppose one of the scientists finds a man who, he concludes, has been alive forever. Logically speaking, the hypothesis that all men are mortal is on very shaky ground. In reality, the problem is considerably more complex. For instance, some of the scientist's colleagues may feel that the newly found subject is not a man at all. Others may question how the immortal's age was determined or disagree on the discovering scientist's interpretation of his tests. Yet another scientist, perhaps a statistician, might note that close to one-third of all people who have ever been born on earth are still alive. He may have a different view altogether. Popper, again, acknowledged these difficulties. He countered by asserting that, in part due to such problems, it is desirable that hypotheses be stated in as unambiguous a way as possible. Supplementally, he stated that a degree of common sense must be maintained by science when dealing with these complexities.

The ability of science to properly interpret a falsifying instance is indeed a complex issue. Most scientific hypotheses rest on a number of auxiliary hypotheses. Once confronted with a disconfirming observation, how is one able to unambiguously determine whether the fault is with the major hypothesis or an auxiliary one? Similarly, how is a disconfirming observation to be distinguished from an incomplete or incorrect one? Here, creativity (of the type Whewell described), ethical neutrality, and reliability of the scientist come into play.

Difficulties involved with falsifying theories through experimentation are addressed in Pierre Duhem's "irrefutability" thesis. Essentially, the thesis states that predictive failure strikes at the whole theory, not just individual components, and, also, that more than one theory may potentially explain an accumulation of evidence since a theory is only a subjective mental construct. A commonly used example demonstrates this point: Newton's theory of planetary motion did not initially predict Uranus's orbital path accurately. This presented an apparent disconfirming observation. However, scientific creativity produced the idea that Uranus's movements might be thrown off by another, undiscovered planet (Neptune), and Newton's theory was saved—even strengthened. The point is that scientists cannot always be certain whether a hypothesis has indeed been falsified or not. Also, it is not always clear if its salvation has been facilitated by a new falsifiable extension, further corroboration, or merely an ad hoc amendment.

To summarize, Popper rejected the idea that the bounds of science are carefully expanded through an accumulation of rational, unbiased observation and experiment. He did not believe that universal truths could be uncovered with positive certainty. However, Popper did advocate and prescribe methodological canons for science to follow and, in so doing, established new and still restrictive demarcation criteria for addressing matters of theory choice.

**Emergence of Theory Choice as a Philosophy of Science Issue**

With the emergence of the hypothetico-deductivism and the realization that the compilation of knowledge is driven by a priori notions, more effort was spent investigating theory-based scientific methods. Before Whewell, science was not commonly viewed as a theory-led activity. As the role of theory as an integral aspect of scientific development became increasingly acknowledged, the issue of appraisal and questions relating to theory choice quite naturally crept into the literature.

This literature featured both descriptive, historical investigations and prescriptive, philosophically oriented ones. Whewell, for one, was extensively historical in his approach and recognized the great diversity in scientific method, both through time and across disciplines. He realized that the scientist's personal character determined, in part, the course of his study. Frequently referring to the practitioner's creativity, he interpreted history to reveal no set rules for developing scientific hypotheses.

Whewell's significant insight derived from his recognition that hypotheses, not random fact searches, were the starting point for science. Whewell seemed most concerned with pointing out the psychological roots of explanation, stressing that ideas manifest themselves, with tremendous variation, from the inventive mind of the scientist. Thus, his message was most directly concerned with the conceptualization of theories, and not with choosing among competing ones. However, given his appreciation of creativity and historical context, we may suspect in Whewell a distaste for strict canons explicating what distinguishes science from non-science and how theories can be objectively ranked. In this way, he anticipated Thomas Kuhn and Paul Feyerabend, discussed in the next section.

The primary objective of the logical positivists of the Vienna Circle was to develop criteria for distinguishing between scientific (meaningful) and non-scientific (meaningless) statements. As discussed above, the group advocated verificationism. The more closely a theory's predictions match the data, the better it meets strength of confirmation criteria—ultimately chosen by the logical positivists as their yardstick for measuring the acceptability of theories (Caldwell 1982, p. 221).

From this rule-oriented methodology springs a prescription for appraising and ranking competing hypotheses. Bruce Caldwell summarizes the Circle's method: First, the whole of a theory, not its individual components, is tested empirically. Results are catalogued qualitatively and quantitatively. Competing theories are compared and ranked according to their strength of confirmation. Given the case when two theories yield comparably successful predictive results, they are subjected to further evaluative criteria, including quantity of favorable outcomes, procedural precision in observation and measurement, and variety of supporting evidence (ibid., p. 222). Post–Vienna Circle positivists (Carl Hempel and Rudolf Carnap) recognized limitations of the verificationist methodology and pointed out that the most highly confirmed theory is not necessarily the true one. They stipulated additional non-empirical criteria for judging theory acceptability, including logical consistency, simplicity and elegance, generality and extensibility, theoretical support and compatibility with existing theories, and heuristic value (Tarascio and Caldwell 1979, pp. 991–92).

Thus, the problem of theory choice was of central importance for logical positivists and their immediate successors. Their aim was not to interpret how past theory choice had occurred, but to establish an unambiguous method of theory choice (based on empirically verifying mathematically and logically based propositions) for the future. Reflecting these intentions, the logical positivists' approach was almost exclusively ahistorical. Instead, they set out to provide prescriptive procedural guidelines that science could follow.

Their method, dogmatic and restrictive, turned out to be unworkable, however. Verificationism's problems, both logical and practical, could not be overcome. The logical inadequacy of verification embodied the age-old problem of induction. Further, the success of other methods (trial and error, falsificationism, ad hoc) left critics asking, "Why is this the method we should follow?" Certainly testing as a means to substantiate ideas empirically remains an important scientific activity; however, a wider range of scientific method characterizes actual work.

Even had scientists wanted to follow prescriptions outlined by positivism (either the Vienna Circle's or Hempel's modified version), it would have been difficult since no consensus existed regarding how to weight the prescribed criteria. Positivists' non-empirical criteria of theory choice (simplicity, elegance, consistency, etc.) were rooted in subjective interpretation. Even the empirical criterion and central demarcator—degree of verification—can only be subjectively determined. Consequently, the most important function their program served was that of straw-man for Popper and other critical philosophers.

Popper, reacting to the logical flaws of verificationism, sought to reformulate a method of appraisal for science. Popper acknowledged (to a greater extent than did logical positivists) the variety of activity in scientific enterprise. However, as discussed above, his vision of "proper" science also proved limiting when applied to studies in the history or philosophy of science. Like logical positivists, Popper's philosophy of science work was largely concerned with prescribing methods for science.[4]

Independent of the abstract nature of Popper's work, he does maintain a clearly specified stance on matters of theory choice. However, there are significant problems with his position, both as subjective prescription and, perhaps even more so, as a historical account of science. Recall that, for Popper, the primary task of science is to falsify theories. The process of choosing a theory to tentatively accept, via corroborative criteria, is secondary. Presumably, scientists concern themselves with "reputable" theories and not with seemingly shoddy or implausible ones. Therefore, a scientist must really choose theories in two stages. First, he must choose which theories in his discipline are reputable (falsifiable and thus scientific). In other words, he must establish what body of work represents his field. Second, he must choose which theories he wishes to challenge and which ones he would like to accept for a while, since surely he cannot challenge all the theories in his discipline simultaneously.

The second aspect, that of choosing one among various corroborated theories, cannot be buttressed by logical argument, and consequently, Popper did not emphasize it. He was, indeed, critical of those who did. Thus, Popper does not have much to offer us regarding which theories we should choose to tentatively accept. He of course emphasized the second aspect of the choice problem—choosing which theories to test. The criteria, as described previously, center around the presentation of a theory or conjecture. A theory stated in a manner that lends itself to easy testing is scientifically valid.

Another problem—in addition to the subjectivity involved with measuring degrees of corroboration and in determining the extent of a theory's falsifiability—is that many aspects of what scientists must necessarily incorporate into their work cannot really be couched in this methodology. Definitions of the form:

a right angle is 90 degrees
or
$(x + y)^2 = x^2 + 2xy + y^2$

cannot be falsified yet serve an important function in science. General existential statements, such as "earth's gravity causes a ball to fall toward the ground," express a portion of the permanent part of science, yet are not represented within the Popperian methodology.

Additionally, Popper's analysis neglects statistical methods. Probability statements or statistical measures estimated from experimental data are not afforded a role. Likewise, there is no clear notion of acceptable error or variance. Consider, as an example, the following statement: "The probability of landing a head with the flip of a coin is .5." Given an outcome that four heads are landed in ten throws, a reasonable scientist can explain the result with probability theory. A strict Popperian would have problems assessing the evidence. What if the outcome were zero heads in twenty tosses? A statistician would probably question the fairness of the coin. What would a Popperian do?

The answer is unclear. In *The Logic of Scientific Discovery,* Popper writes that probability statements are not logically falsifiable since they do not "rule out anything observable." However, "practical falsification" may be possible "through a methodological decision to regard highly improbable events as ruled out" (Popper 1959, p. 191). Mark Blaug suggests that Popper could have corrected this ambiguity in his work by incorporating in it the Neyman-Pearson theory of hypothesis testing. Blaug goes on to suggest that this failure may have been rooted in Popper's "lifelong opposition to the use of probability theory to assess the verisimilitude of a hypothesis" (Blaug 1980, p. 23).

Rom Harre, a noted philosopher of science, is also highly skeptical of the applicability of Popper's method. In general, he is critical of Popper's vision because it does not (and does not even presume to) provide an accurate account of science; it is severely inadequate because it omits so much of what scientists do. Harre concludes that enlisting Popper's "radical demarcation criteria" (so labeled by Harre) would necessitate a complete reinterpretation of how science actually works, since fruitful investigation may—in reality—arise from elements and activities not accounted for by Popper.

Theory choice was a central concern for Popper, as it had been for the logical positivists of the Vienna Circle. His method of appraisal, however, also proved too inflexible to prescribe science, and certainly to describe its history. In a number of respects, Popper had not deviated markedly from positivism and, consequently, many similar problems remained. Commenting on the parallels between Popper's falsificationism and positivism, Harre writes: "Like Popper, positivists conceive of theories as organized only according to the canons of deductive logic, the logic of mathematics and taxonomy. The effect of this is to force them to conceive very narrowly of theory and its ideal logical structure" (Harre 1972, p. 53).

Dissatisfied with their ability to explain how science works, several philosophers of science began to focus attention on the problem during the 1960s. Inability to capture the seemingly diverse nature of scientific inquiry solely within existing prescriptive explanations elicited a growing concern with accurate historical description. This desire for a more adequate explanation spawned new theories of science that diverged from the traditional interpretation more strongly than had Popper's. Popper had instigated the movement away from logical positivism, but remained fairly prescriptive in his outlook. Just as Popper's work was largely a response to the variant of positivism touted by the Vienna Circle, "growth of knowledge" philosophers reacted to Popper's influential work. To these philosophers we now turn.

### Recent Philosophy of Science Developments

The analysis in this section is centered around the theories of Thomas Kuhn, from his book *The Structure of Scientific Revolutions,* and Imre Lakatos, from his book *The Methodology of Scientific Research Programmes.* Lakatos and Kuhn have been chosen for several reasons. First, their efforts generated the most influential and hotly debated literature in philosophy of science during the last thirty years. Their work, at times seen as an extension and other times as a refutation of Popper, has been instrumental in discrediting the positivist philosophy of science in their own field and has rendered the underlying positivist mentality, which persists in various natural and social sciences, outdated. In addition, contemporary economists concerned with methodology (discussed in the next chapter) have turned almost exclusively to Kuhn and Lakatos in their efforts to understand the philosophy and history of science.

During the 1950s and 1960s, there was a substantial movement among philosophers of science to reject the positivist message—that theory choice is a solely mechanical process that occurs according to some universal methodological code. Post-positivists (particularly post-Popperians) introduced time- and discipline-specific elements, as well as a human dimension, into theories on the evolution of knowledge. For some, the new emphasis on relativism legitimized the use of historical example in philosophical discourse. Perhaps most importantly, universal characterizations of science lost considerable influence.

The emerging school of philosophers (which includes Thomas Kuhn, Imre Lakatos, Stephen Toulmin, Paul Feyerabend, and others) was not, however, homogeneous in its perspectives. The differences rather than the similarities—especially between Kuhn and Lakatos—have drawn most of the attention. Much of the debate, especially between Kuhn, Lakatos, and

Feyerabend, centers around the role that "rationality" plays in dictating the processes of science and prescribing how it should proceed.

In the section that follows, the theories of Kuhn and Lakatos will be briefly reviewed and critiqued. One objective will be to show that Kuhn and Lakatos were tackling essentially different problems that ultimately resulted in "incommensurate" approaches and conclusions. The dimensions of the debate become more clear once it is demonstrated that Kuhn (the natural scientist turned historian of science) and Lakatos (the mathematical philosopher turned philosopher of science) constructed explanations suited to different purposes. Subsequently, and of most immediate concern, their contributions to our understanding of theory choice will be considered.

### Thomas Kuhn

The most influential, or at least the most widely publicized, among Popper's critics is Thomas Kuhn. His book, *The Structure of Scientific Revolutions* ([1962] 1970a), provides the most fully developed antithesis to the received view to date and "in many ways initiated the recent revolution in the philosophy of science" (Caldwell 1982, p. 69).[5] Kuhn brings novelty to the debate in that he views science operating as a social structure rather than as an impersonal entity advancing toward epistemological commitment. He gives a human character to science, intending to capture the organic makeup of its creators. Like Whewell, Kuhn de-emphasizes the potential of an overly systematic approach to science and thus rejects the idea that the scientific method exists. Kuhn's analysis is mainly descriptive and is buttressed with assorted examples from the history of natural science. His apparatus provides an analytical tool as opposed to "laws" of theory development.

The notion that science has progressed incrementally via a "process of accretion" or an accumulation of facts is attacked by Kuhn from the outset. Instead, he explains that ideas and theories do not always gain acceptance because they are indeed proven as facts; rather, their acceptance can be the result of a more complex process in which sociological factors play a role: "An apparently arbitrary element, compounded of personal and historical accident, is always a formative ingredient of beliefs espoused by a given scientific community at a given time." Therefore, "The unique character of scientific progress . . . depends upon the characteristics of the scientific community that require additional exploration and study."

Kuhn's interpretation of the history of science is centered around the development of "paradigms." Paradigms, according to Kuhn, are not simply theories but are also "accepted examples of actual scientific practice . . .

(that) provide models from which spring particular coherent traditions of scientific research" (Kuhn 1970a, pp. 4, 8, 10). Unfortunately, much confusion has arisen out of Kuhn's use of the word "paradigm." The various meanings that he attaches to the term range from the particular, such as the introduction of an invention such as the telescope, to the grand, where he might mean an entire worldview held by a profession. The Copernican heliocentric model of sun and planetary position constitutes an example of the latter and is really the important usage of the term within Kuhn's central message. These definitional inconsistencies have been well documented (Margaret Masterman) and will be sorted later. For now, it will suffice to say that this sorting-out process serves to both clarify and limit aspects of Kuhn's theory.

Evolution of science, by Kuhn's interpretation, is characterized by alternating periods of "normal" and "revolutionary" scientific activity, with the periods of normal science—as the label implies—being far more common:

> [Normal science] emerges historically when a universally recognized scientific achievement provides model problems and solutions to a community of practitioners. These achievements, or paradigms ... attract an enduring group of adherents away from random fact gathering and competing models. At the beginning a paradigm is largely a promise of success discoverable in selected and still incomplete examples and an object for further articulation and specification under new and more stringent conditions. Thus from the basic models spring particular coherent traditions of scientific research which develop the promise inherent in the basic model by extending the knowledge of these facts that the paradigm displays as particularly revealing, by increasing the extent of the match between those facts and the paradigm's predictions, and by further articulation of the paradigm itself. (Gordon 1965, p. 122)

There are advantages and disadvantages for the discipline operating within normal science. The advantage of normal science is that it establishes a coherent scientific tradition, thus serving to unify a profession in terms of practice, technique, communication, and worldview (all aspects of Kuhn's term "paradigm"). A commonalty of purpose and accepted base knowledge, as reflected in the incorporation of textbooks, allows practitioners to solve relevant puzzles, previously unapproachable in terms of depth and complexity. Inability to solve the puzzles delimited by the paradigm reflects poorly on the scientist and not on the paradigm.

The primary disadvantages stem from the restrictive nature of normal science. Normal science, as described by Kuhn, is a cautious time. Controversial problems (those addressing questions outside of the accepted paradigm) are not tackled by reputable scientists. Within a discipline, the paradigm itself demarcates science from non-science. Time is consumed in "mopping up activities" of narrow puzzle-solving that do not aim toward novelty. Day-to-day research produces work that essentially attempts to "force nature into the preformed and relatively inflexible box that the paradigm supplies" and is, in this sense, a highly self-deterministic activity (Kuhn 1970a, p. 24).

During normal science, the profession's practitioners are confident and satisfied with the fundamentals of their discipline. Consequently, there is infrequent methodological discussion and little concern for problems that exist seemingly outside the interests of the "invisible college" of professionals.

Despite the stability that normal science imposes, revolutions or paradigm shifts do occur. The social structure of science moderates change but, at the same time, creates inflexibility. It is this inflexibility within a particular science that gives rise to anomalies—occurrences not accountable for by the existing paradigm—and precipitates scientific "revolutions":

> Confronted with anomaly or crisis, scientists take a different attitude toward existing paradigms, and the nature of their research changes accordingly. The proliferation of competing articulations, the willingness to try anything, the expression of explicit discontent, the recourse to philosophy and to debate over fundamentals, all ... are symptoms of a transition from normal to extraordinary research. (Ibid., p. 91)

The discipline's commitment, then, is generally only broken by unmistakable failure of the orthodoxy. The ensuing revolution produces a new paradigm, better equipped to attack the anomalies that precipitated the change. Uncertainty and re-evaluation accompany the transition; questions over proper method, appropriate technique, topical relevance, and problem identification all return to the forefront. The "normal-scientific tradition that emerges from a scientific revolution is not only incompatible but often incommensurable with that which has gone before it" (ibid., p. 103). This idea, that the shift is complete and that all past rules no longer apply, turned out to be one of Kuhn's most controversial claims. This controversy will be clarified below.

The resulting paradigm—with its metaphysical view, theories, hypotheses, and modeling techniques—initially appears in a form not fully developed. Therefore, the new approach cannot be evaluated solely in a rational manner based on the verification of facts; it is still in an infantile state, and therefore, a subjective process incorporating intuition and even leaps of faith must accompany the transition from the old to the new. The interesting result for philosophy of science, and one of Kuhn's primary theses, is that evaluation of the sociological structure of a profession, in addition to the health of its paradigm, becomes a prerequisite to understanding why revolutionary science occurs and why periods of normal science persist.

Kuhn's theory received an enormous amount of attention, but was not overwhelmingly accepted within the philosophy of science discipline. Popper, ironically, questioned whether the conceptual framework of *The Structure of Scientific Revolutions* was descriptively accurate. He asserted that extraordinary science (Kuhn's term)—with the coexistence of multiple paradigms—is the norm, not normal science as Kuhn describes. By Popper's standards, activities comprising normal science are carried out by "research drones" and do not qualify as scientific at all.

Toulmin criticized Kuhn for portraying the distinction between normal and revolutionary periods too sharply. Like Popper, Toulmin accepted the probability that paradigms coexist and, in addition, suggested that continuity is nearly always present during and after paradigm shifts. As Kuhn's ideas developed (as represented by his work during the 1970s), he softened his initial position and acknowledged the possibility that certain types of competing explanations could successfully coexist.

Feyerabend attacked from the opposite side, asserting that Kuhn had not gone far enough in exorcising confining structuralism from his account. Feyerabend rejects the entire genre of theories, such as Kuhn's or Popper's, which hope to explain the workings of all that is considered science, and writes that there can be no universal theory of science that holds across time and disciplines.

Criticism of Kuhn is essentially focused around three aspects of his work. First, his vision of scientific revolution—which stipulates incommensurability of the old theory with the new—was maligned for its seemingly inconclusive historical perspective. Second, his description of normal science (which, by reasonable interpretation, was potentially damaging to the esteemed position that scientists enjoy) evoked emotional rebuke because it implicitly redefined scientific activity. Also, Kuhn got himself into a linguistic muddle by ambiguously using the term "paradigm" in a myriad of ways.

Concerning the usage problem, Kuhn was able to deflect some criticism simply by defining his terms more carefully. This amendment is contained in the postscript to the 1970 edition of *The Structure of Scientific Revolutions.* A new phrase, "disciplinary matrix," is offered as a substitute for "paradigm." Within the disciplinary matrix, new terms are assigned to the assortment of previously undistinguished meanings of "paradigm." Confusion subsides once one realizes that Kuhn's important assertions rarely make sense for more than one or two of the word's usages. If, for example, we equate the terms "paradigm" and "hypothesis," Kuhn's critics appear quite correct, since several hypotheses may be directed toward explaining a particular puzzle that is as yet unsolved. However, if a broader definition such as "worldview" is specified, then the situation changes. Rarely are two views along the magnitude of, say, the Darwinian explanation of man's current physical state versus the creationist explanation compatible.

Another important component of a paradigm involves the similar commitments shared among members of a profession. In Kuhn's defense, it is hard to imagine a scientist with a research agenda addressing heretofore unasked questions attaining any sort of reputability in his field. In most disciplines, the set of relevant puzzles is laid out to would-be practitioners during the formal education process.

The first two criticisms proved more substantive and persist until the present. Initially, perhaps because of the title of his book or its refutable historical nature, Kuhn's treatment of revolutions was given the most attention. In the 1970 revision, Kuhn had to deemphasize some of the bolder claims made in the earlier edition. His softened stance on the incommensurability of theories was seen as quite damaging by some.[6] Blaug's assessment is fairly representative:

> It is evident that these concessions considerably dilute the apparently dramatic import of Kuhn's original message. What remains . . . is the emphasis on the role of normative judgments in scientific controversies, particularly in respect of the choice between competing approaches to science, together with a vaguely formulated but deeply held suspicion of cognitive factors like epistemological rationality, rather than sociological factors like authority, hierarchy, and reference groups, as determinants of behavior. (Blaug 1980, p. 32)

Further, as with almost any general theory applied to history, it proved an easy task to find counter-examples; in this case, Kuhnian revolutions appeared to accurately describe some, but certainly not all, past scientific transformations.

Criticism of Kuhn's revolutions cost him some repute, but it was his perception of normal science that aroused the most emotional and heated retort. What Popper and Lakatos really objected to was Kuhn's implicit demarcation criteria for science. By writing that science had proceeded "successfully" in an intangible and not always rational manner, Kuhn, in essence, was advocating it. Popper and Lakatos insinuated that Kuhn's underlying historically based advice violated a "higher scientific morality" (Lakatos and Musgrave 1970, p. 247). Lakatos argued that normal science, in the Kuhnian sense, is not science at all and therefore is irrelevant to philosophy of science. Popper acknowledged the existence of normal science but warned that it is "a danger to science and, indeed, to our civilization" and stated that such activity should be avoided at all cost (ibid., p. 53). It is evident that, in his early work, Kuhn was unclear (perhaps intentionally) about enunciating how science *should* operate. Kuhn's conception of science, and not his analysis of human behavior, is ultimately what is rejected by Lakatos and Popper.

### Imre Lakatos

Kuhn's hypothesis forced much of the scientific community, and subsequently the philosophy of science community, into a defensive posture. By undercutting the concept of an objective rational foundation for science, Kuhn was rocking the pedestal upon which scientists feel comfortable. Kuhn's most outspoken critic from this defensive front was Imre Lakatos.

Lakatos's work has been viewed by most philosophers of science as an extension and modification of Popper's critical rationalism. Popper, like his positivist predecessors, endeavored to devise universal standards by which theories could be judged. However, he shifted the emphasis of theory appraisal away from verificationism toward falsificationism and, also, created methodological rules—"immunization stratagems"—intended to protect theories from premature refutation. Thus, he followed Duhem's lead and avoided the pitfalls of naive falsificationism (ibid., pp. 18–19).

Lakatos remained in Popper's camp by emphasizing that the aim of philosophy of science should be to prescribe proper methodology for practicing science. This emphasis on delimiting science via demarcation criteria reflected his initial (pre-Kuhn) area of concern—subjective and prescriptive philosophy of science. However, with the publication of *The Methodology of Scientific Research Programmes,* Lakatos moved away from his familiar foundations by transforming the Popperian philosophy of science into a critical tool for generating historical research. His interest in reconstructing history according to "valid" canons of science can be interpreted as a partial return toward positivism. Positivists believe that science does evolve according to these canons; Lakatos believed that one could treat science *as if* it evolves according to them, and produce an accurate characterization. Lakatos proposed the following:

> The appropriate unit of study is not the individual theory, but rather clusters of theories. These clusters, or coherent sequences of theories make up "scientific research programs." An individual research program evolves through its

auxiliary clauses, and renovations occur as one theory eclipses its predecessor in order to adjust to anomaly. This evolution of the program can take on either a theoretically progressive or degenerative character: Let us say that such a series of theories is *theoretically progressive (or "constitutes a theoretically progressive problemshift")* if each new theory has some excess empirical content over its predecessor, that is, if it predicts some novel, hitherto unexpected fact. Let us say that a theoretically progressive series of theories is also *empirically progressive (or "constitutes an empirically progressive problemshift")* if some of this excess empirical content is also corroborated, that is, if each new theory leads us to the actual discovery of some *new fact*. Finally, let us call a problemshift *progressive* if it is both theoretically and empirically progressive, and *degenerating* if it is not. (Lakatos 1978, pp. 33–34)

Lakatos's demarcation criterion follows, as he labels progressive programs "scientific" and degenerating ones "pseudo-scientific." Thus, the importance of empirical content for theory assessment that is so clearly evident in Popper is also present in Lakatos.

Lakatos, however, adds a time dimension that was never explicitly included in Popper's philosophy. The assessment of a program, Lakatos writes, takes time and only becomes clear in retrospect. Therefore, immediate falsification of any kind (or verification, for that matter) is rarely contemporarily possible. This shift away from a universal set of scientific criteria demonstrates the deemphasized role that Lakatos assigned to falsificationism.

Each research program consists of two components, a hard core and a protective belt. By the "methodological decision of its protagonists," the hard core is not open to refutation. All of the action—theory testing and extension, employment of new auxiliary assumptions, and professional debate—takes place in the protective belt. The negative and positive heuristics of the program dictate which paths of research to avoid and which ones to pursue. The negative heuristic indicates the boundaries of the hard core and directs work away from it. The positive heuristic redirects the modus tollens to the protective belt where puzzles of increasing complexity are solved without significantly changing the program's content, which is fundamentally grounded in the hard core (Lakatos 1970, pp. 133–34). Lakatos's philosophy of science incorporates a new brand of methodological falsificationism. Because the protective belt absorbs the brunt of the testing, only small parts of a program are modified at any one time, which makes the role of falsification a much more limited one than prescribed by Popper.

Lakatos ultimately differs from his mentor most markedly by incorporating an explicit theory of history in conjunction with a logical method of theory appraisal. Lakatos contended that his thesis provides not just a philosophy of science, but also a method by which history of science should be studied. In other words, he felt that the history of science could be described in terms of scientists rationally choosing progressive research programs over degenerating ones. This view, that science can be reconstructed accurately from its rational elements, will be of concern in the next section, which considers the critical response to Lakatos's work.

First, it is interesting to note how Lakatos was drawn into the debate because his motives influenced the nature of his argument. Lakatos wrote *The Methodology of Scientific Research Programmes* to express his dissatisfaction with Kuhn's interpretation of scientific development. The book received mixed reviews from within the philosophy of science, while, like Kuhn's before, it was enthusiastically welcomed by methodologists in other fields.

Toulmin provides interesting speculation in his enlightening article, "History, Praxis and the 'Third World' " (1976). Lakatos, he points out, began his academic career as a methodologist and philosopher of mathematics. Not until the late 1960s did he shift away from mathematics and into physics and astronomy. Toulmin convincingly argues that this shift was a response primarily motivated by the controversy generated by *The Structure of Scientific Revolutions* and to the direct confrontations between Kuhn and Popper at the Bedford College Conference in 1965 (Toulmin 1976, p. 658). Toulmin asserts that Lakatos's expertise as a philosopher of math colored his philosophy of science in a distinct way. Lakatos was misled because he failed to fully appreciate the inherent differences between mathematics and science in general.

Philosophers have, since before Bacon, recognized that mathematics is the discipline where the theoretical system can be separated from historical context and the subjective state of the system's creators most cleanly. Mathematical propositions and hypotheses can be judged on their own merits and are timeless. Matters of praxis—"the practical procedures by which we are to identify or generate specific physical exemplars of the entities referred to within the system, whether dimensionless points, equilateral triangles, uniform velocities, or whatever"—have far less to do with the validity of systems in mathematics than in other sciences. Furthermore, it is possible to think of various components of mathematics as existing in their final, definitive form (ibid., p. 663). Thus, mathematical philosophers are apt to overlook the potential importance of praxis and dismiss such discussion as irrational, empirical sociology. The result, in Lakatos's case, was that he did not initially question the applicability of timeless standards to natural science and, more importantly, sought a purely internal interpretation of science.

Clearly, Lakatos developed great disdain for the "irrationalist" implications of a "historically-changing body of praxis" as explained in

Kuhn's work or Toulmin's *Human Understanding*. It was during this time, after the conference, that Lakatos became hostile toward any type of historicism that attributed importance to factors lying outside the actual body of science literature. Yet he had incorporated historical evidence into his own mathematical treatise, "Proofs and Refutations" (Lakatos 1963). Fearing that similarities would be drawn between his own work and Kuhn's, Lakatos retreated back into the protection of a stricter Popperian philosophy. He must have felt that this defensive and distant posture would allow him to avoid any accusations of relativism. Only later did renewed confidence allow him to reject Popper's a priori criteria and to confront the possibility that scientific standards are not immutable.[7]

Lakatos's intellectual displeasure with Kuhn and Toulmin continued, but his strict adherence to Popper eased. His modification of Popperian falsificationism, in the form of "sophisticated falsificationism," greatly reduces the significance—and indeed the possibility—of "program refutation." And, also, his view that rationality only works slowly (i.e., there are no crucial contemporary experiments) injects a time variable that adds a complicating element to the appraisal of science. Despite concessions, Lakatos's vision of science proceeding via research programs remained problematic for many of his colleagues. Ironically, Lakatos fell prey to some of the same pitfalls in which he had caught Kuhn. Choosing historical examples to illustrate his thesis proved interesting but, ultimately, just as inductive and unconvincing as it had been for Kuhn.

As a prescriptive philosophy of science, Lakatos's approach is somewhat immune to tangible criticism because it is not explicit when it comes to methods of constructing criteria for theory appraisal. As a vision of what science should aspire to, the methodology of scientific research programs must simply be subjectively judged worthwhile or not so. However, as an explanation or "rational reconstruction" of actual scientific behavior, it remains unconvincing. How, for example, do scientists select which statements in a program are to be deemed unfalsifiable by fiat—that is, how is the hard core to be delimited? Or, how is empirical content to be measured in order to distinguish between progressive and degenerative programs? The central inconsistency in Lakatos's rational reconstruction is between the idea that the relevant aspects of science evolve according to the methodology of scientific research programs and the idea that research, hypotheses, and indeed programs can only be appraised with time. How can scientists behave, for the most part, according to the canons of the Lakatosian methodology when it is not possible for them to assess what they are doing at any given moment? This ambiguity concerning long-run versus contemporary theory assessment led Feyerabend to charge that Lakatos was presenting nothing more than concealed anarchy (Caldwell 1982, p. 228).

Furthermore, to believe that the only relevant parts of science evolve, and should aspire to evolve, according to his vision of proper science seems, to his critics, confining and pompous. Lakatos described a methodology for "ideal science," not the one practiced by actual, diverse human minds. Kuhn (perhaps biased) explains: "There are no ideal minds, and the 'psychology of this ideal mind' is therefore unavailable as a basis for explanation" (Kuhn 1970b, p. 240). In sum, Lakatos's critics share at least three opinions: that subculture in science is profound and affects theory choice, that science has clearly not maintained universal standards through time, and that Lakatos writes idealized and therefore inaccurate history. Even Blaug, a neo-Popperian and proponent of the Lakatosian framework concludes that:

> Lakatos's effort to divorce appraisal from recommendation, to retain a critical methodology of science that is frankly normative, but which nevertheless is capable of serving as the basis of a research program in the history of science, must be judged either a severely qualified success or else a failure, albeit a magnificent failure. (Blaug 1980, p. 40)

### Philosophy versus History

A considerable portion of the misunderstanding in the Kuhn–Lakatos debate arises from a failure to clearly identify the scope of the problems under scrutiny. Subtle differences in their goals and motives contribute to many of the apparent differences between the two. Kuhn's work is concerned with the history of science first and the philosophy of science second; Lakatos's priorities are the opposite. This assertion requires clarification.

The two domains—philosophy and history of science—are, as their practitioners routinely point out, intricately interwoven. Those methods that have in the past produced "successful" science are likely to be incorporated in a philosophical ideal of how science should operate. In this sense, history provides clues as to what is good and bad science. However, the insights and interpretations are inevitably different for a scholar who constructs a philosophy of science from historical knowledge than they are for a scholar who reconstructs history to support a particular philosophical point. It turns into a battle of the describer versus the prescriber. Each approach potentially serves a different and useful purpose but, too often, these practitioners want to fight the same battle.

Upon reviewing this literature, it does not take long before the different objectives are revealed. With Kuhn, we get the impression that the study of history produced a theory of science from which implicit and normative philosophical beliefs were drawn. Conversely, Lakatos *began* from a normative philosophical position. From there, he produced a philosophy of science, which provides guidelines for historical reconstructions later on.

Kuhn admits his methods: "Unlike most philosophers of science, I began as an historian of science, examining closely the facts of scientific life." By his interpretation, actual behavior among scientists frequently violates methodological canons previously established by philosophers. These failures, according to Kuhn, do not consistently inhibit the success of scientific enterprise. Rather, this "unscientific" behavior seems to fit in fairly regularly and is therefore included in Kuhn's description of normal science (Kuhn 1970b, p. 236). Kuhn's first concern, it seems, is with the actual procedures of science. In contrast, Lakatos and Popper appear more interested in uncovering "proper" method.

As stated above, philosophical and historical approaches to the study of science activity are inextricably connected. Even so, the methodologist's approach will be determined, in part, by which angle he chooses to emphasize. Historical survey is what led Kuhn to his hypothesis, whereas, if we accept Toulmin's interpretation, reaction to Kuhn is what led Lakatos to his. The result was, in Blaug's view, that Lakatos encountered the same difficulty that Popper experienced in "steering a middle ground between prescriptive arrogance and descriptive humility" (Blaug 1980, p. 39).

## Use of Historical Evidence

Each philosopher of science noted thus far—even the "anti-historicist" Popper—employs historical examples to defend his positions. Sometimes the same event is even used, in different guises, to "validate" opposing views. For every example that seems to support Kuhn's interpretation of history, there is one that can be tailored to fit Lakatos's description, another to fit Feyerabend's, and yet another that seems Popperian. Kuhn concedes that no single theory is likely to shed light on all periods of scientific history: "Nothing depends upon my, or anyone else's, being able to respond in every conceivable case, but much depends on the discrimination's being applicable to a far larger number of cases than have been supplied so far" (Kuhn 1970b, p. 251). As it turns out, much of the criticism levied against Kuhn questions both the extent to which his examples can be generalized and the accuracy of the interpretations that he employs as evidence.

Lakatos more vehemently insists that all important epochs in the history of science adhere to his description and can be properly reconstructed from their rational elements. Unfortunately, it is not difficult for Lakatos's critics to find apparent counter-examples in which scientists did not behave in any type of empirically or theoretically "progressive" manner. Furthermore, Lakatos is constantly forced to make value judgments about which historical facts are essential and which ones are not.

Consequently, Lakatos enjoys greater acceptance among prescriptive philosophers; Kuhn seems more popular among historians. Historians tend to fault Lakatos for substituting a set of values in place of reputable historical practice. They argue that Lakatos's "third world" is designed to conform to philosophical ideals of science and that he uses history for no other purpose than to find examples of "good" science (Barnes 1982, pp. 62–63). Thus, Lakatos's insightful interpretation of the shift from Newtonian to Einsteinian physics is no more generalizable as a universal history of science theory than is Kuhn's enlightening re-evaluation of Carnot's contributions in thermodynamics.[8] Each only demonstrates that his thesis contains explanatory power for a specific application.

What we are ultimately left with are two theories that are not as far apart as they may seem. Parallels between Kuhnian concepts (paradigm, normal science, and crisis) and Lakatosian ones (hard core, protective belt, and degenerative phase) are readily evident. In the end, both reject Popper's ahistorical approach to the philosophy of science and are, in a sense, "relativists." Differences arise most acutely during the subjective assessment of philosophy of science aims (i.e., should scholars in the field be more concerned with methodology of science at its best or as it is actually practiced). This debate will not be resolved here, or probably anywhere else, because individuals will inevitably continue to be drawn to both aspects of inquiry.

### Kuhn, Lakatos: Treatment of Theory Choice

Now we come to a major question: Were the new growth of knowledge philosophers able to produce a more satisfactory explanation of theory choice than their predecessors? More specifically, what insights can be gleaned from Kuhn's effort to establish a more "realistic" account of science and from Lakatos's effort to reshape Popper's analysis?

Kuhn's methodology breaks from the traditional hypothetico-deductivist view by denying that scientific activity consists purely of interaction between theory and data testing. He unambiguously rejects Popper's falsificationism as a description of how science works. Kuhn acknowledges the importance of positivist and Popperian criteria (testability, theory construction, predictability, etc.), but contends that external factors characterizing social and intellectual environments also contribute to a discipline's development.

Kuhn points out that few scientists are ever actually called upon to choose among theories in a meaningful way. If normal science is the predominant activity, then most practitioners do not spend their time empirically verifying or falsifying theories for the purpose of choosing among them. Instead, they spend their time working with theories previously accepted by their scientific community. Normal science dictates to practicing scientists which theory structures will be studied.

For Kuhn, true theory choice—that is, picking one among several competing theories—only occurs during periods of extraordinary science. Presumably, the overthrowing paradigm is "progressive" (in the Lakatosian sense) in that it corrects the anomaly created from insufficiencies inherent in the previously dominant paradigm. The new paradigm may yield more accurate predictions or offer a closer match to empirical regularities. However, for Kuhn, there is more to the decision-making process. Because the new theory seldom emerges in a fully developed form, guesswork, leaps of faith, luck, professional attitudes, and a multitude of subjective processes play important roles.

From Popper we received a short list of criteria from which to judge competing theories. The central criteria dealt with the ease with which a theory or proposition could be tested and subsequently falsified. Popper advocated a methodology for science that emphasizes falsification, without immediate concern with replacement. In Kuhn's vision, falsification (or, more accurately, failure) leads directly to replacement.

Unfortunately, Kuhn is unable to identify the components of theory choice clearly. He only directs us toward the complex interworkings of science's social structure, pointing out that to understand why paradigms are chosen requires additional inquiry into these forces. Thus, there seems to be a tradeoff: Kuhn, in his attempt to describe how science works more realistically, loses the ability to clearly identify a limited set of variables that affect theory choice; no easily workable prescription is produced. In unraveling the multidimensional processes of science, Kuhn is unable to maintain a highly structured Popperian system.

Compared to Kuhn, Lakatos's treatment of theory choice seems astoundingly simple. From a prescriptive point of view, Lakatos advocates choosing progressive research programs (clusters of theories) over degenerating ones. Progressive programs produce theories that increase the empirical content of the science. Therefore, according to Lakatos, scientists should choose to work with theories that are part of a progressive program.

Lakatos also finds this methodology acceptable as an account of how science does and has worked. That is, the history of science can be properly explained in terms of scientists rationally choosing progressive research programs over degenerating ones.[9] Unfortunately, further reflection reveals that the shift from a Popperian to a Lakatosian methodology results in a definite loss of clarity concerning the problem of theory choice. Recall Lakatos stated that a research program cannot typically be judged progressive or degenerative until well after its initial presentation. The value of a program cannot be contemporarily assessed, presumably because only time will reveal whether or not the components of that program—its theories—are yielding increasing empirical content. If this is indeed the case, the Lakatosian methodology has basically lost, and failed to replace, the key Popperian mechanism of theory choice—falsificationist criteria.

To compound matters, Lakatos established no method for measuring the empirical success of a theory. His approach implies a certain objectivity of measurement, which has already been shown to be problematic. There is no clear criterion, like that which falsificationism provides, for ranking clusters of theories in order from most progressive (best) to most degenerating (worst). This, along with the above-stated ambiguity concerning the dynamics involved with assessment, leaves Lakatos's methodology of scientific research programs ineffective in dealing with theory choice issues.

Lakatos was far more concerned with modeling the structure of scientific systems. He assigned components of research programs various names—hard core, protective belt, etc.—which is descriptively useful. In this way his work is akin to molecular chemistry models, in that it organizes and labels different parts of a system. Lakatos's methodology serves better as a taxonomic device than it does as an explanation of how science works.

Within the Lakatosian methodology, there is a definite shift away from the question, "When faced with two competing theories, what criteria have scientists invoked to appraise the relative value of each?" Within the rational reconstruction method of historical inquiry, it is not important whether or not purely scientific considerations motivate scientific progress because history can, in either case, be explained properly as if it were. In other words, by the Lakatosian account, it is adequate to say that theory choice has occurred according to rational canons of science. Thus, uncovering variables of theory choice is not an issue, it is a foregone conclusion. The final assessment must point out that, in modifying Popper, Lakatos abandoned issues of theory choice to a significant degree.

## Conclusions

Theory choice did not clearly emerge as a philosophy of science issue until the mid-nineteenth century, after initiation of the hypothetico-deductivist movement. Until then, the advancement of science was predominantly viewed as a pure process of accumulating facts. The received view stipulated that knowledge is acquired via deductive logic or compiled via inductive empiricism. Once it was recognized that hypothesis and theory play an a priori role in science, verificationists and falsificationists set out to establish criteria for appraising and choosing between competing offerings.

The philosophers of the Vienna Circle and Karl Popper established criteria that they hoped would guide theory choice. Despite logical and practical problems with verificationist and falsificationist methodologies, much of their secondary criteria, both empirical and non-empirical, have been accepted as important considerations for choosing theories. It is not controversial to say that variables such as logical consistency, elegance, and generality are important factors in theory choice. However, some philosophers found the treatment simplistic and incomplete.

A growing dissatisfaction with positivist and Popperian explanations of how science works emerged during the 1960s and 1970s. Growth of knowledge philosophers argued that these existing explanations did not adequately characterize the wide variation in scientific activity. The most critical charge was that logical positivists, and even Popper, had failed to provide a realistic account of how science has actually proceeded. Kuhn and Feyerabend, among others, abandoned the idea that scientists behave in an unwaveringly rational and detached manner. Kuhn, in particular, sought to incorporate psychological and sociological factors into the picture. He raised important issues concerning the complexities of science as a human activity.

There seemed to be a tradeoff, however; by expanding his analysis to make it more descriptively realistic, Kuhn was unable to present as structured an analysis of theory choice as had Popper. The message that emerges is that inquiries must analyze specific conditions within individual disciplines in order to produce insights into the workings of science. Kuhn does not presume to have developed a *general* theory outlining what these conditions are for each science.

Lakatos sought to eliminate the extra-scientific considerations that Kuhn, Toulmin, and Feyerabend had introduced into the debate. He advised looking at history of science as if it had been motivated by purely rational factors. Unfortunately, descriptive realism was abandoned in the process. More importantly, Lakatos, in modifying Popper's methodology, lost the falsificationist appraisal criterion and replaced it with a taxonomic device that scarcely addressed theory choice.

### Notes

1. This process closely resembles that described in Immanuel Kant's twelve concepts or "categories."

2. This simple example neglects the additional logical difficulty created by definitions. For instance, what if the trait "blackness" is included in the definition of a crow?

3. The special problems that social science presents are examined in detail in Chapter 2.

4. In fact, despite frequent references to the history of science, he explicitly stated that his concern was not with the actual behavior of scientists (Popper 1959, p. 52).

5. It should be noted, however, that many of the ideas in Kuhn's book were previously explored. The visionary work of Whewell, for example, has already been mentioned. Consider, also, the following excerpt from James Harvey Robinson's *The Humanizing of Knowledge* (1923): "Experimental science is tireless groping and fumbling, or the laborious discrimination and comparison of detail. . . . It often requires years to ascertain facts and to record observations that in the end fill a small abstruse and technical pamphlet" (p. 46).

6. This softened stance acknowledged the possibility of cross-paradigm debate and that paradigm shifts do not necessarily require total discontinuity between the old and the new.

7. This is a paraphrase of the explanation given by Toulmin of Lakatos's temporary hostility toward historically and sociologically dependent methods in science (Toulmin 1976, p. 672).

8. For an extended discussion on this topic, see Barnes (1982), pp. 5–8, and Blaug (1980), pp. 37–38.

9. Note, this is not that different from Kuhn's explanation of new paradigms replacing old ones to overcome anomaly.

# CHAPTER 2

# Philosophy of Science and Economics

## Introduction

The objective in Chapter 1 was to review relevant tenets of philosophy of science literature. This fundamental basis creates a starting point for considering how closely theory selection, and methods in general, in economics correspond to various philosophy of science treatments of the topic. Additionally, to accommodate the purposes of this thesis, it was necessary to make, from this general discussion, two particular points. First, by tracing the evolution of philosophy of science approaches, it was purposely shown that logical positivism has lost considerable influence as an explanation of how science operates. The second point is that the philosophical constructs that have replaced positivism are limited in their ability to reveal how theories in science are chosen.

These points are immediately relevant to this chapter, which considers theory choice explanations offered by economists concerned with methodology. Even though positivist explanations of science are virtually dead in the philosophy of science, and seriously waning among physical scientists, economists have been slow to respond to the now well-established, anti-positivist critique. Similarly, economics remains relatively unaffected by new approaches such as those offered by sociology of science and history of science. This reluctance, or lack of interest, in rejecting an outdated and mythological interpretation of science by mainstream economists has left the field methodologically behind other disciplines.

Clive Beed (1991), in providing a concise overview of positivism's grip on mainstream economics, writes that contemporary "economics is conspicuous among the social sciences for ignoring" the anti-positivist critique of science. This is not to say that economists are indeed following, and refusing to give up, methodological *practices* prescribed under positivism. Rather, it means that economists' claims of what they are doing still sound like the rational, idealized description of science, which was popular with philosophers before the influx of "growth of knowledge" writers.

Nowhere is this lip-service to positivism paid more confidently than in our discipline's textbooks, which initiate potential economists. Beed points to the 1980 edition of Paul Samuelson's *Economics,* which describes its content as "economic science, the newest of the sciences." The economic method, Samuelson writes, is characterized by "patient attendance to the empirical facts of life," and by "systematic reasoning about them" (Samuelson 1980, pp. 1–8). Beed cites the popular text by Robert Lipsey et al. as a bolder submission to the 'received view': "Positive economic science consists of following the scientific method . . . an impersonal set of criteria . . . relating questions, problems, theories or issues to empirical evidence. . . . The idea of an objective, fact-guided science of human behavior (is achievable without regard to) our philosophical, cultural and religious positions" (Lipsey et al. 1986, pp. 6, 3, 5).

In contrast, as discussed previously, the anti-positivist critique is now almost mainstream in the philosophies of the physical sciences. Even in other social sciences, the challenge to positivism has permeated the orthodoxy. In sociology, for example, several introductory texts provide discussions identifying how modified philosophy of science approaches have emerged to replace the old verificationist and falsificationist methodologies (Beed 1991, p. 474).

The first formal assessment of the rejection of positivism and its implications for economics did not appear until Bruce Caldwell (1982), and the movement to open methodological dialogue has only gained momentum slowly. Several new journals (*Economics and Philosophy, Journal of Economic Issues,* and the *Journal of Post-Keynesian Economics*) encourage the submission of articles designed to promote a more comprehensive understanding of economists' methods. Contributing authors articulate shortcomings of the dated positivist explanation but, more generally, such discussion has remained on the discipline's periphery.

Although the relevant literature is not especially deep in volume, interest in theory choice and related issues has increased over the past decade, and there is sufficient material to form a point of departure. But, before turning to the work of economic methodologists, it will be helpful to consider the link between economics and physical science. The anti-positivist critique has a longer history in physical science, and it is from this source that methodological inquiry has infiltrated into the fringes of economics.

## The Physical Science–Economics Link

The task here is to briefly compare economics to other sciences with which philosophers of science have more generally concerned themselves. Lakatos and Kuhn were formally trained in mathematics and physics, respectively, and their work in philosophy was directed accordingly toward those areas (and the level of generality they intended for their theories is not immediately evident). Economic methodologists have, for the most part, acknowledged problems with applying non–social science–specific theories to their field, but have nevertheless attempted to support one particular philosophy of science view or another. It is important to check the logic of extending these theories to fields other than those that they were originally intended to investigate.

Economics has historically borrowed material, methods, and philosophy from the physical sciences. The influence that methods in other sciences have had on economics is well documented. Introduction of marginal analysis, largely originating from practitioners trained outside of economics proper, represents one such occasion. Phillip Mirowski (1989) convincingly argues that economists directly copied mid-nineteenth-century physics, adopting "energetics" as a metaphor and framework for neoclassical price theory.[1]

If economics follows the methodology of physics as closely as it has apparently followed its methods, then the casual lip-service that economists pay to various forms of positivism will eventually fade, as it has already faded in the lead discipline. As of now, however, many economists still cling to positivism (which, incidentally, originated in the very disciplines that now seek to discredit it). Edward Leamer, an econometrician, writes, "Economists have inherited from the physical sciences the myth that scientific inference is objective, and free of personal prejudice." Following the example set by other disciplines has gotten economics in trouble before; "The false idol of objectivity has done great damage to economic science" (Leamer 1983, p. 36). Thus, before advocating economists to abandon positivism only "because other sciences have," a consideration of the unique characteristics that economics displays is required.

Because of the nature of economics subject matter, simple appeals to "fact" become problematic and, consequently, theory tends to be more ad hoc than it is in other fields. Physics, and certainly mathematics, deals with material that is far less time and context dependent. Economists, on the other hand, must concede that the composition of their object of study is ever changing.[2] The distinction is that economics, like biology, displays uniqueness and variability, complexity, indeterminacy, and irreversibility. Ernst Mayr's (1982) work, which argues the inapplicability of "reductionist" methods to biology, should inspire economists to question the validity of their physics metaphors (as Mirowski has done).

Differences between physical and social sciences have become clear at the empirical level with the emergence of econometrics. Special problems arise for econometricians because they must deal with non–experimentally generated, as opposed to lab-generated, data. Extending law-testing methods of physics to evolutionary sciences is problematic because the "laws" are probabilistic and, therefore, take the form of generalizations. In economics, the complexity of the ceteris paribus condition, unparalleled in physical science testing, limits most efforts at testing to what has come to be termed "innocuous falsificationism." Consequently, testing and predictability have never played more than a secondary role in the development of economic theory.

Over the past several decades, a greater effort has been made to at least acknowledge the importance of the testability criteria.[3] The lack of objectivity surrounding testing within economics becomes apparent, however, when one notes the correlation between an individual's policy views and his empirical findings. On this matter, Don Patinkin writes:

> What generates in me a great deal of skepticism about the state of our discipline is the high positive correlation between the policy views of a researcher (or, what is worse, of his thesis director), and his empirical findings. I will begin to believe in economics as a science when out of Yale there comes an empirical Ph.D. thesis demonstrating the supremacy of monetary policy in some historical episode—and out of Chicago, one demonstrating the supremacy of fiscal policy. (Patinkin 1972, p. 142)

A careful check into considerations surrounding "ethical neutrality" is rarely as crucial when assessing the objectivity of applied work in the natural sciences as it is in economics.

Certainly, variability in the context of theory interpretation does exist even in "exact" sciences such as physics. However, this difficulty is magnified enormously when studying human behavior, where virtually nothing can be accurately expressed solely in mathematical terms. Geometry, for example, in no way depends on the actual existence of dimensionless points, whereas physics depends on real electrons and economics on human rationality. Unlike mathematics, the dynamic essence of economic activity forbids construction of hypotheses in a "final form" (Toulmin 1976, p. 664). In economics, it is unlikely that a genius will discover something, explain his findings logically, confirm it empirically for the betterment of all, and then receive immediate and general acknowledgment.

Mathematical economists (even Karl Popper) have pointed to the addition of marginalist tools, or the major extension of mathematical methods beginning in the 1950s, and claimed that the rigor of economics is increasing, bringing it closer to a hard science ideal. This impression is misleading, however, because, as Terence Hutchison explains, "The mathematical 'revolution' in economics has been one mainly (or almost entirely) of *form, with very little or no empirical, testable, predictive content involved*" (Hutchison 1978, p. 186, emphasis added). Mathematicization in economics simply aids in manipulating the descriptive apparatus; it cannot quantify the theoretical results. The difference between mathematicization in economics and, say, physics becomes evident when the predictive power of their theories is compared. The relative stability of physical relationships has allowed engineers to design bridges and buildings based on predicted material strengths, structural design properties, and so on. A comparable level of confidence does not accompany the prognostications of economists.[4]

As with its theories, major shifts in the economics discipline take a different form than they do in physics or chemistry. In economics, the nature of the subject makes anomalies appear less severe, and therefore, revolutions do not spread as rapidly or with as high a degree of consensus. Hutchison contends that there has never been conclusive empirical falsification (or verification) of a theory in economics. For this reason, ousted theories are far more likely to be revived in economics than in the hard sciences (Hutchison 1978, p. 287).

Further, paradigm shifts in economics contain destructive as well as constructive elements because they usually involve a change of emphasis rather than an overthrow of a conventional wisdom. The result is that, for extended periods, entire aspects of economic behavior or phenomena may be neglected. The Smithian, Jevonsian, and Keynesian revolutions can all be characterized as partial paradigm shifts. Adam Smith focused attention on growth issues and emphasized the optimality of a laissez-faire system; William Stanley Jevons's marginal analysis adopted a micro-focus and developed maximization principles for *given* endowments; John Maynard Keynes refocused on the macro-perspective but, unlike classical economists, exposed glitches in the market mechanism. Nonetheless, self-adjusting, maximizing models underlay the whole system (even most of Keynes's) since the late seventeenth century. Because of this, Donald Gordon, Guy Routh, and others applying Kuhn's *Structure of Scientific Revolutions* to economics have, for the most part, agreed that there have been no revolutions, in the Kuhnian sense, in economics.

The inability of economists to assess their theories empirically and quantifiably has also created disagreement about when the discipline experienced periods of intellectual growth. A similar inability to identify growth of "objective" knowledge among physicists, and certainly mathematicians, does not exist (ibid., p. 297).

In economics, there is the added importance of historical relativism. Sir

John Hicks points out that economists cannot easily escape their past: In economics, ideas have risen, fallen, and come back again; "to 'neoclassical' succeeds 'neomercantilist'; Keynes and his contemporaries echo Ricardo and Malthus; Marx and Marshall are still alive . . . [and this historicism] is a consequence of what we are doing, or trying to do" (Hicks 1976, p. 207). Human behavior which, in turn, provides source material for economists, is itself contingent on historical context. The particular configuration of societal institutions presents complex forces that are subject to wide and varying interpretation. Wesley Mitchell was one of many prominent economists to acknowledge that theory responds to major new events and issues: "The growth of our science will be shaped in very large measure by the appearance of new social problems" (Hutchison 1978, p. 299). Such is not the case for disciplines that study "non-evolving" subject matter.

Examples of historical relativism abound in economics. A relatively valid generalization, such as A.C. Pigou's self-adjusting relationship between wage-flexibility and employment, may cease to hold true for some period of time due to unusual circumstances. Such was the case during the interwar years in England. Similarly, the unemployment–inflation relationship posited in the Phillips Curve was considered valid for a period then, more recently, underwent serious modification due to stagflation. And not only does history affect the validity of economist's claims, it also determines the topical emphasis of their investigations.[5] Because the subject matter is altered by social and institutional change, "external" events are far more relevant in economics than in mathematics or physics. Classical economists were concerned with the main problem of their day—growth. Marginalists studied efficiency, after it seemed that growth was inevitable. Similarly, Keynes responded to persistent and unexplainable unemployment, and stagflation stimulated research into supply-side policies and issues.

Frank Knight and Milton Friedman have also identified the role of history in providing source material for economics: Knight maintained that, "The particular trend which the development of economics took in Great Britain after Smith was largely determined by the character of the economic problems which confronted the nation, partly by reason of rapid changes in its own industrial structure (the Industrial Revolution), and partly in consequence of the French Revolutionary and Napoleonic Wars" (Knight 1956, p. 10). Friedman, critiquing the Keynesian revolution, writes, "The basic source of the revolution and of the reaction against the quantity theory of money was a historical event, namely the great contraction or depression" (Hutchison 1978, p. 299). By Mitchell's assessment, "The important departures in economic theory have been intellectual responses to changing current problems" (ibid.). Hutchison too sides with the externalists and finds it "remarkable that leading theoretical economists (e.g., Sir John Hicks, and Professors H.G. Johnson and G.J. Stigler) emphasize changes originating mainly 'externally' " to the profession (ibid., p. 319).

The point is that the complex and evolving quality of economic phenomena make external and subjective factors (which lie outside the scope of positivist or Lakatosian explanations) more pervasive in the development of economics than suggested by philosophy of science literature, which is directed primarily at natural science. Further, a methodologist, even if not "committed to Kuhn's particular sequence of scientific change, [must realize that]. . . causal references to contemporary intellectual or social phenomena [no longer] constitute a respectable explanation for particular changes" (Stigler 1973, p. 318).

One can, then, reasonably assert that ideological factors make for greater tenacity of paradigms or research programs in economics compared to physics and mathematics. We have, in our profession, laissez-faire economists on one extreme and Marxists on the other; ideology certainly dictates, to some degree, what each will study. Ideological differences may exist among natural scientists, but not in as stark a form so directly related to their professional interests.[6]

It is not possible, or necessarily desirable, that economics should fully follow the methodological road paved by physics. Calling economics an "immature science" is misleading because it implies that the discipline will advance and some day operate on the same level as the "mature" sciences. Economists waiting for their Newton may instead be waiting for Godot.

## Economists and Philosophy of Science

This section assesses the productivity of efforts by economic methodologists to apply philosophy of science to investigations of their own discipline. In so doing, a few questions must be answered: (1) Has a detailed breakdown of the theory appraisal process in economics been produced? (2) Can methodologists account for what has actually led to, in the history of the discipline, rejection or acceptance of ideas and theories? And (3), have the criteria changed over time?

In the previous chapter, it was shown that positivism lost much of its influence among philosophers during the first half of this century. More recently, philosophy of science has even rejected much of Popper's early work, which is considered by some to simply be modified positivism in that it maintains, albeit revised, the view that theory appraisal can be largely objective and rational. In an effort to mend the growing rift in philosophy of science during the 1950s, Alfred Ayer, an avid positivist, emphasized these similarities: "The affinities between (Popper) and the positivists whom he criticized appear more striking than the divergences" (Ayer 1959, p. 6).

That a form of positivism remains prevalent among economists illustrates the natural historical trend of the discipline, and other sciences, to lag behind philosophy of science on methodological issues. In fact, economics has remained quite impervious to the anti-positivist critique that destroyed the reputability of the received view elsewhere: "Positive economics, positivism, and positive science . . . weathered the debate within economics largely unscathed and still constitutes an important position in mainstream economics" (Beed 1991, p. 475). As Beed correctly points out, "The first substantive overview of the positivist–anti-positivist debate in physical science, and its relation to economics (did not) appear in a form specifically aimed at the economics profession (until Caldwell)" (ibid.).

Before continuing, it may be helpful to characterize, in more tangible terms, the variant of "positivism" ascribed to by economists. This clarification is helpful since modern economists have derived their espoused methodology from numerous sources, not all of which can be accurately classified as "logical positivists." To a substantial degree, the adopted philosophy of economics can be found in the now famous methodological writings of relative contemporaries such as John Neville Keynes, Lionel Robbins, Terence W. Hutchison, and Milton Friedman. These economists (with the notable exception of Friedman), however, borrowed heavily from John Stuart Mill, Nassau Senior, and John Elliot Cairnes whose work is, in turn, rooted in David Hume, Auguste Comte, and others.[7]

Given this complex methodological evolution, labeling economic philosophy of science "logical positivism" is an unnecessary simplification. The more central concern here is with identifying, rather than labeling, those features that distinguish the modern philosophy held by economists. No doubt, opinions differ as to what exactly this philosophy is; however, in general terms, there is a widely shared mentality within the profession. Rhonda Williams, in an article assessing how closely labor economics actually follows its espoused methodology, writes, "The majority of mainstream economists are self-proclaimed falsificationists . . . unlike their nineteenth-century counterparts, who were predominantly verificationists" (Williams 1984, p. 24).

Mark Blaug agrees: "Modern economists frequently preach falsificationism, but they rarely practice it: their philosophy of science is aptly described as 'innocuous falsificationism,' " because a disconfirming test does not lead to theory rejection (Blaug 1980, p. 128). A case could, however, certainly be made that verificationism, of the sort advocated by logical positivists, has held on as the dominant view. One can easily find numerous applied articles claiming to empirically *support* an hypothesis.

At any rate, whatever the exact nature of the testing mentality (to the extent that it exists) in economics, there persists an adherence to a general view that was dominant in science at the turn of the twentieth century. This view, roughly called "positivism," is capsulated in Alan Chalmers's popular philosophy of science text:

> Scientific knowledge is proven knowledge. Scientific theories are derived in some rigorous way from the facts of experience acquired by observation and experiment. . . . Personal opinion or preferences and speculative imaginings have no place in science. . . . Scientific knowledge is reliable because it is objectively proven knowledge. (Chalmers 1982, p. 1)

Clive Beed has assembled a list giving more detail to the received positivist view. The components of the list are as follows:

1. Scientific knowledge (including logic and mathematics) is the only valid knowledge.
2. Metaphysical claims, normative statements, value judgments, and opinions are not valid knowledge.
3. Human sense experience (empirical data) is the only source of valid knowledge (except for logic and mathematics).
4. Valid knowledge can only be obtained by the methods of natural science, especially physics, utilizing logic and mathematics.
5. Generalizations, principles, and theories in science can only be derived from empirical data (except for theories in logic and mathematics).
6. Generalizations, principles, and theories in science must be verifiable (or falsifiable for Popperians) from empirical data—except for theories in logic and mathematics.
7. Generalizations, principles, and theories should be expressible in mathematical logical form.
8. Normative views, value judgments, convictions, beliefs, and opinions should not enter into empirical data collection, theory formulation, or verification.
9. The methods of obtaining valid scientific knowledge are the same for all fields of experience (= unity of the scientific method). (Beed 1991, pp. 462–63)

The above tenets, upon some clarification, adequately summarize a methodology that is commonly held (but, again, not necessarily practiced) by economists. Points 3, 5, and 6 have often not been emphasized in economics and have in fact sometimes been criticized. The reliance on a priori, deductive methods in the history of economics accounts for this. Economists concerned with the discipline's status as a science have asserted the importance of similar criteria, however, in advocating "proper method" for their science.

Methodology literature indicates general agreement that points 1, 2, 7, and 8 do characterize the dominant view in economics. Disagreement only arises once the accuracy of this view is questioned. Orthodox practitioners, along with methodologists of a positivist or even Popperian bent, have attempted to confirm the validity of the above-listed criteria. "Anti-positivists," on the other hand, contest the assertion that this philosophy prescribes proper method and that it describes actual practice in economics. Beed categorizes the opposing view:

1. The distinction between positive and normative science is untenable.
2. Value judgments play an integral role in all stages of scientific research.
3. No one "correct" scientific method exists.
4. No universally agreed basis to evaluate scientific theories exists.
5. Prediction, explanation, internal consistency, economy in assumptions, and so on, may all be valued in scientific theories, but none of these is decisive for theory selection.
6. Scientific activity can rest on a metaphysical basis. For example, the empirical validity of all assumptions underlying a scientific theory may not be testable; some may be metaphysical assertions.
7. In their practice of science, scientists do not follow prescribed methodologies.
8. Scientists rely on convictions, beliefs, faith rhetoric, and persuasion, as well as mathematical and statistical analysis.
9. In the social sciences, few laws have been discovered that hold in all times and places.
10. In the social sciences, verbal analysis is not necessarily inferior to mathematical and statistical analysis. (Beed 1991, pp. 470–71)

Here, points 4 through 8 are especially relevant for the theory choice discussion at hand. The lists above serve to delimit the two sides of the debate. The next task is to turn to a sampling of what economists have had to say on the issue.

### Growth of Knowledge in Economics—A Challenge to Friedman's Methodology

For a period, economists, when pressed about methodological issues, seemed content to casually pledge allegiance to Friedman's so-called "instrumentalist" variant of Popper's falsificationism. Friedman wrote that the task of economics is "to provide a system of generalizations that can be used to make correct predictions about the consequences of any change in circumstances" (Friedman 1953, p. 4). In this way, evidence could be gathered by comparing predictions with experience. This evidence, although it could not prove hypotheses (it could only fail to disprove them), could be amassed to corroborate them.

Friedman's view, perhaps buoyed by his notoriety within the field, gained widespread attention among economists. Proponents were persuaded, in part, because Friedman's insistence on prediction asserted a methodological bond with physical science, which economists were seeking to emulate.[8] Further, the instrumentalist view did not insist on realism (and therefore accuracy) of assumptions, which, for economists, was palatable for obvious reasons.

Despite this highly contented stance among economists in general, it is now acknowledged by methodologists that economics does not often follow a testability-based methodology, especially not Popper's falsificationism.[9] These methodologists, realizing that testability was not central to the development of economic thought, were drawn into the growth of knowledge debate. Some, like Blaug, appeared motivated by a desire to redirect economics toward a Popperian "program." Others have sought to demonstrate that economics is unique and should not follow prescriptive methodologies (such as Popper's) handed down from physical science.[10] Early efforts to wrest useful information from the Popper–Kuhn–Lakatos philosophy of science debate consisted of fitting, sometimes with the aid of an interpretive shoehorn, the history of economics to one or another view. More recently, methodologists have benefited from the slowly growing pool of critical research, and the debate has taken on a slightly subtler quality.

*Thomas Kuhn and Economics*

Publication of *The Structure of Scientific Revolutions* spawned, in economics, a small wave of articles asking how well the Kuhnian explanation fits the history of economic thought. The role that revolutions have played during the history of economics, in particular, became a hot topic. The debate over Kuhn's book, as it filtered into the economics literature, can be divided into three categories:

1. General applicability of *The Structure of Scientific Revolutions* to economic science.
2. Occurrence of Kuhnian revolutions in economics.
3. The role of normal science in economics.

These three areas of debate are briefly reviewed below; several conclusions are then drawn regarding how and if these studies promote further understanding of the theory choice process. The core of this literature, compiled during the late 1960s and early 1970s, includes articles by A.W. Coats (1969), Donald Gordon (1965), Martin Bronfenbrenner (1971), Michael DeVroey (1975), J. Ronald Stanfield (1974), and contributors to the Spiro Latsis (1976) volume.

*Applicability of Kuhn's Theory to Economic Science.* Reception of Kuhn by economists followed a fairly typical course in that it reflected, in a lagged form, trends in philosophy of science. Articles written in the immediate wake of *The Structure of Scientific Revolutions* were generally optimistic about the usefulness of Kuhn's theory, both as an account of science generally and as a potential interpretation of the history of economic theory. After rebuttals to Kuhn appeared in the philosophy of science literature, most notably by Lakatos, economists again followed and their readings of Kuhn became more critical.

Coats takes the view that the Kuhnian apparatus, if modified (to take into account that crucial experiments, for example, do not arise in economics), is useful:

> It is appropriate to compare the history of economics with the history of the natural sciences, not only because economists have persistently striven to emulate the natural scientists' methods but also because any signs of an anti-positivist movement among historians of science are obviously of interest to those engaged in the interminable debate about "positive" economics, as well as to historians. Moreover, both groups may derive intellectual stimulus from Kuhn's effort to synthesize epistemology, the sociology of knowledge, and the study of science as a profession. (Coats 1969, p. 289)

Gordon also cites similarities between physical theory and economics, which make the Kuhnian theory interesting to economists. He points to the almost exclusive reliance on textbooks during early stages of the training process, along with the degree to which consensus around a basic model exists, as factors that make "us closer to the natural sciences than to some other" social science fields (Gordon 1965, p. 122).[11]

Blaug and Bronfenbrenner were early opponents of applying Kuhn's theory to economics; later, others joined, after Lakatos, in countering Kuhn, drew them into the debate. Bronfenbrenner writes:

> Neither conventional incrementalism or "uniformitarianism" on the one hand, nor Thomas Kuhn's "catastrophic" theory of scientific revolution on the other, fits the broad sweep of economic doctrinal history particularly well. (Bronfenbrenner 1971, p. 136)

Bronfenbrenner opts instead for a dialectical view of the history of economic theory. He chooses to contrast rather than to compare sciences and points out that, because outmoded ideas are longer-lived in economics than in natural science, quick Kuhnian breaks in theory development are inhibited. Blaug, citing Coats and Bronfenbrenner, articulates his agreement: "Some commentators have expressed misgivings about Kuhnian methodology applied to economics, throwing doubt in particular on the view that 'scientific revolutions' characterize the history of economic thought" (Blaug 1976, p. 149).

*Existence of Kuhnian Revolutions in Economics.* The recurring theme emerging from this tract of literature posits that total breaks from the past do not occur in economics. Instead, ideas in economics, once gone, may reappear; they are not always thrown away forever. Even among those favorably impressed with Kuhn, few find more than one or two legitimate candidates to nominate as Kuhnian revolutions.

Coats's conditional application of Kuhn concludes that a single paradigm—equilibrium via the market mechanism—has dominated the formal history of economic thought. However, he writes that, "the Keynesian Revolution of the 1930s possessed many of the characteristics associated with Kuhn's 'scientific revolutions.' " As evidence, he points to economists of the day and their "growing concern about the inadequacy of existing theory," coupled with "a change in psychological outlook on the part of many economists virtually amounting to a conversion experience." The manner in which the movement, led by "a band of youngsters" and fiercely resisted by their elders, was initiated from within the profession demonstrates the importance of sociological factors (Coats 1969, p. 293).

In a slightly different interpretation, Benjamin Ward writes that the Keynesian shift and the formalist movement of the 1950s (toward mathematical model-building and econometric methods) do satisfy the Kuhnian criteria. He goes on to lay out, categorically, Kuhnian aspects of economic science and, thereby, establishes himself as perhaps the leading proponent of Kuhn's methodology. However, in supporting his contentions outlining "what's wrong with economics," he notes that revolutions did not substantially alter the nature of economics. This reasoning, while imperative to the central point of his book, undermines the assertion that the Keynesian and formalist shifts were truly Kuhnian in nature.

Gordon, like Coats, is in the single-paradigm camp. He maintains that Smith's postulate of the maximizing individual in a relatively free market— and the successful application of this postulate to a wide variety of specific questions—is that basic paradigm. It created a "coherent scientific tradition (most notably including Marx)" (Gordon 1965, p. 123). He gets around marginalist and Keynesian shifts by referring to them as sub-paradigms, allowed for by Kuhn in the case of more basic models. From Gordon's perspective, these shifts of emphasis do not qualify as Kuhnian revolutions since the basic maximizing model was not replaced. In fact, Gordon finds it "remarkable . . . that an economist's fundamental way of viewing the world has remained unchanged since the eighteenth century" (ibid., p. 124). Gordon considers attempted rebellions in economics (such as institutionalism or historicism) to have been largely unsuccessful.

What Gordon is getting at, and what other critics point out, is that there is really nothing in Kuhn's theory that adequately describes the type of theory shifts that actually occur in economics. Movements toward, say, a macro-perspective or a mathematical emphasis have always been partial, never affecting all members of the profession or altering economic theory in its entirety. Therefore, it seems at the outset incorrect to say that incommensurability, of the Kuhnian variety, exists in economics.

Two central points emerge from discussions regarding Kuhnian revolutions as viewed in the economics context. First, dramatic, all-encompassing theory changes (of the Copernican or Newtonian magnitude) simply have not occurred in economics. Thus, Kuhn's description of *how* scientific revolutions unfold (involving incommensurability, total theory abandonment, etc.) does not fit economics. The second point is that, despite the apparent absence of revolutions in economics, Kuhn's explanation of *why* change occurs *is* relevant. That is, a sociological, and certainly an extra-positivist, element is influential in determining when and what kind of new ideas will be accepted. This normative element is especially apparent in economics because of its immediate proximity to policy issues.

In separate articles, DeVroey (1975) and Stanfield (1974) both consider socio-political influences within the history of economic thought. DeVroey writes that neoclassical theory was given credence in part because of its ideological palatability. The relative emphasis assigned to capital versus price, or the treatment of profit, shifted over time to keep theory concordant with contemporary political-economic views. He concludes that the transition from classical to neoclassical theory contained Kuhnian elements because there was a political dimension that affected theory and choice and those in power indirectly limited the type of social science that was developed.

Similarly, Stanfield (1974) argues that acceptance and proliferation of *The General Theory* had Kuhnian aspects. Acceptance of Keynes by economists required a change in worldview involving, to some degree, an abandonment of laissez-faire. Additionally, the constituency least receptive to the new ideas contained those members of the profession with the greatest professional and political stakes in the orthodoxy.

Axel Leijonhufvud agrees that Keynes's success exhibited Kuhnian qualities:

> By external, sociology of science criteria, it was without doubt a genuine Kuhnian revolution. It cannot be disputed: ask anyone who was there! The period had a high incidence of "conversions," *Sturm und Drang* among the young, resistance from the old, etc. (Leijonhufvud 1976, p. 83)

Interestingly, in a footnote that follows, Leijonhufvud writes, "Kuhn has been the subject of a bit of a fad in economics (as in other fields)," illustrating—perhaps inadvertently and certainly ironically—another sociological aspect that Kuhn says exists in science.

The message that emerges from this literature reveals admission of the existence of normative, sociological, and "non-ideal" elements contributing to the evolution of economics. This admission, however, does not encompass Kuhn's full-blown catastrophic theory of revolutions.

*The Role of "Normal Science" in Economics.* What is it about economics that has limited the occurrence of major theory upheavals? Paradoxically, more answers may be found in Kuhn's account of normal science than in his account of revolutions. While the majority of Kuhn's economist appraisers were scrambling to determine whether or not revolutions had taken place during the history of economics, a few were noting the more relevant component of *The Structure of Scientific Revolutions*—the treatment of "normal science."

Recall, Kuhn's view is that normal science is the dominant activity for nearly all of any science community's members. Gordon, in his 1965 article, evaluated the role of normal science in his discipline and concluded that Kuhn's description of its activities should strike a familiar chord with economists. Coats, Bronfenbrenner, and even Blaug have followed, admitting (and condoning) to varying degrees, the existence of normal science in economics. For the most part, they agree that an accurate account of the discipline's workings must include aspects that are described as normal science in Kuhn's methodology.

For example, economics has widely recognized, dominant paradigms such as neoclassical micro-theory. Existence of such a standardized orthodoxy permits a uniform teaching agenda across institutions, which, in turn, dictates a tradition of scientific research. This prescribed focus, established during professional training, encourages the discipline's members to perform exhaustive analysis within the accepted framework. "Mopping-up" operations allow established problems to be solved in meticulous detail and with exacting technique. A perusal of leading journals indicates the depth in which narrowly defined questions are able to be studied.

Kuhn argues that a side-effect of practicing constrained normal science is that potentially interesting topics, which lie outside the paradigm's determinate set of puzzles, are given little attention. Such a case can be persuasively made for economics where, currently, certain assumptions and hypotheses (maximizing behavior, rational agents, neoclassical price adjustment, etc.) are not tested and attempts to do so are generally not highly regarded. And, as Kuhn describes, the rigid structure of the discipline's normal state has led to an inability on the part of its members to handle important problems (such as business cycles, the role of the entrepreneur, etc.) that may fall outside the purview of neoclassical economics. These "anomalies," according to Kuhn's theory, have the potential to create instability within the field or, perhaps, to even ignite an abandonment of the faith.

Barry Barnes, applying Kuhn to social science in general, looks at the influence of training on a discipline. He contends that textbook education is, in the sense that it "demands concentration on the component of one tradition to the exclusion of others," indicative of the socio-professionally predetermined "Kuhnian" activity existing in economics (Barnes 1982, p. 19). Barnes is left pondering if the popularity of neoclassicism is based on rational scientific decision-making or on elements that include a sort of religion.

Additionally, the methodological scope of semi-independent sub-fields, largely adhering to identical disciplinary accepted techniques, indicates how far puzzle-solving activities have gone in economics. Alfred Marshall expressed that, in his time, economics was nearly complete and that future activity would consist primarily of useful puzzle-solving—that is, application of the existing model. Support for his prediction can be generated by pointing out that many economists have indeed spent careers finding new applications for (labor economists) or extensions of (economics of the family) the neoclassical paradigm. While these developments can and have been productive, there is a genuine absence of interest in developing entirely new theories and methodological approaches.

Blaug agrees that "most economists are delighted with 'puzzle-solving' activity" (Blaug 1976, p. 173). From a prescriptive perspective, Blaug's judgment is that economists have performed unsatisfactorily because they do not follow methods of falsificationism: "The central weakness in modern economics is in fact the reluctance to produce theories which yield unambiguous refutable implications" (ibid., p. 172). He clearly recognizes the existence of normal science in economics (as Popper admits it in science generally). Implicitly, Blaug wishes economists would change their methods.

Another aspect of "normal science" must also not be disregarded too quickly. Kuhn's version of normal science indicates that disciplinary norms and values evolve out of the common social structure of a particular science community. Thus, sociological factors (such as leaders' political views) or institutional influences (such as the university structure on the publication process) may affect professional practices. Hutchison, for one, cannot dismiss the possibility: "We would hold, for our part, that though economics may not exactly be 'riddled' with fashion and uncontrolled dogmas, and though 'verbalism' may not be precisely 'rampant' in the subject, nevertheless these phenomena are not exactly conspicuous by their absence from economics" (Hutchison 1976, p. 186).

There is, then, some acknowledgment that behavior described by Kuhn as normal science does exist in economics. If there is insight to be derived from Kuhn's methodology, it may well come from his description of normal science rather than from his account of revolutions. What is lacking in economic methodology is a cogent discourse outlining if and how such activity might affect the production of economic ideas. To what extent is the process predetermined by a particular paradigm?[12] Also absent is a structured analysis investigating how sociological variables combine with less normative standards of science to influence theory choices, both at the preliminary stage—during the publication process—or at the secondary and perhaps more complex stage—the path to doctrinal status. Proponents of the Kuhnian methodology suggest that, to understand the history of economic science (which has, in the past, been written largely in positivist terms), one must at least consider new "sociology of knowledge" approaches.

A central idea in the sociology of knowledge approach—that one must go beyond traditional methodological canons to understand the subject of theory choice fully—has been hesitantly acknowledged by economists exposed to Kuhn's ideas. In particular, professional norms and values are important, whether they are established rationally through objective processes of science or other, more subjective and organic influences. This observation is echoed in Caldwell:

> Kuhn proposes that the usual criteria provide a shared objective basis for theory choice, but are criteria which can nonetheless be interpreted differently by individual scientists, who blend together both subjective and objective elements in the process. By positing the scientific community as the primary source of norms and individual scientists as interpreters of those norms, differences between communities and individuals can be rationalized. (Caldwell 1982, p. 226)

And similarly, after considerable criticism concerning the "diluted" message in Kuhn's second edition, Blaug writes:

> What remains [of Kuhn's theory] is the emphasis on the role of normative judgments in scientific controversies, particularly in respect of the choice between competing approaches to science, together with a vaguely formulated but deeply held suspicion of cognitive factors like epistemological rationality, rather than sociological factors like authority, hierarchy, and reference groups, as determinants of scientific behavior. (Blaug 1980, p. 32)[13]

Finally, it must be noted that research into applications of the Kuhnian methodology softly hit a dead end. The directions Kuhn outlined, at least for understanding theory choice, are very general. Furthermore, the prospect of trying to uncover norms and practices of scientific communities is a daunting task, and potential investigators seemed hesitant to venture off into complex sociological studies. Not to mention, economists assume rationality for their subjects; how would it look to admit extra-rational considerations in their own professional practices. Also, Kuhn's relative emphasis on revolutions—which, by most accounts, have not frequently occurred in economics—led some investigators to abandon, perhaps prematurely, the whole message of *The Structure of Scientific Revolutions*. These factors precipitated the move toward a more pliable methodology, that of Imre Lakatos.

*Imre Lakatos and Economics*

With the publication of Lakatos's *Methodology of Scientific Research Programmes* (1978), economists were given another alternative to Friedman's "methodological instrumentalism," which emphasizes predictive accuracy in theory appraisal. A philosophically oriented group of methodologists adopted Lakatos's concern with demarcation and subsequently attempted to determine whether or not economics meets the criteria of "science" set out in *The Methodology of Scientific Research Programmes*.[14] The primary contributions to this literature are Blaug's *The Methodology of Economics* (1980), Latsis's *Method and Appraisal in Economics* (1976), and articles by Alexander Rosenberg (1986) and E. Roy Weintraub (1985).

The issue that methodologists have addressed in this line of research is not wholly comparable to the theory choice question, as it has been delimited here. Instead, the dominant concern among Lakatos's economist advocates has been with appraising their discipline in a *general* way. However, an implicit assumption in Lakatos is that, just as a program can be judged, so too can its components.[15] A second motivation among economists using the methodology of scientific research programs has been to describe the history of economic theory. This section provides an assessment of the extent to which economists, employing Lakatos as a descriptive historical apparatus or as a tool of appraisal, have shed light on the theory choice question.

To begin, it must be pointed out that Lakatos, like Kuhn, was not writing initially for economists. His methodology is conducted against a Newtonian physics backdrop, and as Coats points out, "There is no precisely comparable paradigm or exemplar in economics" (1976, p. 59). The result is that additional difficulties are encountered when attempting to apply Lakatos's schema to economics. Particularly, judging whether a "program" is degenerating, static, or progressive is extremely problematic. Again, a central component of this problem is that quantitative empirical work has a less direct bearing on appraisal of theories in economics than it does in physics.

First, let us consider the accuracy of Lakatos's categorical description of scientific research programs as applied to the structure of economics. Subsequently, our attention will turn to Lakatos's method of appraisal— distinguishing between theoretically (and empirically) progressive and degenerating programs—and its relevance to economics.

*The Structure of Research Programs and Economics.* Recall that the unit of appraisal in the Lakatosian approach is the research program, a cluster of interrelated theories. A research program contains a hard core, accepted by the "methodological decision of its protagonists," which directs a positive and a negative heuristic outlining proper and improper avenues of research. The program also contains a protective belt in which hypotheses are tested and challenged.[16] One question worth raising here is, can the formal economics literature be accurately categorized according to this descriptive device? E. Roy Weintraub's *General Equilibrium Analysis: Studies in Appraisal* (1985) provides a thorough application of the methodology of scientific research programs to an economic program. As the title indicates, Weintraub casts general equilibrium theory in Lakatosian terms, identifying its hard core, protective belt, positive and negative heuristics, and so on. He then provides a "rational reconstruction" of the program's historical development, and finds it to be a theoretically (but not empirically) progressive program.

Weintraub contends that the hard core of the neo-Walrasian program, the dominant program in microeconomics, hardened during the 1950s: "The sequence beginning with the [Karl] Schlesinger paper and continuing through those of [Abraham] Wald, [John] von Neumann, [Trilling] Koopmans, [Kenneth] Arrow, [Gerard] Debreu, and [Lionel] McKenzie should be recognized as a hardening of the hard core of the neoclassical research program." It was by this time that the "program was . . . no longer problematic" (Weintraub 1985, p. 112). It should be noted that Lakatos, himself, writes very little about this hardening process; he only recognizes, in a footnote, that hard cores do not "emerge fully armed like Athene from the head of Zeus" (Lakatos 1970, p. 48). Unfortunately, not all economists agree with Weintraub's assessment of when the neoclassical program matured.[17] Alexander Rosenberg writes, "Others . . . date the current research program in economics from 1874, when Walras's *Principles of Pure Economy* was published, instead of 1953" (Rosenberg 1986, pp. 134–35). Friedman writes that key parts of economic theory—like price theory—were fundamentally sound and well confirmed, having nearly reached their present form in Marshall's *Principles of Economics* (ibid., p. 133). Blaug's view is that "the Walrasian program [failed] to make much progress until [Sir John] Hick's *Value and Capital* (1939) and Samuelson's *Foundations* (1947) provided it with a new 'positive heuristic' " (Blaug 1976, p. 167).

This disagreement over when economics, or parts of economics, matured (became a science in the Lakatosian sense) is indicative of the difficulties in applying Lakatos's concept of the hard core to economics. It is difficult to even argue effectively that hard cores exist—in the form that Lakatos intended—in our field. In fact, it may be equally valid to propose that economic theory lies within an entity more closely described by the "protective belt."

A hard core, as specified in *The Methodology of Scientific Research Programmes,* must contain a body of material (fundamental laws, relationships, assumptions) that is treated as *irrefutable* by individuals associated with the program. Among members of the economics profession, many do not even think of hypotheses in terms of refutability, or even verifiability, criteria. Additionally, fundamental tenets in economics (rationality, maximizing behavior) are far more vulnerable to criticism than are those for, say, physics (gravity). In physics the "core" is constructed of "immutable laws," and in economics of debatable assumptions. Likewise, in mathematics, certain properties are truly outside the realm of controversy for all but the most philosophically minded.

Further, as pointed out above, economists do not agree upon when a hard core came into existence in economics. This in itself can be interpreted as a violation of existence criteria because a hard core, by definition, is a body of knowledge that is professionally accepted—agreed upon by fiat. Let us refer again, for a moment, to Weintraub's application. Included in his list of "hard-core propositions" for the neo-Walrasian program are the following:

HC3:   Agents independently optimize subject to constraints.
HC5:   Agents have full and relevant knowledge.

HC6: Observable economic outcomes are coordinated, so they must be discussed with reference to equilibrium states.

It is inaccurate to suggest that these *assumptions* underlying price theory are analagous to, say, the basic laws of planetary motion in astronomy. Also, it is dubious whether economists judged the validity of these hard-core propositions distinctly differently after 1953 (the time when the hard core supposedly hardened).

Assigning a hard core to the general equilibrium program essentially means only this—that mathematical models of interrelated markets require the imposition of these restrictions in order for them to be tractable (to solve problems associated with negative price results, consistency, etc.). Existence of a common starting point for a group of individuals engaged in a similar endeavor does not, in itself, validate or invalidate their work. Astrologists, for example, attempting to maintain a certain system, seem to have agreed upon a set of preliminary assumptions:

HC1: Horoscopes shall follow the solar calendar.
HC2: Horoscopes shall give predictions to individuals based on their birth dates.
HC3: These predictions should be as general as possible, etc.

One may legitimately conclude that categorizing economic theory, in and of itself, does little to advance an understanding of how economic theory has evolved over its history. Before getting too mired in matters of linguistics and classification, however, let us exit with a final remark, then move on to the more important matter of appraisal. Methodologists have demonstrated that it is possible, if not dubious, to phrase the discipline's history in Lakatosian (or Kuhnian) terminology. If using these terms (whether hard core, paradigm, or whatever) as organizational or heuristic devices facilitates research into how economic science works, then a contribution has been made. However, it is counter-productive to allow these taxonomic frameworks to stand as substitutes for substantive explanations of complex methodological questions.

*Lakatosian Appraisal and Economics.* The purpose of this section is to review Lakatosian appraisals of economics. In order to do so, the term "appraisal" needs to be clarified, as it has been used in at least three distinct ways. First, one may consider appraisal of an entire program. A "program," depending on how the Lakatosian term is to be interpreted, may consist of a fairly broad range of theories (microeconomics), a less broad range (neoclassical microeconomics), or an even narrower range (consumer theory). At this level of appraisal, methodologists and philosophers seek to demarcate science from non-science, to make a judgment on how a body of research is progressing. Certainly this type of appraisal is central in *The Methodology of Scientific Research Programmes* (and in Weintraub's application of it to general equilibrium theory).

A second type of appraisal is performed from a historical perspective. Historians of most any subject, regardless of discipline, must appraise which theories and theorists, art works and artists, symphonies and composers are important in the overall development of their field. For example, when Schumpeter had to decide what material to include in his *History of Economic Analysis,* he necessarily made value judgments concerning the comparative importance of various work. Lakatos, in his "rational reconstruction" methodology, is also interested in this type of appraisal.

A third type of appraisal has to do with the practical workings of a discipline. A contemporary, working perspective type of appraisal must continually occur in order to keep a discipline operating. This type of appraisal involves theorists and practitioners who may claim no particular interest in methodology or philosophy of science. Included here are all the instances where individuals, departments, professional groups, and so on must judge their colleagues' works. Journal editors and referees appraise articles for publication; academic departments appraise job and tenure candidates, in part on their literary contributions; and together a discipline's members, by some perhaps ambiguous process, dictate what future theory will look like in their profession. Lakatos's methodology does not address this type of appraisal as clearly. His work appears more directed at the first type of appraisal, carried out by methodologists, rather than the third type of appraisal, engaged in by working members of an academic community. This third category of appraisal is, however, intimately related to what has been specified here as the theory choice issue. Each of these three types of appraisal will be considered below.

Several attempts have been made to identify economic theory, or a part thereof, as a progressive or degenerating program. These attempts apply the Lakatosian method in order to appraise how far the discipline has gone toward achieving "scientific status," the standard of which is Newton's theory of gravity—which Lakatos regards as "probably the most successful research program ever." Although these efforts have not been terribly convincing,[18] they have nonetheless reiterated commonly perceived accomplishments and shortcomings of the economic method. Also, this literature has provided an approach for reconstructing the "rational" elements of science—to whatever extent they exist.

The initial task in this type of research has been to identify an area of economics as a scientific research program. Next, the investigator sets out to determine whether or not the program is "theoretically progressive"— that is, if it contains "excess empirical content" compared to previous programs and if it predicts "novel, and hitherto, unexpected fact[s]." Additionally the program is judged "empirically progressive" if this "excess empirical content is corroborated" (Lakatos 1970, p. 118). It follows, then, that a degenerating program is not considered scientific. However, an unscientific program may become progressive at some point, and Lakatos finds it reasonable that an individual may stick with a degenerating program for a time, particularly in the case of a "budding research program."

Latsis (1976) undertook the first appraisal of economics using the methodology of scientific research programs. He identifies the neoclassical theory of the firm as a research program. The neoclassical hard core (which is shared by both perfect and monopolistic competition) consists of assumptions: "(i) profit-maximization, (ii) independence of decisions, and (iii) complete and relevant knowledge." Additional "situational assumptions" are included in the protective belt: product homogeneity, large numbers of sellers, and free entry and exit (Latsis 1972, p. 212).[19] Proceeding along Lakatosian lines, Latsis finds the program, which is dominated by "situational determinism," to have been degenerating since Marshall. He argues, "After its initial progress in the theory of perfect competition, [the neoclassical program] was extended into fields in which it failed" (Latsis 1976, p. 30). In particular, Edward Chamberlin's theory of monopolistic competition failed on testability criteria and consequently performed even worse than perfect competition as a qualitative predictor of economic variables.

The underlying premise in Latsis's article is that a modified version of Lakatos's methodology is a useful tool in economics for appraisals of the first type. In the case of neoclassical theory of the firm, it can be used to demonstrate the degenerating nature of the program. Thus, Latsis uses the framework to criticize economic theory. However, the scope of Latsis's investigation is limited to only the first, and possibly the second, type of appraisal discussed above.[20] In other words, Latsis can assert only that, from a methodologist's standpoint, the neoclassical research program may be judged unscientific by the Lakatosian definition.

Latsis cannot, and probably would not wish to, suggest that this type of assessment is what has led to the actual reception of theories in economics, which involves the third type of appraisal. Latsis writes, "Chamberlin himself was quite uninterested in the derivation of testable predictions" (Latsis 1976, p. 28). It seems unlikely that a Lakatosian assessment of theoretical and empirical progressiveness is what motivated Samuelson to call monopolistic competition "the best current model of price theory." Similarly, Robert Bishop wrote, "As I judge the consensus of economists, Chamberlin's *Theory of Monopolistic Competition* and Mrs. Robinson's *Economics of Imperfect Competition* are acknowledged to have touched off, in 1933, a theoretical revolution whose relative importance in the micro-economic area was comparable to that of the Keynesian analysis in macroeconomics" (ibid., p. 30). There is no reason to conclude that Bishop's criteria for "importance" is the same as, or even similar to, appraisal criteria established in *The Methodology of Scientific Research Programmes*. Nonetheless, enthusiasm of the sort expressed by Samuelson and Bishop propelled the theory of monopolistic competition into the textbooks—a sure sign of consensus—where it continues to exist today.

Here we have a program that, by reasonable account (the first type of appraisal), fails to meet Lakatosian standards of science. It has testability problems, is not internally consistent, does not yield precise predictions, and yet was accepted by the profession. The Lakatosian methodology is pliable, however, and can be manipulated to defend degenerating programs by philosophers, historians, or practitioners (corresponding to the three types of appraisers). For example, a Lakatosian may justify his commitment to the neoclassical theory of the firm on the grounds that it is a "budding program" and may therefore be evaluated leniently. If the program had been judged progressive, then it could naturally be defended. Because any outcome can be explained by the methodology of scientific research programs it, in effect, explains nothing at all. The demarcation between scientific and unscientific activity is unclear; it is as Paul Feyerabend describes (and everybody quotes), nothing but concealed anarchism, or anything goes.

Rosenberg, debating Weintraub, argues that the Lakatosian approach is "of little use ... in the 'appraisal' of economic theory (and) the assessment of its scientific status and achievement." His view is that "appraisal is a much more difficult, much less abstract undertaking than has widely been assumed" (Rosenberg 1986, p. 138). Of course, part of this disagreement stems from unclear delineation of what type of appraisal is being pursued.

Even methodologists who are enthusiastic about the methodology of scientific research programs do not seem fully convinced of its merits. Weintraub, by narrowly defining the dominant research program in economics—limiting it to post-1950 neo-Walrasian literature—is able to muster a positive judgment for the work that at least some economists perform. He considers the hard core of this program to be *theoretically* progressive. However, Weintraub admits that theories that he classifies in the protective belt (demand, human capital, etc.) have not proven to be *empirically* progressive. Thus, readers may conclude that Weintraub has found the Lakatosian framework useful in rendering a type (1) appraisal of neo-Walrasian economics; it is scientific because its program is theoretically progressive, but perhaps not as scientific as a program that has been shown to be both theoretically progressive in its hard core *and* empirically progressive in its protective belt.

Weintraub is aware of the Lakatosian program's limitations and his acceptance of it as a tool of appraisal is qualified accordingly. He writes that such appraisals "leave out much that can facilitate an understanding of . . . scientific history. . . . There is no doubt that a full understanding of a line of work in economics requires a relevant social history . . . [and] the Lakatosian approach to the appraisal of work in economics is a starting place, not a final destination" (Weintraub 1985, pp. 111–12).

Blaug is also an admirer of *The Methodology of Scientific Research Programmes,* and particularly of the idea that "scientists [which we presume he means to include economists] are rational and accept or reject ideas for good intellectual reasons." He uses Lakatos's classification system to describe the structure of economics in both his article, "Paradigms Versus Research Programs," and in his methodology book. And, as further evidence of his approval, Blaug concludes that "a Lakatosian 'rational reconstruction' would suffice to explain virtually all past successes and failures of economic research programmes" (1976, p. 177). However, his readers may be taken aback by this conclusion because, while expressing some "tentative misgivings," Blaug actually builds quite a damaging case against applying the methodology to economics.

Blaug argues that what economists do does not exhibit many characteristics of the Lakatosian methodology:

> The central weakness of modern economics is in fact the reluctance to produce theories which yield unambiguously refutable implications. . . . When in the long process of refining and extending the neoclassical research programme over the last hundred years, have we ever worried about "excess empirical content," much less corroborated excess empirical content? (1976, p. 172)

And, showing that his true allegiance is with a Popperian philosophy of science (producing falsifiable *theories*) and not a Lakatosian one (choosing progressive *programs*), Blaug critically writes:

> Much empirical work in economics is like "playing tennis with the net down": instead of attempting to refute testable predictions, economists spend much of their time showing that the real world bears out their predictions, thus replacing falsificationism, which is difficult, with confirmation, which is easy. (Ibid., p. 173)

And finally, Blaug offers:

> The upshot of this long harangue is to suggest that *MSRP* [*The Methodology of Scientific Research Programmes*] may not fit the history of economics: economics may cling to "degenerating" research programmes in the presence of rival "progressive" research programmes while denying that the "degenerating" programme is in need of resuscitation because they are suspicious of hard data, inclined to assign low priority to the discovery of novel facts, accustomed by long habit to deny feedback of evidence on theory, or simply because they are deeply attached to the welfare implications of their theories. (Ibid., p. 176)

Thus, we have what Hutchison calls "Blaug I" who believes in the methodology of scientific research programs combined with falsificationism as the correct prescription for scientific behavior and in rational reconstruction as the proper method for recounting the history of economic thought. We also have "Blaug II" who questions whether economists choose or even try to choose research programs that are theoretically and empirically expanding. To reconcile Blaug's views, one must conclude that he condones using Lakatos's methodology as a tool of appraisal by philosophers while fully knowing that it does not describe the processes whereby economic science actually proceeds.

Similarly, Hutchison writes that rational reconstruction is a fine ideal, but finds that most of what economists have determined to be important in their intellectual history would not qualify for study under the rules of rational reconstruction. He concludes that Blaug I is overly optimistic and that rational reconstruction is not particularly useful in studying the history of economic thought (Hutchison 1978, pp. 296–97).

### Toward an Assessment of Scientific Research Programs

Finally, we must ask, why has Lakatos's methodology been so difficult to apply convincingly to the history of economic thought? The explanation offered here contains two distinct parts. First, economists have run into general philosophy of science problems (as outlined in Chapter 1) before even getting to the history of their own discipline. As Rosenberg points out, "the notion of 'empirical content' of 'novel fact,' of 'corroboration' are among the most vexing in philosophy of science" (Rosenberg 1986, p. 135). No ideal observers exist who can judge the progressiveness of a program. Not unlike the form of verificationism developed by the Vienna Circle philosophers, the methodology breaks down to subjective processes that are still not understood or even frequently addressed. And, even if measuring the "degree of corroboration" or "extent of progressiveness" were not logically problematic, it would remain difficult in practice. The dearth of decisive tests in economics challenges the creativity of methodologists who hope to explain theory transitions in terms of increasing versus decreasing empirical content.

Also, ambiguity concerning the time frame in which programs are judged has created problems in Lakatosian appraisals of economics. According to the methodology of scientific research programs, appraisal takes time, but no one is sure quite how much. Budding research programs must be treated leniently, but no one knows what defines a budding research program and exactly how leniently they should be treated. Hutchison has written that economics produces a high proportion of conjectures to refutations, which has extended the life of its programs. We are still left asking, however, what dictates shorter-run decisions such as those that must be made during the publication process?

Second, the form of appraisal that Lakatos's framework is equipped to execute is typically carried out by philosophers of science and historians (the first and second type of appraisal). These evaluative processes take place post facto—that is, after literature has emerged in a discipline. Weintraub's assessment of neo-Walrasian economics is a case in point. Such studies may ask, is program *A* progressive, or is it scientific, or was it important in the overall development of the discipline?

When methodologists, drawing from this perspective, debate the value or success of scientific theories, they conduct appraisals using a modern set of criteria. Studies of this sort have typically not asked, why was theory *A* accepted *initially*? Or, why did practitioners from a particular period judge theory *A* superior to theory *B*? The type of appraisal (3) that produces these decisions is a completely distinct activity from that which is carried on later by philosophers of science. To put it another way, a methodologist can use a particular framework to appraise a theory, program, or paradigm. He may attempt to distinguish good science from bad science based on his own perception of the relevant criteria. However, to assume that assessment by actual practitioners was based on the same criteria as that established later by philosophers is an obvious error.

As an example, let us again use the theory of monopolistic competition: A methodologist (perhaps Latsis) may pass a negative judgment on an economic theory because it is empirically degenerating. However, a practitioner may have liked the very same theory, either because he interpreted the same criteria differently or because he had an entirely different method of appraisal from the start. This is essentially why one particular vision of how science should work is inadequate when studying how theories are incorporated into a discipline's formal doctrine.

What Lakatos has done is to point out and provide structure for *some* of the variables that may have influenced past and current theory choice. Perhaps science should work to fulfill, as far as it is possible, Lakatos's vision of "rational science." However, to conclude that a rational reconstruction of economics explains theory choice is idealistic and simplistic. Most efforts that seek to explain the appraisal process with a limited set of factors are ideology laden and highly susceptible to critical scrutiny. At one point, Blaug appears to fall into the trap. He writes:

> To be convincing, the externalist thesis in the history of ideas must produce instances of (i) internally consistent, well corroborated, fruitful and powerful scientific ideas which were rejected at specific dates in the history of a science because of specific external factors [meaning any factors besides Lakatos's rational ones], or (ii) incoherent, poorly corroborated, weak scientific ideas which were in fact accepted for specific external reasons. (Blaug 1976, p. 177)

Blaug, at best, provides logic for not limiting historical accounts to *only* externalist criteria. It would be no different to insist that strict internalists, in order to validate their view, must produce instances where a theory that is consistent with professional norms, uses accepted techniques, and is produced by a respected member of the discipline working from a leading institution is rejected because it is not empirically or theoretically progressive, or a theory that does not utilize accepted disciplinary methods, written by an unknown from outside of the profession, is accepted because it is empirically progressive.

Such demands (Blaug's or the externalists') oversimplify and blur the real issues. By Blaug's own admission, it is a difficult task just to produce an empirically well-corroborated, fruitful, and powerful scientific idea in economics. One only needs to find instances where evidence points to both internalist and externalist variables to dispel myths that one or the other explains all. A more interesting question for economic methodologists is, why is one partially internally consistent, not-so-well-corroborated scientific idea accepted over another, similarly qualified one? When faced with this type of puzzle, rational reconstructionists would do well not to dismiss, in total, externalist explanations. Likewise, externalists must not overlook, and, in fact, should probably begin with, appraisal variables labeled "rational."

### Notes

1. Keynes, in creating *The General Theory,* may have been similarly influenced by Einstein's relativity principle (see Galbraith and Darity 1994, pp. 11–16).

2. Two plus two has equaled four since the beginning of time; gravity has "always" been present; however, the capitalist system has certainly not been the dominant economic structure in all places and times.

3. This acknowledgment was expressed most influentially in Milton Friedman's instrumentalist version, discussed later.

4. We reveal a measure of confidence in predicted results every time we cross the Golden Gate Bridge or travel to the observation deck on the 103rd floor of the Empire State Building. If predictions about physical relationships were no more reliable than those in economics, problems of excessive traffic crossing San Francisco's famous bridge and long lines waiting to view Manhattan from 1,250 feet above the streets would cease to exist.

5. Incidentally, this is more or less the theme of J.K. Galbraith's *Economics in Perspective.*

6. The direct effect of ideology on theory choice is examined in Chapters 4 and 5.

7. Readers should refer to Caldwell (1982) or Blaug (1980) for accounts of how positivism rose to prominence in economics.

8. See Mirowski (1989).

9. See Blaug (1976), pp. 172–73, or Hutchison (1976), pp. 202–3, for two of many such acknowledgments.

10. See Benjamin Ward's *What's Wrong with Economics* (1972) on this score.

11. I find this line of reasoning a little perplexing. Gordon's and Coats's point, I suppose, is that economics is close enough to physics to justify our using philosophy of science theories originally written for it. However, if I were promoting Kuhn's theory as an explanation of economic methodology, I would stress the *differences* between the two sciences because, as I have asserted above, those differences can be interpreted as taking economics further from the traditional positivist view and toward a more subjective, sociological—or Kuhnian—view.

12. Here paradigm is being used in its broadest sense, encompassing not only basic assumption of economic models, but also acceptance of an entire methodological approach.

13. In context, the reader will see that Blaug is not necessarily advocating Kuhn's approach as a useful way of learning about theory choice. His own particular view, articulated most clearly in Blaug (1980), more or less adheres to Popper's prescriptions.

14. Alexander Rosenberg considers "the economist's fixation with Lakatos (at least, the idea that science can be distinguished from non-science) philosophically dated" because philosophers abandoned the search for objective criteria of science by the late 1960s (Rosenberg 1986, p. 136). Economists have tried to appraise economics using a Lakatosian approach nonetheless.

15. Refer back to Chapter 1 for a review of Lakatos—particularly logical and philosophical problems associated with using his methodology of scientific research programs for theory appraisal.

16. Again, see Chapter 1 for a full description.

17. This is undoubtedly due, in part, to the fact that there is no formal agreement that the neo-Walrasian program—as defined by Weintraub—should substantively dominate microeconomics.

18. Indeed, the intention of some methodologists has been to demonstrate that the methodology of scientific research programs does *not* apply to economics.

19. Latsis notes that the reasoning in the above assumptions goes back to Smith—a view of the neoclassical program that certainly differs from that of Weintraub.

20. Even in this limited sense, there are problems—as pointed out by Blaug (1976).

# CHAPTER 3

# Rationale for a Broader Interpretation

## Introduction

This chapter contains final arguments appealing for a less abstracted interpretation of theory choice than that which has traditionally prevailed in formal economic literature. Discussion above reveals that a number of economic methodologists have been willing to investigate their discipline's workings by employing relatively recent vintage philosophies of science— particularly Lakatos's methodology of scientific research programs and Kuhn's structure of scientific revolutions. It has also been shown that these approaches, when applied to economics, have not yielded impressive results in the sense that they do not clearly increase the accuracy of historical research or decipher an underlying logic to the development of economic theory. Indeed, application of these philosophies has, by almost all accounts, raised more questions than it has answered.

The task laid out in this book is to uncover and assess the relative importance of criteria that influence research appraisal and theory choice in economics. In this and previous chapters, the idea being developed is that adequate explanation of this discipline-specific process necessitates a broadening of traditional philosophy of science. Recently, several influential names in economics have offered untraditional interpretations of "how economic science works." Much of this work emphasizes the theory development stage more than the theory reception stage, but this distinction is not always clearly drawn.

A short list of the relevant literature includes Neil de Marchi's and Mark Blaug's *Appraising Economic Theories* (1991), D. McCloskey's *Rhetoric of Economics* (1985), Harry Johnson's *On Economics and Society* (1975), and Phillip Mirowski's *More Heat than Light* (1989). These authors seek to explain the development of economic theory or the activity of economists more realistically than has previously been done; all seek to avoid the confining elements of non–discipline-specific philosophies of science. We draw from these references, briefly described below, to close our case that orthodox economic methodology fails to generate an adequate understanding of theory appraisal and selection, and to establish a starting point for the alternative explanation developed in the next chapters.

*Appraising Economic Theories: Studies in the Methodology of Research Programs* is a collection of essays that was projected by its editors to legitimize Lakatosian appraisal of economic theory. However, the theme that emerged instead challenges the premise that a particular philosophy of science can simply be applied, without major modification, to produce a convincing account of the history and methods of economics. Contributors to the collection, most of whom were willing at one point or another in their careers to give the Kuhnian or Lakatosian methodologies a try, echo the sentiment that single philosophies (whether positivist, Popperian, or Lakatosian) fail to capture the diverse scholarly activity, including theory selection, which propels a discipline.

McCloskey's *Rhetoric of Economics* is an attempt to dispel the myth that "modernism" is the operative methodology in economics. Borrowing from established rhetoric theory, he emphasizes the importance of factors (which include aspects of professional communication, the structure of persuasive discourse, and the language of presentation) which are not accounted for in philosophy of science explanations such as positivism. By choice, McCloskey avoids the vexing (and, he would argue, unproductive) debate over what constitutes good science and confronts economics as it is actually practiced.

Harry Johnson, in his famous book *On Economics and Society,* asserts that certain characteristics of a new theory or idea may influence its potential success. He uses the proliferation of Keynes's *General Theory* to illustrate that, among other factors, a work's method of presentation and its degree of difficulty affect the extent to which it will mesh with the prevailing intellectual and sociological environment and, in turn, be assimilated by the profession. In the process, Johnson acknowledges a decidedly non-positivist hue to the events he describes.

Mirowski's *More Heat than Light: Economics as Social Physics, Physics as Nature's Economics* explores the calculating way in which economists adopted the energy metaphor from mid-nineteenth-century physics. In so doing, he seeks to discredit the idea that economists acted out of a positivist motivation to increase testability, empirical content, or "truth" and replaces it with a picture of theorists attempting to legitimize their discipline by creating a more "scientific" facade.

The goal here is to coordinate this literature, which generally does not explicitly isolate the theory choice process, and construct a more systematic account identifying potential theory choice influences. To achieve this end credibly, however, we must first examine what motivates this and other efforts to step beyond positivism, beyond Karl Popper, and beyond Imre Lakatos.

## Critical Response to Lakatos

The recent move to escape beyond limiting philosophy of science explanations of how economics works finds its impetus in the applied Lakatosian literature. Increasingly, the assertion is made that it would prove more useful to expand our understanding of how a discipline actually works rather than to force it into some specific, "proper" methodology.

Nowhere does this theme emerge more forcefully than in the set of essays collected in *Appraising Economic Theories*.[1] What makes the volume's message convincing is not as much the originality or assertiveness of the contributors' arguments as it is the context wherein that message is delivered. *Appraising Economic Theories* is the product of the Capri Conference, which was held in 1989 "to promote the writing of further case studies in the application of Lakatos's *MSRP* [*Methodology of Scientific Research Programmes*] particularly to such intractable fields as game theory, and Sraffian economics" (p. 499). Participants, which included mainly economists, but also physicists, philosophers of science, and sociologists of science, were asked to apply the Lakatosian analysis to various periods of development in the history of economics.

However, the majority of the contributors were unable to take their assignments at face value because, during the course of completion, they developed serious reservations about how useful such studies would be. The result, more often than not, is that the discourse does not simply apply Lakatosian method; rather it challenges the assertion that it *can* be usefully applied. In the afterword to the volume, Blaug assesses the results:

> No one could possibly have predicted how the mixture of people collected at Capri would react to our instructions but I was personally taken aback by what can only be described as a generally dismissive, if not hostile, reaction to Lakatos's *MSRP*. Of the thirty-seven participants, I estimate that only twelve were willing to give Lakatos a further run for his money and of the seventeen papers delivered at the conference not more than five were unambiguously positive about the value of *MSRP*. (p. 500)

In the volume's introduction, de Marchi specifies that the conference was organized because "we wanted to know whether *MSRP*, in the hands of methodologists and especially historians of economics, had shown itself to be an appropriate framework for analyzing what economics is and is not like" (p. 1). Ian Steedman, for example, delivers appraisal of the "Sraffian Research Program" as his contribution toward assessing "the usefulness of the ideas of Imre Lakatos to our understanding of recent developments in economics" (p. 435).

Unfortunately the project was severely biased from the start, undoubtedly due to the editors' previously established and enthusiastic positions on the potential of the Lakatosian methodology. As evidence of this lack of neutrality, Steedman quotes his instructions, which indicate that ideally, his "evaluation of Sraffian economics should employ the Lakatosian apparatus, amending it along the way if necessary" (ibid.). Mirowski, in his comment to Weintraub's "Stabilizing Dynamics" (1991), opines that "the conferees desire a further vindication of the Lakatosian organon" (p. 291).

Steedman's article exposes another problem with the Capri project. As directed, he attempts to appraise Sraffian economics using the methodology of scientific research programs. However, he also feels compelled to appraise the Lakatosian method itself using Sraffian economics as a case study: "Section 3 will present a discussion of what light the Lakatosian methodology and the Sraffian contribution can throw upon each other" (p. 436). It should be quite evident that the "proof" cannot logically run both ways. What we are left with is a picture of the conferees scrambling about searching for cases that provide a "suitable testing ground for Lakatos's *MSRP*" (p. 266).

At any rate, the decisive judgment projected from the conference was that Lakatos's methodology fails in an array of areas as a tool of appraisal. Further, the initial pro-Lakatosian environment that underlay the conference makes this failure even more striking. This volume demonstrates that scholars (historians and methodologists) are not satisfied with the methodology of scientific research programs, even as a means for evaluating scientific progress from a purely philosophical perspective. It leaves the notion that practicing economists have historically employed Lakatosian criteria as a means of choosing among alternative explanations almost an absurdity.

We may then ask, what is the source of dissatisfaction among these historians of economic thought who have evidently given ample thought to methodological issues? In which ways have inquiries inspired from philosophy of science failed to capture the workings of economics? These questions were partially answered in Chapter 2, at which point specific criticisms regarding particular philosophy of science explanations were developed.[2] To these arguments, additional criticisms may be added to form a comprehensive appeal aimed at broadening the methodological study of economics.

**Summary of Philosophy of Science Shortcomings**

As it has been applied to economics, philosophy of science can be generally criticized on the basis of arguments that fall roughly into one of five interrelated categories:

1. The function of philosophy of science is mis-specified.
2. Prescriptive methodology does not generate historically accurate accounts.
3. Philosophy of science explanations do not characterize the underlying theory structure in economics.
4. Philosophy of science exaggerates the role of empirical appraisal in the development of economic theory.
5. Economists preach packaged methodology but do not practice it.

Before synthesizing an alternative, which is the task laid out in Chapters 4 and 5, each of these criticisms requires clarification.

*Category 1.* There appears to be a growing mistrust in the idea that one role of the philosophy of science is to dictate the methods of actual practice in science. The charge has been levied that philosophy of science should reorient its objectives so that less emphasis is placed on prescribing objective guidelines for successful science.

From this perspective, the subject–observer relationship defines the roles of the scientist and the philosopher of science. The philosopher of science (or historian of science) studies the practicing scientist who maintains his own objectives. The scientist's activities are not typically motivated out of a desire to satisfy the philosopher. Just as a consumer does not necessarily base his actions on an economic theory, a scientist does not typically base his on a particular philosophy of science theory.[3]

The implication is not that traditional methodological studies are useless; critical appraisal may indeed lend insight into validity of method. At debate are questions surrounding the appropriate *function* of philosophers and historians concerned with the development of science. Christopher Gilbert writes:

> There is a danger that in discussing methodology one starts with a view of the way scientific activity is or should be carried out and then looks for examples which illustrate this view. An alternative, empiricist, approach is to start from the science and work back to the methodology. Doing this I am impressed by the diversity of our methodological approaches. (p. 137)

Gilbert supports his observation by comparing methods used in demand analysis with those of consumer theory. He concludes, "Examination of these two closely related areas of the discipline suggests that any account of economic methodology that attempts to embrace both will be too general to be useful. . . . Methodologies are to a large extent implicitly defined by the questions being addressed" (p. 159).

Steedman agrees that applying Lakatos's rational reconstruction to the history of economic thought is essentially a misappropriation of philosophy of science. After reflecting on the history of Sraffian economic thought in Lakatosian terms, he confesses his inability to derive any valuable insights using the methodology of scientific research programs that he could not have otherwise arrived at. Further, he explains that his topic could "readily be displayed in Lakatosian style," but that the lesson was essentially misconceived because, among other reasons, it added nothing to the content of the analysis. He appeals instead to Stefano Zamagni's warnings that "each science may need its proper (different) methodology, that methodology follows science rather than leads it, and that it is indeed undesirable that methodologists be permitted to prescribe what is good procedure in science" (p. 447).

Greater acceptance of this natural subject–observer relationship between philosophy of science and science would, perhaps, motivate more efforts aimed at analyzing and critiquing actual science. By abandoning the search for the illusive system of "best method," along with the idea that philosophy of science will ever dictate scientific procedure, methodologists might appear less presumptuous and, perhaps, increase their own influence among scientists.

*Category 2.* The second general criticism of reconstructing economic history according to the guidelines of a particular philosophy of science is that such an approach does not (and does not always claim to) produce accurate accounts. Again, the Lakatosian system, which characterizes scientists continually searching for progressivity within their program, attracts considerable criticism. In appraising new classical macroeconomics (rational expectations), Kevin Hoover argues, "Lakatos's approach does not capture the essential features of scientific progress" (p. 365). He argues instead that Kuhn's explanation of science provides more hints as to how new classical macroeconomics developed. Hoover is, among the Capri participants, with the majority in expressing a desire to explain how economics has historically proceeded in a more detailed and accurate way than can be constructed from a "prepackaged method."

Even Blaug, who has in the past (1980) sought to examine history using rational reconstruction, now (1991), more explicitly than ever, professes the inadequacies of the Lakatosian program. Blaug maintains some confidence by clearly identifying the differences between historical and philosophical methodology. In this way, he preserves the normative position that scientific research programs "should be appraised in terms of excess empirical content," alongside the apparent reality that, because "modern economists preach the methodology of falsificationism but rarely practice it," the methodology of historiographical research programs "is largely false" (p. 503). Thus, Blaug only disagrees strongly with the anti-philosophy of science writers (like McCloskey, Mirowski, and many of the contributors to *Appraising Economic Theories*) on half of the issue. Their views on what the discipline's members should be doing to improve their theories diverge (as will be shown later in this chapter); however, admission that a wide variety of factors influence what actually transpires in the profession is common.

To convincingly argue our case—that is, to explain why a particular theory, model, or idea is appraised favorably and hence selected by a profession to represent its beliefs—the above-noted individuals would all prescribe a broader approach than that offered by conventional philosophy of science. For example, if our goal is to account for "the unprecedented speed with which Keynes conquered the minds of his fellow economists," even Blaug admits we would have to turn to a more historical approach—a "methodology of historical research programs"—which, unlike the methodology of scientific research programs, is not limited to a normative impression of what science ought to be like (p. 504).

*Category 3.* An inadequate capacity to describe the structure and empirical potential of theories in economics underlies this inaccurate historical interpretation. One structural problem—program (or paradigm) identification—arises when methodologists attempt to place economic literature into a particular framework. By Kuhn's initial account (1962), a single, dominant paradigm operates incompatibly with other (previously dominant or rising) paradigms. Lakatos's theory presents scientists attaching themselves to a single progressive research program. It is difficult to explain the existence of interdependent or overlapping areas of research and stay within these visions of scientific behavior.

Rodney Maddock finds the Lakatosian explanation too simple to account for how rational expectations has grown to its position of prominence within macrotheory (p. 337). In his view, philosophy of science applications fail because new classical economics has rejected unrefuted material while it has incorporated many unsubstantiated ideas borrowed from previous paradigms. Economic doctrine, in general, maintains a unique coexistence of theories, which allows scholars to endorse more than one program simultaneously.[4] Robert Lucas, for example, is a pioneer in the rational expectations sub-field and also an orthodox neoclassical microeconomist. And, within the confines of macroeconomics, rational expectations has been incorporated into a variety of theories, not all consistent with a definable program. Hoover points out that Olivier Blanchard's influential text is Keynesian in spirit but more consistent with Thomas Sargent in technique and rigor.

In analyzing new classical macroeconomics, both Maddock and Hoover agree that the Lakatosian framework implies too sharp a distinction between that which is in and that which is out of a program. This problem arises in part because, in economics, there are a number of sub-disciplines that are linked by a variety of common features. Hoover suggests that the philosopher Wittgenstein's schema offers a more accurate description of the underlying theoretical structure of economics. In so doing, Hoover portrays a "school" more as an anthropological family tree than as a Lakatosian research program. Within this context, specialization by macroeconomists results from a natural division of labor, not simply because of conflicting agendas. This division surfaces most noticeably between theorists and empiricists, whose work may seem to be very different, and at times incompatible. However, influence between the two groups appears to run both ways (p. 382).

Alessandro Vercelli, commenting on Maddock's paper, is able to defend the Lakatosian structure by identifying Lucas's rational expectations as merely a "model-building principle" and, consequently, only a respecification of the classical research program (p. 361). Vercelli is not off base; it is easy to make the case that rational expectations work does not meet the necessary Lakatosian criteria to be called a research program. However, this only points to the problem that, because it is difficult to know how narrowly or broadly the term "research program" should be defined, general agreement on what one is or how many there are in economics is unattainable.

Through all of this debate, an important issue gets clouded. Whether or not rational expectations can correctly be called a research program, a paradigm, or neither, it certainly remains important to understand *why* this method of analysis became respected and popular in our profession. Maddock contends, "Lakatos does not prepare us well for the early and formative stage," when presumably a program, theory, method, or idea is selected by a profession (p. 357). His conclusion is that, despite the fact that Lucas and Sargent were more committed to testability than most other major economists in the discipline's history, their "behavior was motivated by ends other than progressivity" (p. 355). Consequently, he adds, our understanding of rational expectations could be more fully understood by looking at other factors of theory choice such as the social aspects of research.

*Category 4.* A major reason, then, that economics does not readily conform to the taxonomies of positivism, Lakatos, or Popper is due to the unique nature of theoretical propositions in economics. Determinants affecting theory choice can, very broadly speaking, be divided into two categories—empirical and non-empirical. Philosophers of science have traditionally focused on empirical appraisal criteria. This focus, while perhaps appropriate for some sciences, limits the applicability of their work to economics (where theoretical propositions are rarely linked directly to an empirical counterpart).

The first two chapters of this book consider the validity of approaches that emphasize, in one way or another, empirical criteria. Chapter 1 focuses on logical problems associated with testing propositions according to particular philosophy of science theory guidelines. Chapter 2 demonstrates why economists who employ these theories cannot account for theory choice in their discipline's history. The conclusion produced by this line of inquiry is that testing (whether motivated by the verificationist, falsificationist, or Lakatosian litmus) does not, and cannot, lead to unambiguous theory choices in economics.

The most common criticism levied against the purely empirical approach (both as prescriptive philosophy and descriptive historicism) points out that economic data is often inaccurate and that testing of "non-lab generated data" is imprecise. Also, as several contributors to *Appraising Economic Theories* note, most economic theories cannot be directly tested because initial conditions as well as predicted actions are rarely observable. Frequently, "economic propositions are presented in such a way as to be irrefutable. What, for example, does it mean to say that utility will *eventually* diminish or that cost functions will *eventually* rise if the points at which those eventualities are supposed to occur are never specified?" (Tarascio and Caldwell 1979, p. 990).

Instead, economic relationships must be represented by models that may or may not be adequate representations of the theoretical assertion. The initial conditions, generally captured in the model builder's ceteris paribus assumption, cannot be easily checked. Thus, apparent disconfirming tests can be attributed to violations of the ceteris paribus condition (ibid., p. 987).

Jinbang Kim uses the case of job-search theory to illustrate the nature of testing in economics. He shows that job-search theory, along with most other economic theories, cannot be directly tested.[5] Instead, empirical models must be derived in order to transform the unobservable (theory) variables into observable ones. The result is that falsifiability in economics, as compared with physics, is more problematic. Because a theory can be represented by many differently specified models, each modified with its own set of assumptions, we may get corroborating and refuting evidence for the same theory. For this reason, economic theories have, historically, rarely been thrown out on empirical grounds. Kim concludes that testing is productive in economics but that it does not perform a Lakatosian function:

> Few economists regard it as necessary for new empirical models to contain excess empirical content in order for them to replace their earlier models. Though Lakatos might see "dishonesty" in this attitude of economists, I myself see "rationality" in it. Many economists are still interested in the truth value of an isolated theory or its predictions although they understand that a conclusive test is seldom available. (p. 128)

Similarly, Blaug argues that general equilibrium *theory* contains "no empirical content whatsoever." General equilibrium *models,* on the other hand, are geared toward testing. Unfortunately, these models, usually constructed as systems of simultaneous equations, are only a representation of the theory, which means that direct hypotheses about the economy go untested. Blaug writes that there is no proof that the end state implied by general equilibrium theory is an accurate representation of any phase of a capitalist economy's workings and that "all-round multimarket equilibrium is a feature of certain models of the economy and not necessarily a reflection of how the economy is constituted" (p. 506). He then refers to Frank Fisher and posits that, perhaps, it is the power and elegance of general equilibrium analysis rather than its relevance that attracts economists, because "it rests on uncertain foundations, . . . is of little help, and is perhaps a positive hindrance in explaining the true merits of competition" (p. 508).

Additionally, one must identify when in the sequence of scientific process testing actually takes place. If, as Johnson asserts, theories are really chosen on a priori grounds, then testing of hypotheses is merely a euphemism for "ceremonial adequacy" (Johnson 1975, p. 92). Thus, even when testing does occur, and it surely does, we must still ask what role the tests are playing. Perhaps, after an appropriate period of time, a methodologist can look back on a program and gather some evidence to claim that the program was or was not theoretically or empirically progressive. However, if this testing took place after the program was already integrated into the economic literature, then this assessment does not help us understand why it was initially identified by practicing economists as something worthwhile.

For a simple example, models representing the law of demand have been tested in an effort to substantiate the inverse relationship between price and quantity demanded. The results in this case—regardless of verdict—are unfortunately not relevant to our understanding of why the theory evolved to doctrinal status in economics. The basic premise underlying the law of demand was accepted long before it was ever tested, mainly on a priori and intuitive grounds.

Similarly, the proximity of testing in relation to the analytic core of economic theory limits the value of empirical research in economics. With the development of applied sub-fields and econometrics, the scope of economics has widened to include some types of empiricist thinking. However, Richard Whitley notes:

> The results of empirical research do not seem to feed back into the dominant orthodoxy or become integrated into its theoretical development. Instead, this core is partitioned off from empirical work and seems remarkably unaffected by the latter's uncertainties and ambiguities. Such a strong separation is maintained by the strong prestige hierarchy in economics which accords analytical work the greatest status and relegates most empirical research to what Hutchison has termed the "suburbs" of the field, not least because analytic precision and elegance are idealized as the hallmarks of significant contributions. (Whitley 1991, p. 23)

Additionally, legitimate empirical work is constrained by theory—the centerpiece of economics. To be judged valid, empirical research need not pertain to actual phenomena associated with the market economy. Favorable assessment does, however, generally require that puzzles be generated from and conform to the existing analytic framework (ibid.).

Another problem, exposed in Harry Collins's essay, is that evidence frequently looks very different "here and now" than at other times and in other spaces. He points out, "What might look like a clear piece of novel empirical content *now* might look like a mistake in a decade; what looks like a piece of novel empirical content *here* might look like a mistake from over there" (p. 495). The implication is that the Lakatosian system is not very helpful, if our interest is in understanding decisions by scientists "here and now" (as opposed to appraisals by philosophers of science later on).

Scientists must also make decisions about problem-solving techniques that are not inherently testable. For example, Roger Backhouse (in reviewing Mary Morgan's "The Stamping Out of Process Analysis in Econometrics") explains that the simultaneous equations method associated with Trygve Haavelmo's work (and the Cowles Commission) was chosen by econometricians over Herman Wold's process analysis research program even though it was no better at enabling economists to predict novel facts. Why then, in the absence of compelling empirical evidence, was one program chosen over the other? Morgan asserts that the Cowles Commission "pursued the simultaneous equation approach because it posed interesting mathematical problems." This plus "the evidence for the failure of Wold's group and Cowles to communicate effectively with each other" leads Backhouse to recommend employing McCloskey's rhetoric approach to the work of John Muth and Paul Samuelson as a method for uncovering why the simultaneous equations technique was chosen over process analysis (pp. 268–69).

If we are persuaded by comments of the economists cited above, we will conclude that frameworks exist for empirical work in economics but, perhaps because of the very nature of economic phenomena, they do not allow us to directly test the validity of theoretical propositions about the economy. And, given the type of testing that does occur in economics, it must be acknowledged that theories have historically been accepted into economic doctrine long before empirical assessment has had time to accumulate. Kenneth Arrow, when asked what criteria he would consider in evaluating the soundness of an alternative theory, replied, "persuasiveness," and added, "it is foolish to say we rely on hard empirical evidence completely" (p. 505). Thus, we are still left with unanswered questions: What makes a theory attractive to economists? What makes it persuasive? And, what are the criteria for choosing one over another?

Of course, this reasoning does not imply that testing economic models is useless or that testing is incapable of yielding influential results. Rather, we can convincingly argue that empiricism has not historically provided the sole, or perhaps even the most important, criteria for evaluating theoretic assertions in economics. Recall that proponents of broader accounts, such as those offered by sociology of science, do not generally dispute the existence of positivist or Lakatosian empirical criteria. McCloskey, or even Kuhn, is unlikely to challenge the assertion that a theory that apparently corresponds to empirical evidence is more likely to be selected than one that does not. The debate, instead, concerns the *extent* to which such "rational" criteria has and potentially can dictate such decisions.

In deciphering "what made the multiplier effect so telling in *The General Theory*," for example, it is undoubtedly relevant that the "consumption function turned out to imply . . . novel facts about saving behaviour and the relationship between saving and investment which, in turn, were corroborated by empirical studies" (p. 503). However, we must also realize that, as Blaug asserts, whether or not this is a valid contention, "It does not by itself begin to account for the Keynesian Revolution, that is, the unprecedented speed with which Keynes conquered the minds of his fellow economists" (p. 504). As Pierre Duhem wrote in *La Théorie Physique*, there is something vague about the way economists choose theories (Duhem 1954, p. 319). The task here is to account for why certain works conquer the minds of fellow economists and to clarify the vagueness surrounding how economists choose theories.

*Category 5.* A fifth factor motivating the anti-philosophy of science movement has materialized from the belief that economists do not practice what they preach. That which economists preach is usually a variant on one or more of the "rational" accounts of science. De Marchi claims, "Economists see themselves very much as Lakatosian methodology would imply" (p. 5). Most of the contributors to this literature would perhaps agree with de Marchi, but would add that economists view themselves rather uncritically and with the aid of a badly warped mirror.

The alternative position holds that research into the nature of methods that are actually available and put to use by economists would be far more constructive to the discipline than the current research that attempts to fit economics into some ideal model of science. McCloskey has become a leading proponent in the move to abandon methodological prescriptions offered by philosophy of science. He argues that the "official rhetoric" of economics, which he terms "modernism," was established during the 1930s and 1940s and contains elements of positivism, falsificationism, and verificationism: "Modernism views science as axiomatic and mathematical, and takes the realm of science to be separate from the realm of form, value, beauty, goodness, and all unmeasurable quantity" (McCloskey 1985, p. 6).

The theme of McCloskey's 1983 article (and subsequent book), "The Rhetoric of Economics" is that the *actual* rhetoric—which includes the way a discipline's members converse, communicate, argue, and so on—of economists is very different from this official rhetoric. Economists could not follow the tenets of modernism and still discuss economics. Economic discourse is, out of necessity, much wider than any one philosophy of science theory would indicate. McCloskey goes so far as to say that economic science would cease to function if it had to follow the prescriptions of positivism. He concludes that modernism is impractical and that methods prescribed by philosophy of science theories such as positivism or the methodology of scientific research programs are limiting and in fact arrogant.

McCloskey's solution is to study the actual rhetoric of economics because orthodox models of science do not explain, among other things, why economists accept the theoretical propositions that they do. To illustrate the failure of the modernist version of science, McCloskey cites a survey of economists to identify a number of issues where near consensus exists.[6] Concerning these "truths" in economics, McCloskey writes, "The factual experience of the economy, certainly, has little to do with their [economists'] confidence. No study has shown in ways that would satisfy a consistent modernist, for example, that high tariffs in America during the nineteenth century, on balance, hurt Americans" (ibid., p. 493). Why then do economists remain quite confident about various assertions that are only supported by obscure evidence? To uncover the answer to this question, McCloskey argues one must first investigate the nature of the "unofficial rhetoric" in economics, which (as of 1983) remained largely unexamined by methodologists (ibid.).

Details of this argument will be critiqued and, where appropriate, incorporated into the next chapters. What is relevant here is that McCloskey directly opposes prescriptive philosophies of the type that Blaug endorses.[7] Clearly a theme of *Rhetoric* is that such attempts are futile. McCloskey is able to call upon one great thinker to support his contention—Einstein once remarked, "Whoever undertakes to set himself up as a judge in the field of truth is shipwrecked by the laughter of the gods" (ibid., p. 490).

## Methodological Considerations and Conclusions

At this point, we may reasonably assert that, to understand the process of theory choice in economics, we must look beyond a purely rational, empirically based description. A complete explanation must include the *non-empirical* aspects of the processes of appraisal and selection. This is, however, a far-ranging and broadly defined category: Popper offered advice on how to assess non-empirical theories in *Conjectures and Refutations: The Growth of Scientific Knowledge* (1968); Carl Hempel, along with Paul Oppenheim, suggested that, in addition to empirical confirmation, certain non-empirical criteria could aid the theory choice process. Their work investigated the limited extent to which observation (empirical verification) can logically confirm general statements and they sought to soften the strict verificationist criteria established by the logical positivists. Kuhn and the "growth of knowledge" philosophers have gone much further to bring historical accuracy to philosophy of science by looking more closely at actual episodes of scientific inquiry and integrating sociology of science into their methods.

The discourse in Chapter 4 will incorporate aspects of Hempel's "rational" science, which emphasizes traditional non-empirical criteria. These non-empirical criteria, "which are used to evaluate aspects of theoretical structure and form, include logical consistency, simplicity, elegance, generality, theoretical support, and others" (Tarascio and Caldwell 1979, p. 984). However, as Tarascio points out, logical problems arise when theory choice is predicated solely on these rational, non-empirical criteria. Essentially there is no method for weighting, then ordering the various criteria in terms of importance, and thus, even from a prescriptive standpoint, they provide an incomplete method of appraisal. Pertaining to the "rational canons of non-empirical" theory appraisal criteria, Tarascio writes:

An ... important barrier to the application of these criteria is the fact that no theory exhibits all of the criteria listed above. Some hypotheses are fruitful and suggestive but are insufficiently formalized; thus they do not meet the criteria of, say, logical consistency or elegance. Others may advance our understanding of a particular problem but may do little to satisfy generality or extensibility. That no theories meet all of the criteria makes theory choice [based only on these] non-empirical grounds problematic, for competing theories may be incommensurable in terms of those criteria. (Ibid., p. 994)

This line of reasoning provides a partial rationale for including, in the present analysis, other non-empirical criteria, extracted from much broader versions of the history of economics. Additionally, the approach here reflects recent trends within philosophy of science proper. In contrast, the general view held by economists on methodological issues is still based on an outdated, modernist version of logical positivism.[8]

Recall from the first chapter that philosophy of science, as developed by the Vienna Circle and more recently by Lakatos, was motivated from a desire to demarcate, by a modern standard, science from metaphysics or non-science. Proponents of the new historical trend contend that philosophy of science, as practiced by positivists, Popper, and Lakatos, "follows the wrong track by searching for non-existent things, i.e., methodological rules" (Mokrzycki 1983, p. 20). Additionally, Ernam McMullin posits that these philosophers used history, not to generate accurate accounts of science, but to make a philosophical point: "Though names of scientists and general references to their works may dot the narrative, what is really going on (in the sense of where the basic evidence for assertions ultimately lies) is not history" (ibid., p. 15).

The publication of Kuhn's *Structure of Scientific Revolutions* in 1962 created profound turmoil among philosophers of science by undermining logical positivism, as well as Popper's methodology. It replaced prescription and demarcation with realism as the focal point of attention, which meant that historical, rhetorical, and sociological arguments were given much greater consideration. Although Kuhn's questions may have been generated from fairly traditional philosophy of science underpinnings, as Edmund Mokrzycki argues, he changed the raison d'être for the philosophy of science. In his concern for accuracy, he "does not so much introduce the historical approach to the philosophy of science as show the significance of the study of science's past for philosophical reflections on science" (ibid., p. 21).

This transition toward a new point of emphasis has profoundly affected the way philosophers of science portray the theory choice process. The type of methodology they practice will be determined, to a considerable degree, by the types of question they ask. If the goal is to appraise a theory according to a list of currently drawn criteria, then it may be deemed acceptable to delete much of its actual history and footnote the rest, as Lakatos suggests. However, if the goal is to uncover why a theory was appraised as it was at the time of its acceptance, then the investigator must transport himself back to that period. These are two very distinct—and often confused—objectives of methodology. The position maintained here is that the latter question is more relevant to the development of science itself.

The traditional interpretation, which is a by-product of the first methodological objective, portrays scientists choosing among competing hypotheses according to probabilities represented in a Bayesian-type decision matrix. Philosophers developed this type of decision theory from the theory of games, which assumes rational agents basing decisions on known probabilities. The scientist can then be viewed as a rational agent who maximizes his utility by choosing theories that maintain the highest probability of satisfying his quest for truth.

The current history-oriented trend portrays the scientist conducting investigations, but constrained by his own biological, intellectual, and sociological context. Additionally, Kuhn contends that the norms and values of a science community, which rest on a wide range of subjective factors, alter the traditional criteria of theory choice and account for methodological diversity across disciplines. Within this context, the scientist may still be viewed as attempting to maximize his utility. However, his utility is functionally dependent on a humanistic set of variables, which may include professional, sociological, and even financial considerations. Proponents of this interpretation posit that a better understanding of what science actually does gives a better indication of what is possible in the future.

The analysis here acknowledges this trend toward accurate historicism and away from demarcation philosophy, which limits, or defines, science as a purely rational process. All of this is not to say that there are no problems associated with supporting an explanation of theory choice with historical evidence. Such an approach inherently relies on interpretive and inductive method, which cannot establish conclusive proof. Additionally, one cannot escape the fact that the historian begins with a philosophy, or prior conception, of science. Lakatos himself provides an extreme example of this; his rational reconstruction dictates which historical "evidence" may be included to the point where his conception "completely ceases to correspond to research practice in the history of science and at which using that term becomes merely a *façon de parler*" (ibid., p. 18).

It is thus acknowledged that normative methodology underlies historical analysis and, in that sense, complicates such projects. To make the historical evidence convincing, one must avoid common pitfalls and appreciate its limitations. Paul Feyerabend, for example, has on more than one occasion been accused of abusing historical method. McMullin has demonstrated in convincing detail that "what Feyerabend wrote on Galileo's cosmology, selects facts in a way which is not substantiated by historical data, formulates generalizations based on atypical cases, interprets events without taking into account the historical context, and finally, distorts the sense of historical events by presenting them in a dramatized form" (ibid., p. 20).

For the present purpose, historical documentation may support a contention concerning how or why a theory became popular in economics. However one must be extremely careful before asserting that a particular case is representative of events in the history of science, or even social science, or even just economic science. Perhaps the best that can be hoped for is a convincing case that criteria *A*, for example, was critical in promoting the acceptance of theory *B* and it is possible that this criteria may again be important in future disciplinary choices.

## Notes

1. Unless otherwise noted, page-number references in this chapter refer to this source.

2. For example, Kuhnian revolutions rarely occur in economics; it is difficult to define and operationalize terms such as hard core or protective belt; there are no objective methods of measuring criteria such as theoretical progressiveness or degree of corroboration.

3. This, of course, does not mean that scientists have no philosophical basis for their work.

4. The current coexistence of theories would, in some cases, appear quite improbable in the context of earlier historical periods. For example, models of imperfect competition were originally put forth as challenges to the model of perfect competition. Now, of course, they can be found within the confines of the same introductory texts. Also, new theory can arise without destroying old theory, especially if the new work asks essentially different questions. The marginal "revolution," for example, did little to refute classical economics as developed by Adam Smith and David Ricardo. Instead it changed the focus of study (from issues of growth and distribution to problems of optimization, given fixed resources). For reasons such as these, upheavals in economics cannot be accurately described in terms of "Kuhnian revolutions."

5. Consumer theory provides another clear example of the problems associated with testing economic theory. See Homa Katouzian's book, *Ideology and Method in Economics,* for an excellent discussion on why consumer theory is an untestable proposition. He consequently finds consumer theory to be inconsistent with positivist or Popperian methodologies of economics.

6. The poll was conducted by James R. Kearl et al. and was published in the article, "What Economists Think. A Confusion of Economists?" One example of this type of consensus is: "Only 2 percent disagreed with the assertion that 'a ceiling on rents reduces the quantity and quality of housing available.' "

7. In his methodology book, Blaug writes: "What methodologists can do is to pro-

vide criteria for the acceptance and rejection of research programs, setting standards that will help us to discriminate between wheat and chaff."

8. McCloskey's pliable term "modernism" is used here because there is, of course, some variation in the way economists view themselves. Some may espouse Friedman's instrumentalism, some positivist verificationism, and others Popperian falsificationism. Generally, however, the "official rhetoric" emphasizes rational aspects of economists' behavior and falls within the context of one or a combination of these explanations. Refer back to Chapter 2 for a more careful characterization of the variant of positivism adopted by economists.

# CHAPTER 4

# Prepublication Appraisal and Editorial Selection

## Introduction

We are now in a position to build a case outlining how research appraisal and theory selection occur in economics. As our starting point, we assume that the discipline has had to and will continue to integrate a small percentage of new work into its formal body of literature (which, of course, requires dismissing a far larger percentage). Further, determination of which research constitutes a contribution is based on a unique, discipline-specific evaluative process. This chapter argues, first, that there is a significant subjective—and hence largely non-positivist—component inherent in this process and, second, that it is of a multidimensional character.

Until this point, it has been shown that, in general, methodological accounts fail to accurately depict economic method. Philosophy of science approaches, which economists have historically derived their methodology from, do not typically focus on actual practices of science. Short-run appraisal, for example, which culminates in the publication of journal articles, has been largely ignored. Instead, philosophy of science has been used as a vehicle to prescribe or define "correct science," using physical science as the prototype. The task here is to shift the analytic emphasis away from an abstract ideal and toward the concrete practice of science. By utilizing evidence from doctrinal history, a more relevant account can be constructed, and insights into current and future method can reasonably be drawn.

In the first section of this chapter, pre- and post-publication periods are defined. Literature appraisal is conducted both before and after publication, each in a distinct context; therefore, the two periods are addressed sequentially in Chapters 4 and 5. Next the essential differences between philosophy of science appraisal, as performed by methodologists, and evaluation, as performed by a profession's decision-makers, are identified. As demonstrated in previous chapters, methodologists have experienced major difficulties in their attempts to tailor standard epistemological approaches to the economics case. In contrast, the profession's journal editors and referees are, generally speaking, not concerned with abstract appraisal of this sort.

The third, fourth, and fifth sections form the chapter's central contribution. In "The Role of Subjectivity in Publishing," the distinction is drawn between objective and subjective appraisal criteria. The hypothesis that determination of a work's significance and, hence, publication decisions must ultimately be based on individual value judgments is supported. Evidence is drawn directly from surveyed referee comments, which serve to illustrate the diversity that characterizes academic reviewing practices. In the fourth section, sources of bias in research appraisal are categorized and discussed. Here it is argued that ideology and sociology—certainly "non-positivist" components of research appraisal—are relevant. Also, the uniformity with which disciplinary standards can realistically be applied toward publication decisions is estimated. "Norms and Trends in Economic Research" reviews current standards and practices prevailing in the academic literature. In the process, some of the features that distinguish successful economic research from the majority, which is ignored, are discussed. Of course, these features vary across and even within sub-disciplines, reflecting the fact that no singular, universally recognized model of social science method exists. The chapter's final section offers summary remarks and conclusions.

**Pre- versus Post-Publication Appraisal**

Theory choice, and its appraisal component in particular, should not be viewed as a homogeneous process. Two distinct stages of activity can be delimited, with publication marking the transition point.[1] Organizing the evaluative process in this manner is in no way meant to imply that a document is typically only appraised twice. Prior to actual publication, an author may solicit comments on his paper from colleagues, either informally or through structured outlets such as seminars and conferences. Later, the paper may be submitted for evaluation by journal editors and referees. Appraisal, as carried out by publishing institutions, must obviously take place before a work reaches the transition point (acceptance or rejection) and is, therefore, categorized in the prepublication stage.

This two-stage classification also serves to contrast early appraisal, which dictates the likelihood that a work will be chosen for publication, and longer-term appraisal, which shapes the basic theoretic apparatus. Although prepublication and post-publication processes are propelled by different forces, they are also inextricably linked. Through time, the published body of literature provides a menu of potential research paths and, via this channel, influences a discipline's long-run evolution. The analogy has been made that editors and other decision-makers at academic journals are the "gatekeepers of science."[2]

This chapter focuses on prepublication appraisal, which, as pointed out above, maintains a shorter-run perspective where practical matters are necessarily of some concern. Editorial policies define the scope of individual journals;[3] however, each is also constrained by limited resources—manuscript space, competent referee time, publishing deadlines, costs, and so on. A reference guide to publishing opportunities in economics points out that "little is known about (publication) criteria of a refereed journal," in part because there are "no formally agreed upon standards" (Miller and Punsalan 1988, pp. viii, xii). A complete inquiry into the process requires specification of how professional standards, sociological norms, political ideology, and institutional affiliation, as well as more traditional criteria (both empirical and non-empirical) figure in the evaluation by an author's colleagues of a work.

Over a longer-run period, a different evaluative process emerges, which constrains or expedites a work's rise to prominence. It is during this stage—when the profession collectively identifies from the mass of literature those articles and books that they find promising—that economic doctrine evolves.[4] This second component of theory choice, where the competition is among literature that has already attained status afforded by publication, is the focus of the next chapter. At that point, the post-publication evaluative process can be compared to the prepublication process and inferences about the efficiency of academic journals as tools for accomplishing the goals of economic science can be drawn.

### Journal Appraisal: Philosophy or Practicality?

To understand the methods of appraisal and the criteria for selection that economists employ, we must first recognize the nature of publication in economics. The publication process, which provides a formal system for submission and evaluation of research, plays a two-dimensional role in theory choice: First, and most obviously, it legitimizes research and systematically produces candidates that potentially contribute to the evolution of economic literature. Publication marks the first major screening stage of doctrinal development. Second, the dominant publication system enforces disciplinary standards, which, in turn, influences the type of work that will be produced in the first place. In both of these ways, journals play a substantive role in determining the course that economic inquiry will follow.

For some time now, publication in economics has been a self-sustaining and highly insulated process. The intended audience for the majority of articles are colleagues (as opposed to other social scientists, politicians, or lay persons).[5] Appraisal is also carried out *internally,* in the sense that journal editors and referees are usually professional academic economists. In the modern context, leading journals not only reflect, but also define, best practice in economics.

The type of appraisal that is a basic component of daily journal operation is a completely distinct activity from that which is attempted later by methodologists.[6] For those entrusted with evaluating contemporary research, the feasibility of making quality judgments based on empirical criteria becomes even more remote than for methodologists. Unlike historians or philosophers, journal editors and referees do not benefit from hindsight, which may generate additional evidence of a work's validity.[7] The verificationist (or falsificationist) criterion cannot be universally invoked to evaluate journal submissions because (along with the logical and practical difficulties inherent in the proposition) the majority of articles do not even employ empirical evidence as a means of persuasion. Similarly, since only a small percentage of published work claims to penetrate the theoretic apparatus of economics, 'theoretic progressivity' of the sort Imre Lakatos discusses is inappropriate as an evaluative tool of *individual* research papers.

Rendigs Fels examines regularities in recently published economics articles and, in so doing, indirectly demonstrates why positivist and Lakatosian tools are insufficient for practical research appraisal. His study, which relies on a sample of articles appearing in nine mainstream journals,[8] indicates that very few authors present new theory: "[There are no] major breakthroughs in the 127 papers. The sample represents normal, everyday science at work" (Fels 1994, p. 46). Since creating new theory is not the dominant activity of authors producing and submitting scholarly research, theory appraisal (as traditionally discussed by methodologists) is obviously not the primary task facing journal editors and referees.

If Fels's survey is a fair representation, then testing—even of existing theories—also occurs infrequently in economics. This is no doubt related to the finding that "there are no articles devoted primarily to increasing the stock of data" in his sample. Rarely is the validity of one hypothesis challenged by testing it against alternative hypotheses. Work selected for publication more often attempts to modify a model to fit a particular case or to develop an econometric method that, in itself, has nothing to do with actual economic problems. Most often, however, "Economists are . . . engaged in telling more or less plausible stories . . . and very little gets proved beyond a reasonable doubt" (ibid., p. 57). It may be reasoned that the range of criteria that must be implemented when executing day-to-day publication decisions

is far broader (and more variable) than that implied by prescriptive methodological approaches such as positivism.

### The Role of Subjectivity in Publishing

In the abstract, positivism implies an objective system for appraising and ranking the value of competing theories. In reality editors and referees, as "status
judges," must determine whether or not research submissions are of sufficient
interest and quality to warrant their inclusion in the limited pages of a journal.
In this section, it is argued that publication decisions cannot be executed on the
basis of objectively drawn criteria of the sort emphasized in positivist prescriptions. The goal here is to demonstrate that subjective elements figure prominently in the process. More specifically, it is shown that, in assessing the
significance of research in economics, referees and editors are forced to make
numerous judgment calls. Hence, even in a critically neutral environment,
article quality ratings will vary from reviewer to reviewer.[9]

In fact, it is unclear how economists in general evaluate literature and
choose research paths to pursue. This uncertainty motivates one line of ques-
tioning in Arjo Klamer's popular and provocative *Conversations with Economists* (1984). Klamer interviews prominent economists to argue, among
other things, that empirical evidence and pure logic cannot settle disputes
between competing macroeconomic schools (new classical, neo-Keynesian,
monetarist, and non-conventional). What is more, he uses the comments of
such luminaries as James Tobin, Robert Lucas, and Alan Blinder to indicate
that social, political, ideological, and personal preferences and biases may
rule out the possibility that certain macro-questions are ever settled.[10]

In an earlier paper, Tarascio and Caldwell explicitly address the issue of
theory choice as it relates to publication in economics. They recognize that
the evaluative process is objectified, to an extent, by existing disciplinary
norms and by standards of science in general:

> A researcher is free to cast his research, theoretical or empirical, within the
> framework of his subjective state of knowledge, but he is also constrained to
> observing the disciplinary norms obtaining in his science. Minimum stan-
> dards of professional competence and training exist in every science and are
> a necessary condition for favorable evaluation of research. . . . To the extent
> that the evaluation of research is confined to such norms, it may be called
> "objective." (Tarascio and Caldwell 1979, p. 998)

However, it is further reasoned that establishing a work's significance
entails subjective elements:

> Nevertheless, acceptable professional workmanship does not in itself assure
> an acceptable contribution to the literature. . . . There is, in addition, the
> requirement of *significance*, which is interpretive and hence subjective in

nature. A research paper may be "technically correct" and at the same time lack significance. (Ibid.)

To illustrate this subjective–objective distinction, consider again the editorial policy of *Econometrica,* which states that submissions should "advance application of mathematics and statistics to economics." Judgment calls on the part of a referee are not important in implementing part of this criterion. Mathematical and statistical rules allow referees to check that theoretical and applied results are technically correct. In addition, the journal's scope is well defined; we would not expect an article on the economics of developing countries, for example, to be appropriate for publication in *Econometrica.*

However, determining which submissions advance the application of mathematics and statistics to economic study entails interpretive aspects. The judgments of referees and editors will be affected by their own personal interest in or knowledge of the relevant literature, as well as current topical interests prevailing within the discipline. Angus Deaton reports that it is not at all uncommon for co-editors at *Econometrica* to alter criteria, or institute temporary publication guidelines; for instance, papers in "overworked" areas are of less interest and are generally "held to higher standards" than are other papers (Deaton et al. 1987, p. 205). One only need look at the history of econometrics to observe that the significance of various research programs has not always been uniformly recognized.[11] In fact, the extent to which mathematical and statistical technique can advance our understanding of economic problems is among the most vexing methodological questions of the last half-century.

Another prominent journal, the *Quarterly Journal of Economics* (*QJE*) seeks "significant advances in economic theory." Determining a submission's significance is, unfortunately, no easy task; it is doubtful that a single reader (especially one from the University of Chicago) would judge all articles appearing in *QJE* as significant to the development of economic theory. Klamer's interviews, in many instances, provide evidence of the potential for this kind of disagreement. For example, new classical economists, who emphasize precise and rigorous model-building (at the expense of realism of assumptions), have found work that advances innovative application of certain mathematical techniques significant. Other groups, neo-Keynesians and certainly post-Keynesians, often object to the basic premises of these modeling exercises and find little interest in such research.

Inconsistency in appraisal arises because predicted theoretic relationships between economic variables cannot be simply verified (or falsified) in a positivist (or Popperian) manner. Frequently, mathematical and statistical techniques can only be applied to the presentation, not confirmation, of theories. As a result, one group cannot simply demonstrate the superiority of their program by testing their hypotheses against their rivals'. In social sciences, controlled experiments can rarely be repeated time after time as in physical science, and individual cause and effect relationships are difficult to isolate. These empirical limitations escalate the role of interpretation, and hence subjectivity, in determining the value of economic research.

Naturally, the extent to which standardized criteria can minimize the role of individual value judgments or otherwise aid the publication decision-making process varies from case to case. Profound differences in the levels of rigor practiced by academic journals undoubtedly exist both across and within disciplines. Nonetheless, statistical evidence from the journal review process suggests a role and also illuminates the character of non-positivist evaluative criteria. Data on rejection rates, in particular, make a striking initial impression. A 1971 article, "Patterns of Evaluation in Science: Institutionalisation, Structure and Functions of the Referee System," by Harriet Zuckerman and Robert Merton provides a case in point. The primary objective of their study is to assess trends in acceptance rates for the leading physics journal. Data is gathered from the Physical Review archives in order to examine correlations between author and referee rank and publication decisions. A secondary objective is to define the function of referees and identify some problems inherent in the academic journal system.

Additionally, and most relevant here, Merton and Zuckerman compile rejection rates for eighty-three major journals ranging in origin from the humanities to the physical sciences. Based on 1967 data, the sample indicates the following mean rejection rates: history (three journals)—90 percent; philosophy (five journals)—85 percent; sociology (fourteen journals)—78 percent; economics (four journals)—69 percent; biological sciences (twelve journals)—29 percent; physics (twelve journals)—24 percent.[12]

Within disciplines, a similar pattern materializes. Among Merton's and Zuckerman's findings are the following two examples:

> The *American Anthropologist,* devoted largely to social and cultural anthropology, approximates the high rejection rates of the other social sciences with a figure of 80 percent, while the *American Journal of Physical Anthropology* with a figure of 30 percent approximates the low rates of the physical sciences. (Zuckerman and Merton 1971, pp. 76–77)

And,

> The journals of language and literature in the humanistic tradition have an average rejection rate of 86 percent, whereas the journal, *Linguistics,* adopt-

ing mathematical and logical orientations in the study of language, has a rejection rate of 20 percent, much like that of the physical sciences. (Ibid.)

Based on this and similar evidence, the following conclusion is drawn:

> The pattern of differences between fields and within fields can be described in the same rule of thumb: the more humanistically oriented the journal, the higher the rate of rejecting manuscripts for publication; the more experimentally and observationally oriented, with an emphasis on rigour of observation and analysis, the lower the rate of rejection. (Ibid., p. 77)[13]

What, if anything, do these trends tell us about article appraisal and selection in economics? The above data informs us that the physics profession has more journal page–space per author submission than does economics, which, in turn, has more than philosophy or history. From 1950 to 1965 the number of pages published annually in the *Physical Review* increased at nearly twice the rate as membership in the American Physical Society. In contrast, the professional membership of sociologists increased more rapidly than did their journal space. It appears that journal editors in humanities and social sciences have simply been forced to reject more articles out of necessity, due to space constraints, than their counterparts in physical science.

Closer examination, however, reveals a more complex and informative story. It is by no means coincidental that the amount of space available for print varies across disciplines. Articles in physics journals, for instance, are relatively short. One is hard-pressed to find a paper that runs eight pages in the *Physical Review;* most are three or four pages long. In economics, on the other hand, it is not uncommon for journals to allow thirty-five or even fifty pages for an article. Actual length tends to fall in the fifteen- to thirty-page range.[14]

On the practical side, this means that the cost (both dollar and opportunity) of publishing an additional article is lower in physics than it is in economics. This permits editors of the *Physics Review* to take the attitude, "when in doubt, publish." Editors at the *American Economic Review (AER)* and other high-rejection, high–page-consumption journals are more likely to take the attitude, "when in doubt, reject" (ibid., p. 78). These contrasting research environments arise because physicists are able to express their ideas more succinctly than their social science counterparts. The fact that, in physics, articles are significantly shorter corroborates the assertion that its standards regarding method and communication are more clearly established. Consequently, potential contributors are able to accurately predict whether or not their work will be judged a legitimate contribution by editors and referees. Given that the most prestigious journal in physics must only reject 17–25 percent of submissions, it seems apparent that physicists know when they have an article that meets those standards and when they must submit to one of the many lesser journals.

Merton and Zuckerman also point out that, based on the testimony of editors, the rates of "unsalvageable manuscripts" submitted in the humanities and social sciences are much higher than in physics. This, they write, "suggests that these fields of learning are not greatly institutionalized in the reasonably precise sense that editors and referees on the one side, and would-be contributors on the other, almost always share norms of what constitutes adequate scholarship" (ibid., p. 77).

Levels of inter-referee agreement directly reflect the interpretive nature of article appraisal across disciplines. This type of evidence suggests, again, that subjectivity is more conspicuous in economics than in physical science. Michael Polanyi (1946) was among the first to express views on matters of this sort. He observed that, historically, a high degree of agreement usually exists between referees of scientific journals. Zuckerman's and Merton's data for the leading journal in physics corroborates this observation:

> In a sample of 172 papers, each evaluated by two referees for the *Physical Review* [for the 1948–56 period], agreement was very high. In only five cases did the referees fully disagree, with one recommending acceptance and the other, rejection. For the rest, the recommendation decision was the same. (Ibid., p. 67)

In contrast, appraisal appears to take on a more stochastic character outside the confines of physical science. For example, Michael Mahoney (1977) reports a remarkably low level of correlation between ratings in behavioral psychology journals when different referees review the same article. Similarly, data from *AER*—the leading journal in economics (based on citations)—reveal that consensus of the sort between referees at the *Physical Review* is absent in economics. Rebecca Blank reveals that, in cases where there were exactly two referees, agreement between them was low:

> The correlation between the theory ratings of two referees on the same paper is 0.28; it is 0.24 for empirical ratings, 0.23 for contribution to the field, and 0.24 for overall paper quality. This seems to indicate a relatively low degree of referee agreement. . . . The evidence from this sample appears to indicate that there is quite a bit of randomness in the ratings any paper receives from referees. (Blank 1991, p. 1059)[15]

Thus, despite considerable formalization of economic methods, a level of ambiguity continues to exist as to what constitutes significance in research.

This ambiguity would not exist if work could simply be judged by its empirical content or by its theoretic "progressivity." Unfortunately, the stamp of approval cannot be administered exclusively on the basis of these, or any other set of formally established standards. Editorial tasks are not directly aided by grand epistemological constructs such as Lakatos's methodology of scientific research programs or positivists' verificationism. Consequently, recently developed methodologies (based on philosophy of physical science ideals), which seek to eliminate uncertainty from methodologists' appraisals of economic programs, remain largely irrelevant to the discipline's actual workaday evaluative processes.

### Decision-Makers' Testimony: A Survey of Referees

If objective guidelines with which authors can gauge the value of their work are limited, how do they establish credibility in the judgmental eyes of referees and editors? Alternatively phrased, what distinguishes successful scholarship from that which is judged a non-contribution? Thus far, it has been reasoned that common versions of the discipline's methodology—as represented, in abbreviated form, by textbook treatments—have traditionally emphasized empirical components of the appraisal process while virtually ignoring the far more difficult, "subjective" ones. In order to identify and characterize these other aspects of appraisal, we must turn to referees themselves and ask what, in their view, makes an article significant enough for publication. This task has been facilitated by means of a mailed survey.

### Format of the Survey

Economists for this survey were randomly selected, primarily from referee lists published in the following journals: *Journal of Political Economy, Quarterly Journal of Economics, Econometrica, Journal of Post-Keynesian Economics,* and *Rand Journal of Economics.* A few more from the *Journal of Economic History* and *Economics and Philosophy* were included for variety. The response rate to the survey was 52 percent, as 62 of 119 surveys originally sent out were returned.[16]

Referees were asked the following questions:[17]

1. Approximately how many articles have you refereed for economics journals during the past two years?
2. In appraising the value of an article, do you find it helpful, harmful, or irrelevant to know the author's identity?

3. What, in your view, are the three most important criteria when determining the significance of an article?
4. If one exists, what is your most common criticism of articles that you recommend not be published?
5. When *you* submit an article for publication, what are the three most important considerations in choosing the appropriate journal?

Due to the open-ended character of the questions, some interpretation was required when categorizing answer "types." Compiling results would have been simpler had a set of choices been offered.[18] However, the point of this survey was to get a sense of the diversity in reviewer appraisal criteria; a preset list of responses would have made this next to impossible.

*Results from the Survey*

*Question 1.* Referees reviewed, on average, 9.7 articles *per year* during the two-year period in question. The median referee reviewed 9 articles per year. The number of articles reviewed during the two-year period ranged from 80, for the most active referee, to 3, for the least active. (Some of the referees surveyed were also editors and acted in that capacity—but not as referee—for more than eighty papers).

Rarely does an individual review one or two articles a year. As the data show, members of the profession who participate in journal refereeing do so on a regular basis.

*Question 2.* Most referees surveyed (about 56 percent) claimed that knowledge of an author's identity is irrelevant, or usually irrelevant, in their appraisal of an article. The remaining 44 percent responded (in approximately equal proportions) that this information is either usually helpful or usually harmful.

Many of the responses were made with qualification. Several referees who claimed that an author's identity is irrelevant to their recommendations noted that they like to know, or are "always curious" anyway. One remarked that he or she is "willing to give better-known authors more leeway to make their case, but [is] perhaps more supportive of efforts by less prominent authors." Another referee wrote that, although "irrelevant," it "saves time to know the identity [because it] is easier to correlate with previous work, etc."

A number of referees prefer knowing the identity of an article's author. One reason was that it makes it easier to make suggestions for revisions. One referee wrote, "As a good Bayesian, I think the information is relevant, e.g., to the question of whether I reread something." Another wrote, "If the article is badly written, it can help to decide how much effort to invest in untangling the article to see if it's worth fixing and publishing."

Those who find author identity harmful typically suggested that it potentially creates additional biases about work ("I prefer not to know because knowing might influence my decision"). One referee wrote that, under blind refereeing, "One is less apt to make assumptions (positive or negative) about the author's underlying thought processes, etc." Others responded that it is "harmful but inevitable" and "harmful if the author has a name and the article is weak."

The implication here is obvious: 44 percent of the referees openly admit that knowledge of an article's author potentially alters their review in one way or another. And, of course, we cannot be certain that referees who claim the information is irrelevant in fact remain unaffected by author identity.

*Question 3.* This is the key question in the survey. The responses suggest that a remarkably wide range of criteria are invoked by referees when determining the significance of an article's contribution.

The most commonly cited criterion is novelty; more than 50 percent of the referees listed one or more responses that fit into this category. Twenty-nine percent explicitly state that ideas or methods in an article need to be original, novel, creative, or innovative to establish significance. Thirteen percent of the surveys reported that, specifically, "obtaining new results" (usually empirical) is one of the top-three criteria. Other forms of novelty cited (there is some overlap as a few surveys list more than one "novelty" criterion) include technical innovations, new tools (8 percent); conceptual or theoretical innovations (3 percent); new data or new uses of data (5 percent).

On the opposite extreme, many surveys (about 32 percent) indicated the importance of conformity in one way or another: 8 percent reported that articles should be relevant to current discussions or contribute to an ongoing argument; another 8 percent indicated that authors need to show an awareness of or be consistent with ("properly situated in the context of") past literature; 3 percent indicated that an author must demonstrate a clear understanding of economic theory to establish competence; 5 percent pointed out that, for a paper to be appropriate, it must fit in with the journal's policies, instructions, and topical interests.

About 22 percent of the surveys included a response that suggests the importance of finding a balance between novelty and conformity. These referees recorded that, to be significant, an article must advance existing knowledge or research programs (by relaxing assumptions or finding new data). Research that offers new insights into old problems should, in their view, be recommended for publication.

Many surveys commented that scholarship needs to be of a "high quality." At least 32 percent of the surveys contained at least one comment to the effect that articles must be carefully presented and contain a clear statement of thesis. Arguments must be "coherent," "well-written," and demonstrate "clarity of expression" and "tightness of logic" in order to be persuasive.

Additionally, according to the survey, articles must possess a basic level of general research quality: Accurately documented empirical results and high data quality (11 percent); internal consistency (3 percent); use of "high quality research" tools (5 percent); correct statistical technique and appropriate use of data (8 percent) all count in favor of a submission's chance for acceptance.

Some surveys indicated the importance of traditional empirical criteria: Thirteen percent cited a form of the verificationist criterion as crucial to establishing significance. In these cases, referees reported that authors must "prove" their conclusions (empirically or theoretically) or otherwise convince readers that their results answer questions posed.

Several referees (again, about 13 percent) implied an important role for falsification. Among this subset, it is important that articles force reconsideration of previously accepted work, change ways in which we think about problems, force us to reject previous work, overturn results, break traditions, or make us rethink old issues.

Quite a few referees (23 percent) are impressed by articles that are relevant to real economic problems. These referees indicated that policy implications and insights into actual market, or "real world," phenomena make articles significant.

A large number of respondents gave extremely vague answers, which indicates high levels of subjectivity. For example, 18 percent of referees wrote that the topic should be "important" or "significant"; 11 percent wrote that papers should be "interesting" or "meaningful." This ambiguity indicates that referees do not approach their reviewing duties with a preset, formalized system for evaluating article quality. Their judgments would appear to rely largely on intuition.

A hodgepodge of other responses round out the reported criteria: Six percent wrote that articles should stimulate further work or open up new areas of research; almost 10 percent cited generality (breadth of impact or application) as a criterion; 6 percent cited simplicity or elegance (generally with respect to mathematical elements, such as proofs); 3 percent of the surveys indicated that first-rate or creative literature reviews are significant; only one referee reported that thoughtful cross-theory comparison is important; and one referee (perhaps jokingly) judges the significance of a paper by how many of his own articles it cites (or, more diplomatically, how it relates to his own work).

The responses to this question indicate that referees invoke at least thirty distinct criteria when determining the significance of an article. Most of the criteria require subjective estimation on the part of the referee.

The majority of referees did not explicitly list positivist verificationism or Popperian falsificationism among their three most important criteria for judging an article's significance. Only one referee specifically stated that comparing the performance of different theories is a key element of appraisal.

The essential tension between novelty and conformity is reflected in the answers to this question. Many respondents want to see "something new"; however, most referees (often the same ones who want a form of novelty) indicate that work must show continuity with existing methods and, more specifically, conform to the journal's specific views and guidelines.

*Question 4.* Most of the responses to this question fall roughly into one of ten categories. The leading criticisms of manuscripts not recommended for publication are the following: The article produces no new insights; it is poorly written; or, it is not interesting, is of low quality, contains insignificant results, or other vaguely expressed comments.

Eighteen percent of the referees reported that their most common criticism of articles is that they are stylistically unattractive—either poorly written, too long, badly organized, incoherent, or demonstrate "terrible prose."

Others (23 percent) offered extremely general responses indicating that papers they reject are simply "of low quality." They may also phrase this type of criticism in the following ways: Papers are "unimportant," "not interesting," or "offer only minor contributions."

Sixteen percent cited a lack of originality, newness, or innovation as the leading reason for rejection. These were usually the same referees who cited novelty as a leading criterion for determining significance in Question 3.

Eight percent of the surveys indicated that a "lack of scholarship" leads most frequently to article rejection. This criterion is usually defined as an "insufficient knowledge of facts or of related work." In a similar category of responses, 13 percent indicated that poor technique or methodology is the most common problem. These referees often reported "bad econometrics." Six percent of the survey's respondents stated, more specifically, that theoretical or modeling errors are the most frequent cause for rejection. A small number (about 3 percent) of referees wrote that the most typically encountered flaw is that articles are too technical relative to the advances they make.

Almost 10 percent of the referees indicated that their most common criticism of articles is that authors do not support their contentions or conclusions. Most often the article does not "prove" what it states it proves because of empirical problems such as faulty or misinterpreted data.

Other reasons warranting article rejection include the lack of logical consistency (5 percent), bad assumptions (5 percent), and too little contact with reality, or lack of relevance (3 percent). About 5 percent of the referees reported that problems with articles are too varied to isolate a "most common criticism."

Again we see limited notice being paid to empiricist appraisal criteria. Only occasionally do referees cite a lack of proof or disproof as the leading reason for rejecting articles.

Also the tension between novelty and continuity is again clearly present, reinforcing the theme that emerged from the responses to Question 3. Many referees want new, or original results. However, they expect knowledge of existing work and consistency with accepted methods.

Method and effectiveness of literary presentation also appear to be important in this category. Comments to the effect that poorly written work is rarely persuasive or significant lend support to contentions made by rhetoric scholars.

*Question 5.* Answers to this question suggest that economists seek to submit to journals that "demonstrate a suitable topical and methodological history," "are prestigious," and "are likely to publish the article."

With only two or three exceptions, respondents to the survey indicated that they try to submit research to journals that are appropriate in terms of audience, subject matter, quality level, and technical sophistication.

Over 40 percent of the referees ranked "reaching the proper readership base" as a top-three consideration. They articulated a desire to communicate with other economists who care about the particular issue at hand.

In a similarly motivated response, 76 percent of the referees reported that they submit to journals with the "proper historical record." This means that the journal must operate within the appropriate sub-field, have the same topical and methodological focus, and cover "related work" ("suitable subject matter"). These referees explained that their own article's characteristics must "fit in" with ongoing programs and discussions prevailing at the journal. One referee asks, "Does the journal publish papers like mine?"

Eleven percent of the respondents indicated that the quality of their article, however subjectively determined, must match the quality of the journal to which they are submitting. Most select the best journal among those of which they feel their paper meets the standards. Others (about 8 percent) specified that they submit to journals that accommodate the levels of technical and empirical sophistication demonstrated in their work.

This search for the "appropriate venue" is motivated, in part, from a desire by practitioners to increase their probability of acceptance. Almost 18 percent of the referees explicitly listed "likelihood of acceptance" as a top-three consideration when deciding on a journal. For an additional 5 percent of the surveys, a personal history of publishing in the journal ("a strong track record") is listed as a plus. Only once does a respondent list diversity (publishing in a wide range of journals) as a top-three consideration.

In a similar vein, over 20 percent of the individuals in the survey wrote that it is in their best interest to submit to journals where they either know the editor personally, or are familiar with his "propensities" or "revealed preferences." Others mentioned that knowledge of referee and editor tastes, as well as composition of the editorial board is helpful.

Journal quality appears to be very important to research economists. Almost 60 percent of the surveys indicated that journal prestige—as measured by circulation, reputation, visibility, rankings, and so on—is a top-three consideration when deciding where to submit an article. Turnaround time—or a journal's reputation in that regard—is also very important; 35 percent of the surveys stated this as a key variable.

About 11 percent of respondents indicated that it is a top-three priority to submit their work to journals where the quality of refereeing and editing is high; they hoped to receive useful comments through the submission process. Five percent reported that it is important to submit to journals with a broad orientation; the greater breadth that the journal demonstrates, the better.

An overwhelming number of responses to this question indicated the importance of conformity in the submission process. The referees surveyed realize that it is crucial to submit their articles to journals that publish similar work. More than half indicated that probability of acceptance hinges on their ability to fit in with the current trends at a particular journal. This calculation is viewed as important enough to warrant, in several cases, investigating the tastes and propensities of editors.

*Survey Summary.* Specific aspects of this survey will be drawn upon at appropriate points during the remainder of the chapter. Within the context of this section, the most important result is that referees' publication recommendations (rejection or acceptance) are based on a complex and highly variable set of criteria. Respondents to the survey differ significantly in their views concerning what legitimizes research in economics. Their answers indicate that determining an article's "significance" is driven by considerations that take on a myriad of different orderings. In this environment, it is inevitable that theory choices diverge, that research is unevenly appraised, and that methodological differences abound in the social sciences. From this perspective, it becomes understandable why the fate of economists' ideas, hypotheses, and theories is determined more by critical debate than by decisive tests.

## Sources of Bias in Research Appraisal

### Ideological Components

As pointed out above, a conscientious and ethically neutral reviewer must still make subjective calls when assessing the value of an article. Although critical approach may be shaped by a conceptual view of what constitutes legitimate research, a reviewer may be impartial regarding a particular topic. However, when appraisal ultimately depends on subjective evaluation, it does become possible for personal or group preferences to influence the process. In such cases, the presence of bias may lead to systematic (and, hence, predictable) responses by reviewers or to a tendency to prejudge work in a particular manner. Intellectual bias, in this context, presents a significant barrier to the practice of positive science. In this section, we turn to this subtly different aspect of prepublication appraisal and selection. It is argued that ideology (both political and intellectual), as well as sociological factors, can add an element of bias that potentially plays an influential role in theory choice decisions.[19]

### Rise of the Journal System

To adequately understand these much-avoided areas of methodology, one must begin with the observation that practices and regularities in economic literature are constantly being redefined. The publication format, and hence the discipline's system of appraisal and selection, has undergone substantial transformation over the life span of economic science. The profession arrived to its present state, characterized by an almost exclusive emphasis on journal articles, only during this century. Since much of the core of economic theory was established prior to the modern period of journal dominance, it would likely prove erroneous to assume that economists chose to accept, say, the theory of perfect competition and rational expectations models for the same reasons.

Eighteenth- and nineteenth-century political economists emerged from diverse intellectual backgrounds. They were formally trained in fields broadly ranging from moral philosophy, to engineering, to physics. Thus, communicating new ideas generally required extensive development of an analytic framework. Today, economists are more likely to share similar training that emphasizes a theoretic orthodoxy and highly standardized approaches. Additionally, as the number of economists has increased and distinct sub-fields have emerged, communicating groups have become increasingly specialized. Within these sub-fields, matters of method and scope are settled and motions to question or rationalize underlying assumptions have been suspended. The earlier environment was not conducive to a journal-dominated publication system; the modern situation is. In Kuhnian terms, instillation of a dominant paradigm—which standardizes knowledge as well as communication—during textbook-intensive graduate training allows today's economists to present their ideas in a relatively concise, structured, and often formal mathematical way. These features, which distinguish modern economics from political economy or from some other social sciences, make the journal system appear appropriate.

Before the proliferation of academic journals, proceedings of Royal Societies served the similar function of advancing and communicating scientific literature. In addition to meeting the scientific standards of the day, contributions also had to conform to additional criteria. Royal patronage demanded that politics and religion, for example, not be debated in the public forum offered through the published proceedings (Whitley 1991, p. 8).[20] Rules for proper scientific conduct originating from "external" sources have affected the manner in which knowledge has been compiled throughout history. In cases where powerful institutional forces seek to define the range of satisfactory research (as when the church "censored" Galileo's astronomical revelations), this effect is obvious.[21]

*Contemporary Sources of Ideological Bias*

Today, science has gained autonomy from state and religious institutions. Nonetheless, a power hierarchy continues to exist. Those practitioners who are judged superior according to the profession's current standards are assigned to prominent positions within their fields. These elite individuals and groups are in charge of resources, such as grants and journals, and are leaders of organizational institutions, such as universities and research centers. They maintain substantial control over the subject matter and methods prevailing in the published literature—just as patrons set guidelines for the Royal Academies.

An author who wishes to publish in a reputable journal must produce work that editors and referees will judge a "contribution" to economic literature. The criteria from which credibility is established varies from journal to journal and, as the survey in this chapter's third section indicates, among individual reviewers. Articles that receive favorable review generally conform to a technical standard and, more importantly, to the range of topics regulated by executors of the journal. If an author fails to recognize these constraints, he will not qualify to share in the benefits that the leaders within his science community allocate. These benefits, which help motivate research in the first place, take the form of peer recognition, as well as financial reward. Given that career advancement decisions are based largely on publication records, successful scholarship improves a practitioner's probability of acquiring (or keeping) a reputable, secure, and high-paying position.

More directly, monetary awards provide an incentive mechanism that allows granting institutions to promote those research areas that they wish to develop. Vincent Tarascio (1986) notes that sponsored research, which has become especially prevalent in applied fields of economics, "reflects the problem orientations and priorities of those who award grants, and who are external to the discipline." In some cases, grants from special interest groups are "awarded with the expectation that research results will be supportive of the views or interests of the grantors" (ibid., pp. 9–10).

When government agencies, private research institutions, international organizations, or even academic journals establish a topical range of interest, an ideological component is almost inevitably present. In such research environments, financially influential groups can add an extra bias to the already subjective, a priori element, which exists in all scientific work. Forty years ago, Gunnar Myrdal recognized, in general terms, the inherent ideology that helps shape the formative stages of inquiry:

> Facts do not organize themselves into concepts and theories just by being looked at. . . . Questions must be asked before answers can be given. The questions are an expression of our interest in the world, they are at bottom valuations. Valuations are thus necessarily involved already at the stage when we observe facts and carry on theoretical analysis. (Myrdal 1954, p. vii)

Funded research, by prioritizing interests of the granting institution, alters the valuative process that initiates doctrinal development. In particular, Tarascio points out, "Such research, which has tended to be directed towards short-run specific policy issues, is not cumulative in nature and adds little to the stock of scientific knowledge over time" (Tarascio 1986, p. 288). Similar observations, made by others, corroborate Tarascio's claims.[22] Also, Fels's survey of articles indicates that economists tend to think "in terms of their own research projects rather than an ongoing research program to which they and many others are contributing." He concludes that the discipline would benefit if practitioners would choose research projects according to their potential to advance unified programs rather than choosing projects "because they have a data set nobody else has or they know of econometric methods superior to their predecessors" (Fels 1994, p. 58).

In modern economics, institutional affiliation has also subtly influenced research paths and publication criteria. A journal associated with a particular intellectual tradition may not tolerate papers with divergent political implications.[23] Whenever policy questions are present, different world-views seem to lead to divisive intellectual approaches and fragmented schools of thought. Consequently, political beliefs have most frequently been a source of methodological disagreement in macroeconomic fields.[24]

The monetarist–Keynesian debate of the 1960s and 1970s serves as a case in point. The two groups were divided ideologically and, in turn, over fundamental philosophical issues concerning scientific inquiry. In the Klamer interviews, Tobin (a Keynesian) states that Friedman (based at Chicago and leader of the monetarists) "had a crusade that he was pushing all over the world, not just in the profession. He saw the big picture, and the big picture was right for him" (Klamer 1984, p. 106). Franco Modigliani concurs: "Friedman is driven by the idea that whatever the government does is bad. He has a mission and seems to be willing to sacrifice some intellectual honesty for that" (ibid., p. 120). The development of Friedman's political and intellectual beliefs seems natural given his proximity to the events of World War II. His emphasis on broad ideals concerning individual freedoms and opportunities (most clearly evident in *Capitalism and Freedom*) dictates, to some degree, his approach to economics as well as that of many of his followers. Critics like Tobin and Modigliani imply that Friedman's instrumentalist approach facilitates the type of latitude he needs to maintain a specific intellectual stance and to pursue a particular ideological agenda.

In contrast, the Keynesian ideological basis is shaped by post-Depression political and economic events and maintains a more optimistic view toward active government policy. Keynesians, like most policy-oriented researchers, are more likely to espouse concerns over the applicability (and hence realism) of economic models and to object to instrumentalist methods. Tobin, for instance, reasons that economists "are not so good at testing hypotheses . . . that we can give up any information we may have at whatever stage of the argument. . . . Any evidence you have on (assumptions), either casual or empirical, is relevant" (ibid., pp. 105–6).[25]

The history of economics shows that intellectual differences reflecting subjective, but basic ideological beliefs (such as those that split macroeconomists during this period) are very difficult to reconcile because rarely in such cases can appeal to fact be decisive. The case at hand is no exception; during the 1970s, Keynesians (whose leaders in the United States were based at Harvard and MIT) were not receptive to monetarists (based at Chicago) and vice versa. Robert Lucas's anecdotal account of an early professional experience is indicative of the ideological barriers that separated the two groups:

I'll tell you what happened in those days—it's ridiculous in retrospect. There was a kind of Chicago faction and a non-Chicago faction at Carnegie [-Mellon University]. Meltzer was the Chicago leader, and Mike Lovell, a Harvard guy who had been at Yale, was the non-Chicago leader. (Ibid., p. 33)

Lucas goes on to explain how the intellectually segregated environment strained relationships to the point where individuals were persuaded to leave. He also explains how this atmosphere prevented him from talking with Thomas Sargent, a future collaborator, during their two overlapping years at Carnegie-Mellon (ibid.).

Since journal editors and referees are members of the profession in which these ideological divisions occur, publication practices are also potentially affected. Two cases in point are *QJE* (affiliated with Harvard) and *JPE* (affiliated with Chicago). Both of these leading journals seek to "advance theory" that appeals to a "general audience." This editorial objective does not, in itself, imply any sort of political, philosophical, or institutional preference. However, between 1950 and 1959 Harvard authors dominated *QJE* (their work occupied 14.5 percent of the journal's pages, while second-place California occupied only 7.2 percent). Similarly, Chicago authors dominated *JPE* (their work occupied 15.6 percent of the journal's pages, while second-place Stanford occupied only 4.4 percent) during the same period. Neither Harvard nor Chicago was even in the top dozen contributing institutions in the opposing school's journal (Yotopoulos 1961, pp. 665–70). Most reasonable observers would surely admit that, in addition to nobler criteria (such as empirical rigor, degree of corroboration, and predictive adequacy), ideological factors created personal ties, political alignments, and intellectual bonds that also influenced publication patterns during the period.

Of course, the intellectual landscape has changed since then. The monetarist–Keynesian debate has subsided, or at least taken a different form. The rift that existed between Chicago and Harvard twenty years ago is no longer as clearly defined. Over a more recent period (1984–89), Harvard-based authors were almost as conspicuous in the pages of *JPE* as Chicago authors. Similarly, the number of Chicago-based authors appearing in *QJE* has increased since the period that Dan Yotopoulos catalogued.[26] Furthermore, disciples of monetarist and Keynesian traditions have dispersed as the number of professional economists has expanded. Over the years, Chicago's and Harvard's graduate students have moved on to other schools (Carnegie-Mellon, Minnesota, Western Ontario, Hoover Institute/Stanford, etc.; or Princeton, MIT, Yale, etc.). This dispersion of talent is reflected in the journals, as the number of institutions represented has grown with the profession.[27]

Yesterday's monetarists and Keynesians have evolved into today's new classical and neo-Keynesian economists. According to Blinder, fundamental beliefs continue to present significant barriers between schools:

> A lot of the disagreement is ideologically based. . . . I see this by talking to people. Certain people have a capacity for ignoring facts which are patently obvious, but are counter to their view of the world; so they just ignore them. . . . Some of the new classical economists are extremely ideological. If you give them evidence, for example, that anticipated money matters, evidence counter to their worldview, they say you're wrong. And if you say their evidence is wrong, they'll say you're wrong again. (Klamer 1984, p. 159)

New classical economists view post-Keynesians with even less tolerance; Lucas says, "Post-Keynesian economists, well, I don't know whether to take them seriously (laughter)" (ibid., p. 35).

The end result is that communication between schools is more often defensive than cooperative. Contrasting beliefs, passed on by the leaders of different intellectual traditions, instill incompatible methodologies. The sources of this incompatibility stem, in part, from sincere epistemological differences, such as the importance of employing testable assumptions. However, there is also an element of gamesmanship that accompanies intellectual debate. Robert Solow frankly admits, "It is very hard to communicate seriously" with other economists:

> It may be that we have come to recognize that we have different sources of evidence. Sargent does not believe that people could possibly behave the way I believe people behave. The other reason is that in any conversation between say Lucas or Sargent and me, there is an element of game playing. There is a tendency to grab a debating point whenever you see it. . . . I suppose each of us has self-respect to maintain. . . . We have positions and we want to defend those, not merely seek truth. (Ibid., p. 145)

Ideological battles continue to split individuals into separate camps today. Post-Keynesians, new classicalists, and neo-Keynesians respond by maintaining their own publications. Certainly, the raw volume of academic research production mandates that many journals operate in highly specialized niches, promoting detailed work in specific areas. However, (as with the *QJE–JPE* example from the 1950s), there are journals operating within common sub-fields that do not share readership because each is promoting an agenda that is incompatible with the other's. High submission rates at the better journals make it possible for editors to increase selectivity and reject papers that do not conform with their tacit philosophical stance.

This is not to say that all referees and editors are dogmatically bound to doing economics one particular way. As the survey above clearly demonstrates, some referees are favorably impressed by creativity; hence, novelty in research is valued. However, that which is rewarded is a conditional sort of novelty—it is novelty within a given framework. Influential work must successfully mesh idea creation with existing analytic method. It must not sever the thematic continuity that establishes a journal's *raison d'être*. Research conducted on or outside the periphery, which challenges the accepted program, will generally not be published. Thus, authors must be cognizant of ideological undercurrents and methodological norms prevailing in their fields. Richard Whitley labels journals "conservative novelty generating organizations" because they demand innovation close to the theoretic core and, at the same time, conformity with accepted methods and continuity with existing doctrine. Some latitude is restored to practitioners since competing schools offer journals that employ editors and referees who emphasize different sets of criteria. Nonetheless, the journal-dominated academic environment, by institutionalizing a bias in favor of work that contributes to ongoing debates, does not facilitate "revolutionary" approaches to solving economic problems.

### Sociological Factors

The social infrastructure of academic professions, and of society in general, also affects research appraisal and selection. Communities of scientists, like other groups, have their own traditions that institutionalize rules, hierarchies, and structural relationships. As discussed earlier, a discipline is often segregated into several groups that may or may not interact effectively. Intellectual partitioning, whether created by ideology, philosophy, or even geography, often leads to social separation, which can affect the practice of science.

The socialization of economists begins immediately, during graduate training. Premier institutions standardize curriculums by placing their graduates in positions at peer or lower-rank institutions. This "trickle down" effect promotes the creation of traditions, such as "Chicago economics" or "Cambridge economics."[28] Students build intellectual capital, and thus a vested interest, in economics as practiced at their school. Graduate training defines the types of problems (as well as the methods for addressing those problems) in which students are likely to become interested. In this sense, the educational process produces a largely predetermined research agenda.

Alliances and divisions arise in this academic climate. Alliances are formed among colleagues who share similar training since, in the process, they develop common views as to what constitutes appropriate method, attractive presentation, and correct worldview. Unifying doctrine is represented by the journals in which each group of practitioners publishes. Conflicts between groups also exist, which potentially creates barriers in journal communications. Yotopoulos's study, cited above, illustrates a case in point: little cross-publication occurred between Harvard and Chicago economists and their respective journals during the 1950s. Each school, convinced of the superiority of their own methods and worldview, avoided interaction with the other.

Novelty in research is generally only rewarded by a group if it occurs within the purview of their existing research program. Consequently, work that exhibits a bold shift in methodology is never immediately recognized and is often dismissed altogether. For example, early efforts by new-classical economists to redefine the role of expectations were not favorably received by mainstream Keynesians of the time. Again, Klamer's conversations with macroeconomists capture the divisive character of the sociological influences at work. Lucas mentions how, at a conference at Yale in 1977, Keynesians were "throwing darts at him" during a presentation of early rational expectations research (Klamer 1984, p. 34). New-classical economists confidently persisted and did, of course, eventually gain influence. However, one must wonder how complete their success would have been had they not been linked to the highly respected economics department at Chicago. A similar historical development—the proliferation of Keynes's ideas—is described in Harry Johnson's *On Economics and Society*. Johnson argues that Keynes's prominent status within the academic community was a major factor allowing him to effectively challenge the orthodoxy. He also offers insights of a sociological nature into why Keynes's domination was not as uniform in the larger and more eclectic U.S. academic environment. These phenomena occurred largely during the post-publication phase of theory choice, however, and can therefore be more appropriately discussed in the context of the next chapter.

Aspects of the orthodoxy have, then, been overturned in such a way that the profession was capable of assimilating. Historically, these were extraordinary events, however. Inspection of journal literature indicates that, anomalies notwithstanding, new work does not have to challenge anything. Under normal circumstances, academic success—defined by journal publication—is much easier for practitioners who gain entry into a reputable group than it is for those who choose an isolated research path. Structured professional outlets, both intellectual and social, exist for research economists aligned with established traditions. Neoclassical microeconomists and neo-Keynesian (or new classical) macroeconomists—and to some extent less conventional schools such as institutionalists, Marxists, or post-Keynesians —have large-enough followings to maintain their own communities. Each group generates productive resources (such as journals and grants) and provides intellectual, political, and financial security to its members.

Very few scientists are willing to risk losing these benefits by voluntarily breaking from the safety that membership in a scientific community affords. Naturally, there are exceptions, such as Leonard Rapping. Klamer's interview with Rapping painfully illustrates the personal and professional costs associated with abandoning or being abandoned by one's scientific community. During the late 1960s, Rapping became disenchanted with the neoclassical economics that he and his Chicago School colleagues practiced. Subsequently, he chose to disassociate himself, both intellectually and socially, from that group. He describes this difficult period, when he found himself operating in an "intellectual vacuum":

> The reconstruction of a worldview is a long, slow process . . . (and) a wrecking experience. . . . I was intellectually exposed. I disassociated myself from a whole set of personal friendships developed over a twenty-year period. Every time I made a move I was accused of inconsistency or disloyalty. I was frozen out of the "money river." (Ibid., pp. 227–28)

Needless to say, after such a gestalt switch, publication in the respected journals was no longer an option.

Given these types of professional constraints, it is not surprising that most young economists, who are already under pressure to publish, generally choose research paths that do not challenge the dominant literature. As Tarascio observes, the professional structure in economics, "rewards conformity, and there is little incentive, and indeed, great risk, for young researchers to pursue new avenues of inquiry outside the conventional framework of economic theory" (Tarascio 1986, p. 14). Doctrinal history indicates that conformity of the sort seen in economics is not exclusively detrimental. Enforcement of disciplinary standards, in particular, tends to advance technique-oriented activities by instilling in young practitioners the value of analytic rigor. However, this system—which encourages exhaustive utilization of existing tools and theory—constrains idea creation, which is an intellectually oriented activity, by discouraging research into alternative scientific approaches (ibid.).

*Sociological Factors and the Application of Standards*

Journal institutions, as part of the profession's sociological unit, are not exempt from the influences described above. This further complicates matters of theory choice in two ways. First, in fields such as macroeconomics where competing approaches coexist, the critical basis for research appraisal varies between journals. Secondly, even when a group shares a common ideology and agrees on a system of standards, evaluative criteria may not be uniformly applied.

One might expect these sociological factors to have more conspicuous effects after publication, when author identity and location in the academic hierarchy are fully exposed to potential critics. In contrast, prepublication appraisal is easier to monitor because it is so formally structured. The systematic nature of the journal process allows measures to be taken that objectify article selection. In an effort to minimize subjectivity originating from sociological (and other) sources, a journal's editorial staff generally prints guidelines concerning the purpose, scope, and audience of their journal. Other bias safeguards (blind reviewing, evaluation criteria forms, signed comment sheets, and multiple reviewers, and so on) systematize the process further. Despite these safeguards (all of which have problems),[29] concerns over fairness in the journal system persist. For instance, Blank's article (1991) was facilitated by the American Economic Association because of concerns expressed by the Commission on the Status of Women in the Economics Profession that the *AER*'s traditional non-blind reviewing practices might adversely affect acceptance rates of articles authored by women.

Additionally, skeptics frequently charge that an author's position in the academic stratification system affects evaluation of his work. Data certainly does indicate that high-status authors enjoy higher acceptance rates than their colleagues based at mid- or lower-rank institutions. Their work is also reviewed by more prominent referees and they are informed of publication decisions more quickly.[30] Unfortunately, these assertions do little to shed light on the author-bias issue. It is not possible to unambiguously determine why articles from high-status individuals are accepted at higher rates. The disparity may be attributable to "reputation effects," or simply to the fact that top universities select the best from the profession, allocate more time for research, provide better staffs, and attract superior graduate students.[31] Zuckerman and Merton show that other factors—age of author, age and interests of the editor, and academic background of editors and referees— are similarly correlated with acceptance rates obtaining in scientific journals. Because there are many collinear determinants of publication decisions, assertions that high-status authors receive recognition disproportionately to the value of their contribution remain highly speculative.

Caveats aside, evidence still indicates that uniform application of standards does not exist in the journal appraisal process. Blank's 1991 article is the most clearly specified investigation into structural referee bias based on author attributes. An experiment by *AER* created a unique opportunity to assess some affects of single-blind versus double-blind journal reviewing practices.[32] Blank's paper does not seek to determine the wide range of factors on which research appraisal is based. Instead, she raises some very specific questions to ascertain whether or not journal standards are systematically biased by author or referee gender and institution rank.

The most important result from the survey is that single-blind and double-blind reviewing practices lead to significantly different patterns of acceptance. This simply means that a referee's evaluation can be influenced by knowledge of the author's identity.[33] Specifically, when the author's anonymity is maintained, Blank finds that referees are more critical, which results in lower acceptance rates under double-blind reviewing. Additionally, this effect varies according to the rank of the author's institutional affiliation. Those who benefit most from non-blind reviewing are authors based at academic institutions rated 6 through 50 and at U.S. non-academic institutions.[34]

On the other hand, author gender does not seem to be a significant factor in publication decisions. The data show that female authors *in this survey* did not benefit as much as their male counterparts from non-blind reviewing. However, the results were not statistically significant, which means fears that a bias exists against females in economics are, at this point, unfounded.[35] Blank does demonstrate a statistically significant difference in article ratings based on *referee* gender; specifically, "female referees rate blind papers more favorably, while male referees rate non-blind papers more favorably" (Blank 1991, p. 1058).

Needless to say, we are in no position to fully understand the psychological forces at work that influence referee appraisal. To explain Blank's general result that non-blind reviews tend to be more favorable than blind reviews, we might guess that it is easier to criticize an anonymous author than it is to criticize the work of a known colleague, who may be a friend or acquaintance. The trend that authors from mid-range universities (6–50) benefit most from having their identities known may stem from the fact that many referees (46.6 percent) are also based at these institutions. Blank's paper corroborates, in a general way, Michael Gordon's (1979) results for physics, which show that reviewers rate papers more highly when they are written by authors originating from institutions similar to their own.[36]

The important information contained in Blank's findings is that blind and non-blind reviewing lead to different acceptance rates of articles. This merely brings to light a reality that should never have been in doubt: There is humanistic, sociologically based subjectivity in academic appraisal that even a highly systematic publication process cannot eliminate. That perfectly rational world, where research can be judged independently of an author's identity is not the academic world. Many economists undoubtedly know this, but rarely discuss its ramifications.

## Norms and Trends in Economic Research

In economics, both topical interest and methodological approach are subject to trends, cycles, and fads.[37] The study of population economics, for example, was prevalent in 1830 and markedly absent in 1930; research in economic growth was active in 1825, dormant in 1900, and resurgent in the 1960s (Bronfenbrenner 1966, p. 539). Similarly, certain techniques, such as rational expectations modeling, or comparative statics, do not experience uniform popularity among practitioners through time. Such fluctuations no doubt relate to the contemporary appraisal of research. As disciplinary norms evolve over time, the measure of an article's worth is subject to change; in other words, research appraisal is carried out within a context.

Ever-changing economic systems and phenomena promote some of this cyclical response by practitioners. However, research seems, in many instances, to be dictated more by largely independent disciplinary trends, which may or may not reflect actual economic problems. Guy Routh points out that, even during the depths of the Depression, economists were preoccupied with abstract theoretical problems such as "conditions of maximization under perfect and imperfect competition and the distinction between cardinal and ordinal utility," and not with creating new theory to address anomalies exposed by changed economic conditions. Publication patterns at the time support his contention: "In the *Economic Journal,* during the years 1932–35, only three papers appeared on the subject of unemployment" (Routh 1989, p. 266). Because journal trends, as much as topical relevance, dictate the discipline's research agendas, a practitioner who wishes to publish work on a subject that is not "hot" may have to exercise considerable patience.

In a similar way, methodological standards evident in journal literature reflect the range of acceptable *approaches* to scientific inquiry. These standards, or regularities in method, have evolved from innumerable sources. For example, a priori philosophical views concerning rationality and free will underlie much of the abstract, reductionist method common to economics. Propositions, based on "self-evident truths," generated natural assumptions from which entire theoretic systems were built. More recently, the importance of testing, as stressed in positivist methodologies, has philosophically legitimized econometrics as a methodological approach. Additionally, techniques have been borrowed from other disciplines. Phillip Mirowski, for example, has argued that the rigorous and elegant mathematical methods of physical science were adopted by economists, in part, to enhance the verisimilitude of their own work.

Each methodological norm, even if it is arbitrarily drawn or ideologically driven, takes on an objectified life once it becomes integrated by a discipline's practitioners into the mainstream. In combination with one another, these norms define "acceptable scholarship." Work that does not adhere to contemporary topical and technical standards is likely to be viewed with suspicion by members of the profession. Similarly, when editors and referees appraise articles, they check for acceptable levels of rigor and scholarly competence. The criteria they invoke reflect the discipline's set of collectively determined and constantly evolving scientific norms. Thus, to understand prepublication appraisal in economics, we must identify characteristics common to successful work, and trends evident in the literature.[38]

Rendigs Fels's paper (1994) on research strategies employs an inductive approach to comment on norms currently prevailing in economics. His survey of recently published work indicates that, conceptually, most articles begin with a set of assumptions, then draw logical conclusions for a particular application. A range of objectives—theory alteration, explanatory modeling (with and without testing), and the search for regularities, to name a few—motivate research. Additionally, Fels's article supports contentions that deductivism (in the tradition of William Stanley Jevons and John Stuart Mill), as opposed to Friedman's much-praised instrumentalism, is the scientific method of choice in economics. Testing of models occurs infrequently; tests of economic theories are even more scarce.[39] Again, a lack of interest in uncovering new data is indicative of this preference. Of the 127 articles in Fels's survey, only 8 present new data. Thus, the litmus for judging the validity of research is not predictive success, or even predictive content. Friedman's method of testing by prediction, exemplified in his 1948 classic, "Utility Analysis of Choices Involving Risk," remains a rarity in contemporary economics.

Econometric approaches are also part of the current standard in research. A practitioner can establish credibility by demonstrating a mastery of sophisticated, up-to-date statistical techniques. However, in many cases, simply the presence of econometric analysis—as opposed to the evidence derived from it—is the key to an article's success. Fels's sample indicates that those articles that employ the most sophisticated mathematical and statistical methods do not test models by their predictions. In fact, the types of articles that require the greatest technical expertise are modeling exercises that are the "remotest from reality" and are assigned the lowest empirical relevance ratings. Solow appears to agree with Fels's assertion. He states that the motive behind much of the econometric work conducted by new classical economists, and some others as well, is "to get across the message that it can be done technically; that's all" (Klamer 1984, p. 143).

Because results from econometric applications are "often nugatory," Fels concludes that "economists rely too heavily on [econometrics] and devote too little effort mobilizing other kinds of information" (Fels 1994, p. 52). Solow has remarked that econometrics is not a "powerful or useable enough tool" to settle macroeconomic arguments (such as those between monetarists and Keynesians over the Phillips Curve); "you can always provide models to support your position econometrically, but that is easy for both sides" (Klamer 1984, p. 137).[40] Thus, a major reason other types of evidence are mobilized is that statistical and mathematical approaches rarely result in verification or falsification of theories as described by many philosophy of science accounts.

### Importance of Presentation

A new idea only becomes a candidate for the evaluative stage of selection, where it is judged by others, after it is set in a communicable form. Since there is no definitive empirical litmus for demonstrating an article's validity, economists must be cognizant of other research standards that offer effective means of persuading colleagues of an idea's merit. The unfeasibility (and subsequent absence) of simple proofs or disproofs elevates the role of effective "storytelling" in economics. Because it is impossible to perfectly convey that which he is thinking about, a writer must pay careful attention to the *way* in which he constructs his argument. Good ideas that are poorly expressed may be given short shrift, while mundane ones, presented with panache, may raise eyebrows.

The language and tone embodied in an author's writing can enhance or detract from the underlying content and, hence, influence its reception. A work may be presented in a confrontational or in a conciliatory style; it may offer new technical methods or it may utilize existing ones. History of science reveals many instances where new systems were strongly resisted because of intellectual, social, and even financial interests of a scientific community. Bernard Cohen, a noted historian and philosopher of science, argues that, depending on the particular environment, scientists have increased or decreased their chances of approval by casting their work in a conciliatory or revolutionary tone.

One example of this rhetorical tactic is examined in Alan Gross's detailed study of Newton's *Opticks*. Gross describes how Newton, after sustaining critical attacks over initial drafts, softened his stance considerably in order to quell resistance and convey a more diplomatic, conciliatory persona. He couched his new discoveries within the preceding optics tradition by employing "a Euclidian arrangement to create an impression of historical continuity and logical inevitability. . . . He initiated a cascade of rhetorical questions, whose cumulative effect was both to sanction his science and license his speculations" (Gross 1988, p. 10).[41] Not unlike Keynes in economics, Newton was a pioneer of new ideas but also maintained an interest in preserving his place in a scientific community.

Consider, also, the rhetorical approach of Thorstein Veblen. His flamboyant prose and creative terminology is commonly recognized to have had an impact on the reception of his work. More recently, Phillip Mirowski's writing style has been described as polemical, brash, and contentious. By adopting this literary approach, most notably in *More Heat than Light,* he has perhaps evoked more emotional response than he would have otherwise. There are disciplinary norms associated with literary presentation; next, we consider how—in the context of these norms—an author's stylistic approach is capable of altering the probability that his work will be favorably judged.

### The Rhetoric of Economic Discourse

There is a growing literature that analyzes how communication technique is used as a tool of persuasion. This literature, commonly labeled "rhetoric," asserts that, because scientists can rarely know how their ideas will be received, they formulate communication strategies and tactics to enhance their chances of acceptance.[42] Question 5 from the referee survey reveals that practitioners do think in terms of "likelihood of acceptance" during the journal submission process.

Lawrence Prelli, a scholar of rhetoric, writes that scientific rhetoric is "strategically created with a view to securing acceptance as reasonable by a special kind of audience" (Prelli 1989, p. 119). He argues that methods of persuasion are much subtler and more complex than traditional interpretations of science imply. A major assertion in the rhetoric literature is that shared values and convictions of a scientific community will dictate which research themes are acceptable and which tactics of communication will be persuasive.[43] Rhetoric studies point out that scientists are, out of necessity, also writers. To positively affect their works' reception by peers (including editors and referees), scientists must convey competence—the "scientific personae"—by effective and appropriate use of literary devices such as examples, analogies, and metaphors. Thus, rhetoric studies strive to clarify that which makes scientific argument, in the absence of positivist criteria, plausible and convincing.

Rhetoric findings should be of interest to active researchers who seek to pose their ideas in an influential manner. The professional literature indicates that creating convincing accounts, as opposed to proving propositions beyond a reasonable doubt, is the dominant activity engaged in by economists. As Klamer points out, "Mere presentation of highly abstract and mathematical models, uninterpreted, is incomprehensible and lacking in persuasive power." Convincing research usually incorporates effective storytelling and plain language—such as Lucas's use of the island parable to establish an intuitive basis for his assumptions—to convey the meaning of new work (Klamer 1984, p. 249).

The most thorough application of rhetoric study to economic literature is D. McCloskey's *Rhetoric of Economics,* briefly discussed in Chapter 3. His central thesis is that economists, in part to advance a particular vision of their science, maintain an "official modernist rhetoric" while their discipline's actual rhetoric goes unexamined.[44] He writes:

> Even in the most narrowly technical matters economists have shared convictions about what makes an argument strong, convictions which they have not examined, which they communicate to graduate students only tacitly, and which contain many elements embarrassing to the official rhetoric. (McCloskey 1985, p. 138)

In other words, certain norms that exist are not examined because they do not square with the positivist methodology in which most economists are indoctrinated. Modern researchers know, for example, that empirical methods such as regression analysis can be used to deceive as well as to enlighten. They may even recognize that their discipline employs particular models that cannot be empirically rationalized (verified or falsified). However, the same practitioners fail to discredit (and even espouse) the textbook rhetoric that portrays economists proving and disproving theories.

McCloskey's point is that the job of an economist, or any other scientist, is to persuade his colleagues who are, generally speaking, reasonable people—but not logicians or philosophers. And, although only a very limited set of criteria can influence a true modernist (say, a positivist), there exist a wide variety of methods for swaying reasonable people. Doctrinal history reveals that most successful theory transitions have, in fact, not been prompted by appeal to empirical evidence. McCloskey approvingly quotes Ronald Coase who asserts that, only after enough economists believe in a hypothesis will a demand for tests evolve. Kuhn's claim that "the road from scientific law to scientific measurement can rarely be traveled in the reverse direction," seems valid for the specific case of economics.

Accordingly, publication decisions are not generally made on the basis of empirical criteria. In economics, as in other fields of study, discourse takes place predominantly in a priori, Bayesian terms. Testing occurs much later, if at all. Based on this observation, McCloskey prescribes "an examination of the workaday rhetoric which leads to (these) prior beliefs" (Mc-Closkey 1983, p. 495). Initial views concerning a theory's validity may be shaped by a variety of evidence types—generated from common sense, anecdotal accounts, personal observation, or political views—which are inconclusive but still persuasive.

Rhetoric scholars are particularly interested in the inherent methodological diversity of argument and in literary devices used in forming those arguments. McCloskey randomly samples from Paul Samuelson's *Foundations* to illustrate the variety of literary techniques that can be found in even a single dominant work. For example, "Mathematics is presented in an offhand way, with an assumption that we all can read off partitioned matrices at a glance." McCloskey argues, "The air of easy mathematical mastery was important to the influence of the book" in the sense that Samuelson was able to create a convincing scientific persona. McCloskey follows by adding, "virtuosity is some evidence of virtue," indicating that such rhetoric is not, in itself, bad or "unscientific" but merely a part of our practice (ibid., p. 500). Additionally, he points to instances where Samuelson effectively employs other literary techniques—appealing to authority, imposing assumptions, and illustrating with hypothetical examples or analogies. Again, modernism does not acknowledge these types of influences in science. However, if McCloskey's account is credible, such factors are important.

Another point made in *Rhetoric* is that reasoning in economics is similar to reasoning in law, which allows for methods of discourse that are rarely mentioned in philosophical treatments of scientific method. McCloskey writes, "modernists have long faced the embarrassment that metaphor, (historical precedent), case study, upbringing, authority, introspection, simplicity, symmetry, fashion, theology, and politics apparently serve to convince scientists as well as other folk, and have dealt with the embarrassment by labeling these the 'context of discovery' " (McCloskey 1985, p. 43). In truth, we present, convince, and critique as well as possible—not as our introductory texts describe, but by a myriad of literary techniques. Additionally, a practitioner may be compelled to write an article for "extra-positivist" reasons; he may wish to make a political point, engage in hypothetical problem-solving, advance his own prestige, or simply earn a living. McCloskey, like Kuhn, warns that economists pay a price for this intellectual dishonesty. By ignoring non-modernist motivations and methods underlying science, we limit critical perspective, delete an avenue of appraisal, and inhibit the art of communication.

The value of rhetoric rests in its ability to extend our understanding of the interpretive component of research appraisal. Investigating methods of communication refocuses attention on actual, not idealized, factors that affect the reception of ideas in science. Analyzing literary technique reveals the existence of disciplinary standards, such as mathematical expression of theory, and also subtler aspects of persuasion, such as the use of metaphors or appeals to authority. It should also be noted here that rhetorical tactics continue to influence selection processes after publication. These affects, as well as the limitations of rhetoric methodology, will be considered in Chapter 5.[45]

## Summary and Conclusions

It is crucial to recognize that appraisal of scientific work takes place on a number of different levels: Journal editors and referees are assigned the responsibility of reviewing new research; practitioners, in general, are frequently called upon to assess already-published work; and appraisal is also conducted by historians and philosophers of science. Failure to distinguish between these distinct activities leads to muddled and incoherent methodological discussion.

This chapter is directed toward characterizing the journal review process, which is the key component of prepublication literature appraisal and selection. The journal system is central to theory choice because it provides the mechanism whereby a subset of new research is legitimized; for economists, it provides a formal method of screening research conducted by their profession's members. Additionally, publishing institutions establish and reinforce standards that influence the course of future work.

The critical basis of decision-making, in this context, is shown to operate quite independently from that which dominates prescriptive philosophy of science. Indeed, if referees and editors were limited to publishing articles that passed strict verificationist, falsificationist, or Lakatosian criteria, their journals would be reduced to, if anything, pamphlets. The nature of research in economics requires that individual value judgments take a visible role in the day-to-day practice of economics.

During the review process, editorial decisions regarding publication of manuscripts are guided, in part, by a designated set of discipline and journal-specific standards. In economics, as in other sciences, articles are made attractive by satisfying generally recognized criteria. Highly valued work demonstrates knowledge of and competence in the methods explicitly endorsed by the profession's members. Additionally, a researcher's choice of analytic framework, terminology, and symbolic representation must conform to implicit guidelines obtaining at the journal to which he has submitted. Although there may be an arbitrary component in the creation and implementation of these standards, they objectively exist and affect the course of research. For example, an individual journal may decide that all submissions must be double-spaced to be considered for publication. This decision, although perhaps based on valid reasons, remains somewhat arbitrary. However, if any submission that is not double-spaced is automatically rejected, then the criterion has obtained an objective status.

These clearly defined, thus easily enforceable, rules can affect doctrinal development in more substantive ways. For instance, to satisfy space requirements, submissions must typically be confined to a length of twenty or thirty pages. Work that does not start with a field's established theoretic structure, mathematical tools, and symbolic representations is unlikely to conform to this regulation and would therefore be inappropriate for journal publication. Thus, as the journal format has evolved into the primary communication mechanism in economics, it has served to formalize, and also narrow, acceptable analytic method.

When viewed in this light, the journal-dominated academic system appears to provide little incentive for economists to tear down and rebuild theory anew. This carries obvious ramifications for the development of economic thought. The modern research environment promotes full exploration of existing theory, but appears to reduce the probability that intellectual upheavals will occur. Requirements of the journal system, coupled with textbook education, generate an abundance of competent practitioners but redirects intellectual capital away from alternative problem-solving research programs. Non-conformist approaches have historically required extensive intellectual development that is time and space intensive. Consequently, new analytic frameworks, such as Keynesian macroeconomics or marginal analysis, have not typically been produced via the journal mechanism. This line of reasoning (which we will return to in the next chapter) implies that the probability of major theory shifts becomes more remote as dominance of the journal system expands.

Nonetheless, in the current context, a practitioner must measure up to designated disciplinary standards if he hopes to gain access to publication resources. Assessment of many basic requirements (such as proper use of mathematical or statistical techniques and proper language usage) typically entails minimal levels of subjectivity on behalf of a reviewer. Therefore the validity of enforcing these criteria is largely uncontroversial. However, many submissions are technically correct and stylistically acceptable. A demonstration of competence is usually, in itself, not sufficient to warrant publication or professional recognition. An author has the additional burden of establishing significance; hence, the evaluative process must, at some point, be completed on the basis of individual value judgments.

Empiricism of the type frequently described in philosophy of science accounts represents only one among many techniques that may be used to convince reviewers of a work's significance. Since only a small percentage of economics research actually tests hypotheses or models in such a way as to establish credibility, there is clearly more to article appraisal than positivism implies. The survey results reported in this chapter indicate that referees allow a wide range of variables to enter into their assessments of research quality; novelty, technical innovation, empirical rigor, extensibility, clarity, elegance, and logical consistency are just a few characteristics that count in favor of a potential publication. Clearly, there exists no objective method for measuring many of these criteria.

The subjective element of appraisal (absent in positivist accounts) correlates positively to the methodological latitude practiced within a discipline and is therefore more conspicuous in the humanities and social sciences than the physical sciences. Academic journals indirectly reflect this trend, as those operating within more humanistic fields of study tend to reject a higher proportion of submitted manuscripts. This is due, in part, to the fact that journal resources are more abundant in physical sciences. However, greater standardization of method allows physics articles to be written within the confines of a few pages, which frees up available space.

To compensate for lower degrees of standardization in the social sciences, authors must often clarify underlying assumptions and concepts, which is space intensive. Even in economics, where formalization is highly valued, articles are much longer than they are in physics. Additionally, there seems to be a more nebulous designation of what demarcates legitimate scholarship in the social sciences. This increases the degree of uncertainty for potential submitters and produces an element of randomness in reviewer evaluations. Comparatively higher submission rates of unsalvageable manuscripts, and lower levels of referee agreement are symptomatic of these trends. Data of this sort are indicative of the increased role of judgment calls in these fields.

The critical basis underlying publication decisions is, out of necessity, much more complex than rationalist accounts of science would have us believe. It was argued above, for example, that the appraisal process can be colored by personal and group biases. Systematic proclivities are instilled and reinforced by professional training, institutional affiliation, and by political and social views. As a result, individual journals (and reviewers) seek to fulfill sets of objectives that appear inconsistent and employ potentially incompatible appraisal criteria.

Thus, to make research attractive, practitioners must tailor their presentations with the appropriate audience in mind. They must pay careful attention to ideological currents, methodological standards, and sociological norms obtaining at the journals to which they submit their research. Responses to Question 5 of the referee survey suggest that this is, in fact, the case. A significant percentage of referees report that knowledge of ongoing debates, as well as of editor and referee tendencies, helps them to calculate the likelihood that their manuscript will be accepted.

The structure of the academic community itself also carries with it the potential to alter publication practices since different components of this community maintain discordant traditions and policy perspectives. As practitioners build stock in their own group's intellectual positions, biases against outsiders may develop as mainstream professionals attempt to protect their interests. In this sense, sociological factors enter the picture and assert an influence on the creation and reception of research. Political orientation, for example, seems especially important in areas of macroeconomics, where scholarly activity is distinctly grouped into several schools. In *Conversations with Economists,* Klamer creatively exposes the impregnable rifts that divide macroeconomists into isolated "research programs." We would not expect that all articles published in the *Journal of Post-Keynesian Economics* would be acceptable submissions for the *Journal of Political Economy,* and vice versa. Journals generally operate under the premise that specific, existing frameworks are superior for tackling issues that fall within the purview of their publication. This serves to establish a common ground for subscribers and allows contributors to express their ideas within the confines of a journal-length article. It also reflects the presence of ideological biases among academic publishers.

Also, as Blank's study reveals, other sociologically based biases may lead to irregular *application* of standards. Although far from conclusive, some evidence indicates that author identity, by revealing position in the academic hierarchy, subtly alters article acceptance rates. Reasoning of this sort is frequently articulated in advocation of blind reviewing practices by journals. More importantly, the mere existence of this debate indicates that members of the profession are cognizant of the fact that reviewer bias is something which potentially reduces the value of academic research.

Through time, a discipline's practices evolve into standards that further guide theory choice decisions. Fels's research helps to reveal that norms prevailing in the discipline's methodological approach are not all positivist in hue. Establishing legitimacy is as much a literary art form as it is a process of proving or disproving conjectures. Similarly, rhetoric studies reveal that common practices of science derive from an array of non-traditional scholarly tactics. Inspection of leading journals reveals that economists employ a broad variety of techniques to persuade colleagues of their work's validity. Arguments may be enhanced, for example, by employing acceptable literary tactics (such as skillful use of rhetoric, well-constructed stories, and appeal to authority). This places an inevitable burden of interpretation on reviewers and explains why critical debate, as opposed to decisive test, plays the crucial role in the development of economics. In the context of academic environments, general methodologies—such as positivism or the methodology of scientific research programs—which ignore the subjective components of appraisal, consequently appear inconsistent with the realities of research evaluation.

A recent increase in critical literature is indicative of the growing awareness of, and impatience with, this inconsistency. Dissatisfaction with the discipline's prevailing methodological perspective establishes common ground for several of the articles cited in this study; most critique some specific deficiency in the way economists report on the practice of their science. While much of this critical literature is valid, it seems to lack persuasive force. Perhaps this is attributable to the disjointed nature of the critique, which gives it the appearance of "nit-picking," rather than of offering a unified alternative to positivism. Consequently, economists remain largely unfazed, and in general, the mentality that continues to dominate casual methodological discussion remains unchanged. Members of the profession do not openly recognize the inherently flawed logic of basing inferences about actual practice on *prescriptive* philosophy of science. This chapter is intended to initiate a more systematic overhaul of the way in which we represent our approach to economics. In this light, the effectiveness of our scientific methods can be viewed from a more direct perspective.

## Notes

1. Tarascio and Caldwell (1979) originally make this distinction.
2. This label originated with Alfred de Grazin's 1963 article.
3. For example, the policy of the *Quarterly Journal of Economics* is to publish, "significant advances in economic theory that appeal to a general audience; original research." Other journals seek research in more narrowly defined sub-fields. Submissions to *Econometrica,* for example, "should advance application of mathematics and statistics to economics. They should be original, well-crafted, and should contain new and correct theoretical or applied results."
4. Judging from citation patterns, only a small percentage of articles published in economics journals become influential. According to David Laband (1986), 90 percent of all articles are cited fewer than twenty times. Only .3 percent are cited more than 100 times.
5. Leading journals most frequently specify their intended audience as academic and professional. The notable exception, which will be discussed in the fourth section, is externally funded research, which has recently become more prevalent—especially in applied areas such as public policy or development economics.
6. It also appears to be more central to the scientific process since there is little evidence indicating that practicing scientists actually follow the advice prescribed by methodologists or philosophers of science.
7. It was shown in Chapters 2 and 3 that, even in retrospect, empirically based appraisal of economic research is seldom conclusive.
8. Journals sampled include the *American Economic Review,* the *Journal of Political*

*Economy, Econometrica,* the *Economic Journal,* the *Review of Economics and Statistics,* the *Journal of Economic History,* the *Review of Economic Studies,* the *Brookings Papers on Economic Activity,* and the *International Journal of Industrial Organization.*

9. The distinction between bias and subjectivity, in this context, was made clear to me by Vincent Tarascio. Many editors, I suspect, accept that subjectivity—or the need for individual judgments—is a necessary component of the journal review process. However, most editors would probably avoid assigning articles to referees who reveal a *bias* toward an article or author for some reason. The problem of reviewer bias is discussed in the next section.

10. It should be noted that Klamer has chosen to study one of the most volatile areas of economics. In a survey of economists, James R. Kearl et al. (1979) show that responses to macroeconomic questions display the lowest level of consensus of any subfield. He attributes this normative element to the ideological nature of many macro-debates.

11. I have in mind here some of Tinbergen's and Haavelmo's work, which sought to incorporate the effect of policy variables on a system's structural parameters. This line of research was initially snubbed by economists but later revived by Lucas's now-famous critique, which, in turn, inspired the rational expectations literature.

12. The age and limited sample size of the survey diminish its persuasive appeal; however, the variance in rejection rates across disciplines is impressive and potentially tells an important story.

13. *Within* economics, it is not possible to discern this trend (if it exists). Instead, a "prestige effect" seems to dominate; the top ten journals (based on citations from core journals) all have acceptance rates of less than 19 percent, well below the disciplinary average of around 25 to 30 percent (Garfield 1989; Zuckerman and Merton 1971).

14. Page limitations in *QJE* and *AER* are thirty-five and fifty pages respectively and are unspecified for *Econometrica* and *JPE.* In 1991, the mean length of articles (excluding short papers, comments, and book reviews) in *AER, Econometrica,* and *QJE* was 18.3, 22.4, and 19.1 pages respectively (total pages divided by number of articles).

15. Referees were asked to rate the quality of the papers they reviewed from 1 (first rate) to 5 (seriously deficient). It should also be pointed out that this has little, if anything, to do with the question of whether or not editors heed the advice of referees. In fact, Blank's study shows high correlation between *mean* referee ratings and editorial decisions.

16. Relative to other surveys, this response rate is comparable. For example, Kearl et al. (1979) "were delighted with a better than 33 percent return," adding that they "were concerned that hostility toward questionnaires among economists might limit the response" (p. 29).

17. The order of the questions has been rearranged here for organizational clarity. See the appendix for an exact copy of the survey.

18. For example, in the Kearl survey, economists were asked if they disagree, agree with provisions, or agree with a number of different propositions. Numbers 1, 2, and 3 were assigned to these responses, which made it very easy to calculate descriptive statistics for each proposition.

19. While an effort has been made to discern and address these aspects of research appraisal individually, they are inherently interrelated. Thus, some overlap of material is unavoidable.

20. Gordon Tullock's *Organization of Inquiry* and Charles Weld's *A History of the Royal Society* provide detailed accounts of the early history of academic journals.

21. From the researcher's perspective, this represents an objectively existing constraint to his own practice of science and communication of ideas.

22. Robert Solow (1990) and Paul Diesing (1991), among others, have discussed the

detrimental effects of a disjointed literature on the discipline's development.

23. This was particularly visible in the early days of academic journals. For instance, the *Quarterly Review* was established in 1809 for purely political reasons. Tory leaders needed a venue to challenge Whig views (articulated in the journal *Edinburgh*) on issues ranging from corn trade to cash payments for the poor (Fetter 1958, p. 47).

24. Kearl's survey of economists, cited above, reflects this generally recognized trend. He finds that statements such as "a ceiling on rents reduces the quantity and quality of housing available" generate considerably more agreement than do statements such as "inflation is primarily a monetary phenomenon." The survey indicates that consensus among economists "tends to center on micro issues involving the price mechanism," while disagreements involve macroeconomics, where the normative nature of many issues "allows ideological considerations to become important" (Kearl et al. 1979, p. 36).

25. Of course, Friedman only rekindled what has been a long-running debate over assumptions. Jevons, writing in 1879, corroborates this claim: "The conclusion to which I am ever more clearly coming is that the only hope of obtaining a true system of economics is to fling aside once and for ever the mazy and preposterous assumptions of the Ricardian School" (Jevons [1879] 1970, preface).

26. By my count, Harvard authors had fully two-thirds as many contributions as Chicago authors (who still had the most) in *JPE;* Chicago authors had half as many submissions as Harvard authors (who still had the most) in *QJE.*

27. For example, the number of institutions represented in *JPE* doubled from approximately 74 during the 1955–59 period to approximately 151 during the 1984–88 period. This trend holds even if we control for the fact that the number of articles published per year increased from about 36 to 67. For random samples of 100 articles, the number of institutions contributing increased from a mean of 49 (1955–59) to a mean of 74 (1984–88).

28. It would be interesting to examine placement patterns at prominent graduate programs and compare them to paths of research development.

29. For example, reviewers can often identify the author of an anonymous paper (about 45 percent of the time, if Blank's sample is representative); further, an author who wishes to be recognized can do so easily through citations, writing style, etc.

30. Statistics of this sort can be found in Zuckerman and Merton (1971), Blank (1991), Crane (1967), and almost any other article on the subject.

31. Stephen Ceci and Douglas Peters (1982) make a persuasive case that the "reputation effect" is large in psychology. They re-submitted thirteen previously published articles with fake names and low-status institutions back to the top journals. Of the ten not recognized as previously published work, nine were rejected overwhelmingly. No clear evidence of this sort of institutional bias has been generated for economics.

32. Over a two-year period, submissions to the *AER* were randomly divided so that approximately half were reviewed single-blind and half double-blind. In single-blind reviewing, the author's name is identified to referees. In double-blind reviewing, the referee is not supplied with the author's name and therefore may or may not know his identity.

33. Some editors think that an author's identity *should* be taken into consideration. In "Econometrica's Operating Procedures", Angus Deaton writes, "Conditional on the honesty and good will of the referee, the identity of the author may be useful in making the assessment, and referees should be given all relevant information" (Deaton et al. 1987, p. 204).

34. Manuscript acceptance rates increase from the blind sample to the non-blind sample at the following rates: universities ranked 6–20, 7.5 percent; U.S. non-academic institutions, 5.9 percent; and universities ranked 21 through 50, 4.9 percent. Top-5 universities and colleges were largely unaffected by type of review system (Blank 1991, p. 1052).

35. Two bits of explanation are important here. First, the number of women in economics

is small, which means the sample size of female-authored articles is small. This, in turn, means significance is harder to establish (statistical means, for example, must show a larger percentage difference to establish significance in smaller samples). Also, it is possible that women are treated differently than men in the profession. Perhaps discrimination is simply offset by male referees who are *more* sympathetic to female authors.

36. Of course, the possible explanations are endless. For example, we could speculate that authors from the top five universities do not benefit as much from name recognition as we might guess because referees are envious or hold the profession's leaders to higher standards. This line of inquiry, while interesting, is not of immediate concern here, as a psychological analysis of scientists' behavior is quite beyond the scope of this research.

37. See Martin Bronfenbrenner (1966) for a survey of how topical interest (as represented by journal entries) has fluctuated through time.

38. Unfortunately, it is difficult to compare the characteristics of published work with those of articles that are rejected. As far as I know, no journals maintain files containing rejected manuscripts.

39. Theories do not always (or even usually) contain observable variables. Thus, testing of models, which bridge the gap between data and theory, occurs more often than does testing of actual theories. See Christopher Gilbert's "Do Economists Test Theories" (in de Marchi and Blaug, 1991) for a clear explanation. In the article, he argues specifically that demand analysis cannot be directly tested and that rejection of demand models has not damaged demand theory. On the other hand, consumption analysis contains observable variables and is, in principle, testable according to Gilbert.

40. This reflects the distinct "confirmatory bias," which exists in economics and other sciences. Despite Popper's assertion that negative experiments carry heavier logical implications, economists overwhelmingly engage in supportive empirical work combined with selective reporting. Although many economists have expressed the need to generate more negative results, the discipline has failed to adopt this philosophy. Little has changed since Francis Bacon noted this tendency in scientific inquiry almost 400 years ago: "The human intellect . . . is more moved and excited by affirmatives than by negatives (Bacon [1621] 1960).

41. Gross begins his article with the observation that there are "two sorts of rhetorical masterpieces: those powerful enough to provoke revolution, and those ingenious enough to avoid it." Darwin's *Origin of Species* is identified with the first type and Newton's *Opticks* with the second.

42. This is certainly the case in economics. Articles periodically appear in the profession's literature outlining "publication tactics." For example, the American Economic Association newsletter *Committee on the Status of Women in the Economics Profession* (May 1990) recently included two such contributions, "Strategies for Publishing Journal Articles" and "More Thoughts on How to Get Published."

43. This line of inquiry clearly has antecedents in the Kuhnian perspective.

44. As Fels points out, the term "official methodology" is misleading since there is no one sanctioned method of science. A variant of the term is used here, in quotes, to indicate the inadequacy of attempts to prescribe one. Similarly, when McCloskey uses the term "official rhetoric" he is not implying that there is an officially designated method in economics; rather, he is caricaturing the methodological approach that is most frequently espoused.

45. At which point it will be explained that McCloskey does not adequately recognize these limitations. His view that rhetoric analysis should replace all aspects of methodological study is misleading and, at times, overly simplistic.

# CHAPTER 5

# Post-Publication Appraisal and Theory Choice

## Introduction

Evidence presented in the previous chapter indicates that a broad range of evaluative criteria are invoked by journal personnel during the formal review process. Although the complexity of actual article appraisal precludes us from portraying this process in a simple and formula-like manner, it has been shown that relevant methodological questions can still be seriously addressed without forcing them into a positivist or Lakatosian framework.

However, only half the story, or perhaps even less, has been reported. As most economists know, publication of a work does not in any way guarantee that it will attract the attention of colleagues or stimulate further scholarship. In fact, citation patterns indicate that only a tiny percentage of published work becomes influential—in the sense that it affects the development of economic theory. Thus, our discussion of the process that promotes certain works to prominence and relegates others to obscurity remains incomplete; inquiries from the last chapter must be extended to include trends that may become evident only over longer periods. To this end, the chapter at hand provides a cursory analysis of post-publication appraisal and selection.[1] Specifically, further attention will be given to the themes emphasized in Chapter 4.

### Characterizing Post-Publication Appraisal and Selection

It is no simple task to systematically study what happens to literature *after* publication. Because of its high degree of formalization and clearly delimited time horizons, the prepublication stage of appraisal and editorial decision-making (as defined in Chapter 4) is a conceptually concise topic. Post-publication research appraisal and theory choice, on the other hand, designates a much more nebulous set of activities. Both the dynamics and the individual components of post-publication processes appear, from a historical perspective, to be highly variable.

In contrast to the structured schedules with which journal operations must adhere, there is no timetable dictating how and when a profession's members will select (or adjust) the set of work that best represents their collective beliefs. During the doctrinal development of economics, some theories and ideas rise to prominence quickly, while others remain dormant for years before attracting proponents. Historical examination of the literature reveals that certain articles and books became "hits" almost immediately; others had to be resurrected long after their completion and publication.

For example, Hermann Heinrich Gossen and Johann Heinrich von Thunen's treatments of marginal utility—in *Entwicklung der Gesetze des menschlichen Verkehrs* (1954) and *Der Isolierte Staat in Beziehung auf Landwirtschaft und Nationalokonomie* (1826, first volume), respectively—were almost entirely neglected at first. However, it was from von Thunen's book that Alfred Marshall reported to have derived his own theory of marginal productivity. Even ideas articulated in William Stanley Jevons's Theory of Political Economy (1871) initially fell prey to hostile reviews (including one by Marshall). His methodological approach had been publicized as early as 1862 in a paper delivered to the British Association for the Advancement of Science, and as late as 1874, he wrote in a correspondence to L. Bodio that "this work was very unfavorably received in this country, and almost the only English economist of importance who noticed it, namely Professor John Elliot Cairnes, repudiated it altogether" (Jevons 1886, p. 323).

In contrast, some articles generate enormous interest practically overnight. For example, Thomas Sargent and Neil Wallace's (1975) rational expectations paper was cited over 200 times by the top forty journals during the five years immediately following its publication. It had an instant impact.

Factors that are both external and internal to the discipline can influence the volume and tone of recognition bestowed upon a particular work. As was pointed out in the last chapter, journal review is largely an internalized process. Editorial decisions are carried out within a narrow context that reflects current norms and trends obtaining both within the discipline and at specific journals. However, after publication (that is, after achieving an objective existence), a work may grow either more or less relevant to economists. Favorable reception at one point does not guarantee indefinite legitimacy. As conditions change over time, the emphasis of questions that economists ask—and hence the credibility of individual works—tends to shift. For example, in light of the stagflationary climate of the 1970s, the theoretical relationship stipulated by the Phillips Curve (both the Keynesian and monetarist interpretations) lost considerable validity in the aggregate view of the profession. Similarly, during a severe recession, a theory that allows for non-clearing labor markets might appear more appropriate than it had previously. Universal modeling is simply not possible in an ever-changing environment. Recognizing this, Robert Solow has stated, "If economics is limited to doctrines which are true forever . . . then there is nothing to economics" (Klamer 1984, p. 136).

Factors that influence the discipline's basis for appraisal are, however, not limited to such external stimuli. Methodological or topical shifts can also be instigated by strictly intradisciplinary developments. For instance, the rational expectations movement directed intellectual capital toward investigating new kinds of mathematical modeling problems. These problems were created largely out of abstract puzzle-solving activities rather than in response to direct observations about the economy. In applied fields, the development of new econometric techniques and the improvement of computers has also shaped the character of economic method from within.[2] Access to computers has dramatically increased the range of empirical questions that a typical professional is capable of exploring. Events such as these indicate that the emphasis of economic study, and hence theory choice criteria, would evolve even if the subject matter did display consistency through time.

Further complicating studies of post-publication theory selection is the fact that literature from several format categories has contributed to the evolution of economic thought. Although clearly the most prominent today, journal articles dominate only one component within the realm of academic publication. Historically, at least three distinct types of literature—syntheses, extensions, and challenges—have been instrumental in the discipline's doctrinal development.

Syntheses digest, formalize, and streamline the existing array of literature; works that fall into this category have often proved influential in designating the discipline's topical boundaries, defining acceptable method, and indirectly sanctioning research paths for the future. Alfred Marshall's *Principles of Economics* (1961), Adam Smith's *Wealth of Nations* (1976), and Paul Samuelson's *Foundations of Economic Analysis* (1947), all contain elements that served to unify the course of economic study. Such tomes are frequently recognized for setting a standard at the time of their publication. They are also heavily drawn upon in the construction of textbooks, which represent the discipline's distillation of a body of theory to the fullest extent.

Another distinct type of research—extensions—seeks to tailor existing theory to accommodate new applications. Gary Becker's economics of the family, which created new applications for neoclassical microeconomics, is a prime example of this type of literature. Much of the influential research published in modern journals falls into this category. As discussed earlier, promoting full development (or, some would argue, exhaustion) of existing analytical frameworks is what the journal system does best. Indeed, a journal's philosophy regarding appropriate material and method is what defines its niche. Readers and submitters are unified by the belief (or self-preservationist rhetoric) that they are on the right track and that persistence will lead to correct solutions to the puzzles that they wish to solve.[3]

A third type of literature—challenges—confronts some aspect of the orthodoxy and, in the process, changes the types of questions that are asked by the profession's members. In the history of economics, such works have generally shifted the methodological or topical emphasis, as opposed to instigating full-fledged Kuhnian revolutions (which require a clean and complete overthrow of the orthodoxy).[4] The most frequently cited examples of challenges to economic theory are Keynes's *General Theory* and the assorted marginalist writings that appeared during the latter half of the nineteenth century. Léon Walras, Karl Menger, and William Stanley Jevons directed orthodox inquiry away from wealth and growth and toward exchange and efficiency issues, essentially offering a superior analytic framework for dealing with Ricardian distribution questions. In returning to an aggregate perspective, John Maynard Keynes partially reversed the trend, although he abandoned the classical supply-dominated approach in order to emphasize behavior of the economy's demand-side components. In both of these cases, as well as with the monetarist and new-classical responses later on, the fabric of economic study was altered but, in the long run, there was no wholesale rejection of the previous body of work.[5] Challenges that have mandated in no uncertain terms more destructive overhauls, such as those mounted by Thorstein Veblen or by Marxists, must be judged less successful as they permeated mainstream theory only indirectly.

Works from each of the three categories defined above have influenced the research path that economics has taken. Authors, motivated by varying philosophical visions and seeking to fulfill different intellectual goals, have produced landmark literature. However, the evaluative processes that underlie the selection of these different types of published literature each displays distinct qualities. In other words, because the contexts in which theory choices occur are different, the process itself is variable. For example, we would expect extensions of the orthodoxy to be less sternly resisted than challenges. Historically, challengers have had to out-maneuver defensive tactics employed by the profession's unified majority. Syntheses that are regarded as classics serve to define the orthodoxy and are often guarded with religious zeal. Thus, heterogeneous literary genre, like inconsistent historical context, creates difficulties for methodologists interested in cataloguing the determinants of theory choice in economics. Even a most casual exploration into this diversity exposes why positivist versions are entirely too simplistic to reflect, in a meaningful way, what economists do.

### Post-Publication Theory Choice—What Do We Already Know?

Fortunately, historians of economic thought have, at times, probed more deeply into this issue than positivist guidelines would warrant. Consequently, topics relating to post-publication research appraisal and theory selection have not been entirely neglected. While the bulk of historical work takes the form of chronological narratives—which often portray economics as a steadily improving science—the question of why certain theories prevail over others has received some scholarly attention. History of thought standards, such as those of Joseph Schumpeter (1981), Mark Blaug (1985), and H.W. Spiegel (1983), which primarily explore the lineage of economics theory, certainly provide hints about theory choice. Additionally, as reported previously, some research has dealt specifically with appraisal and even theory choice issues more directly. This body of literature, when viewed in composite, uncovers no distinct pattern to or implicit formula for achieving long-run influence in academic economics. Practitioners, like referees and editors during the publication process, appear to perform their duties without the aid of a uniform and timeless set of appraisal criteria.

Empirical considerations that distinguish prescriptive positivist methodologies have certainly not been consistently invoked as the litmus for discerning "valuable" (not to mention "true") economic theory from that which is not. Instead, as with the origin of economic ideas, their proliferation is propelled by an array of sources. Existing research reveals that unique, or at least atypical factors figure into almost any instance of theory success. Each case, whether it is the rise of econometrics, the popularization of rational expectations, or the "marginal revolution," requires extensive study to be understood. Any attempt to estimate and rank the relative importance of long-term evaluative criteria must inevitably be based on case-study evidence. Inductive methods of this sort can easily be exploited, via selective reporting, to support a particular vision of theory choice in economics.[6] Thus, the intent here is not to catalogue all of the influences that potentially play a role in long-term theory choice. The work of others has shown that characterizing this process, even for a single theory, may constitute an entire research project unto itself. The topic's nature requires that this chapter take the form of a suggestive essay; the points of emphasis are, out of necessity, limited to several specific aspects of post-publication theory appraisal and selection.

## Scope and Organization of the Chapter

The thematic developments initiated in previous chapters will be renewed here. It is argued below that the post-publication phase of research appraisal and theory choice contains numerous elements that are subjective in nature. As with the publication process itself, this renders traditional, rationalist accounts of science inadequate as explanations of how economics works. The rigid philosophical ideal that suggests that a list of criteria can be or has been invoked to execute theory choice decisions is, again, argued to be unrealistically optimistic.

Here, as in previous chapters, effort is directed toward explaining how a variable subject matter, characterized by time-specific relationships, creates instability in theory appraisal. Essentially, confidence in the explanatory potential of a theory tends to fluctuate as external conditions change. In this context, a theory's level of abstraction and its proximity to policy issues can affect both its initial reception and its longevity.

Finally, the sections below offer further assessment of how the discipline's current reliance on journals for the production of new literature influences doctrinal development. In this vein, we consider the strengths and weaknesses of an academic system in which a journal-driven methodology dominates.

In addressing these and other topics, the remainder of the chapter is organized as follows: "Post-Publication: A Second Process of Elimination" assesses how the basis of theory choice, specifically the relative roles of subjective and objective appraisal criteria, changes after publication. Comparatively speaking, certain "objective" criteria logically diminish in importance over a long period since much work that is error ridden or redundant is upended at journal editors' desks. However, some types of persuasive evidence, such as empirical corroboration or refutation, continue to accumulate after publication. What is certain is that the perspective from which professional appraisal is conducted must naturally change over the life span of any work.

In the next section, the impact that sociological, political, and ideological biases have on longer-run evaluative processes is discussed. Many bias safeguards that serve to regulate journal practices, such as blind reviewing, can no longer be utilized after publication. This potentially elevates the role that sociological currents prevailing within the profession play in literature appraisal. For example, prominent individuals generally operate from highly visible positions within the discipline's hierarchy. Accordingly, they are able to tap into grant money more easily, promote their research agendas more vigorously, and generate support more quickly than the average practitioner. The distribution of the profession's resources is such that the work of its leaders is all but guaranteed instant exposure.

The section that follows assesses further the ways in which a theory's structural characteristics and literary form affect its reception and digestion—extending a discussion initiated in the last chapter. Here, we return to familiar themes—method of presentation, level of abstraction, and proximity to policy—to see how each affects appraisal of work after it has been published. The concluding section integrates this chapter into the context of the book's more general themes.

## Post-Publication: A Second Process of Elimination

After publication, a subset of the "approved" literature captures the profession's collective attention and becomes the subject of more prolonged and thorough critical debate. The majority of articles (and books), however, undergo no significant appraisal after editors and publishers are through with them. One purpose of this chapter is to identify features that distinguish work which rouses further consideration from that which does not. Additionally, since initial high visibility does not ensure prolonged influence, the discerning characteristics of theories that have displayed various levels of staying power are discussed. Indeed, a theory's success, and particularly its longevity, is also a function of how well it stands up against, or avoids, critical challenge over the years. First, however, full clarification of the themes at hand requires an explanation of the ways in which the appraisal and selection process changes through time.

In shifting the focus from publishers and referees to general disciplinary appraisal, it is helpful to have an idea of the extent to which post-publication selection processes narrow the field of relevant research.[7] David Laband (1986) correctly points out that these processes and, specifically, the "causes and consequences" of article popularity have been largely ignored by economists. In this context, he generates descriptive data that shed some light on this intensely competitive aspect of professional academic activities.

Laband employed a sample of almost 6,000 articles that appeared in forty major economics journals between 1974 and 1976 to demonstrate that only a tiny minority of research exerts long-term influence on the formal literature and, in turn, on future research. This was accomplished by measuring the relative popularity of articles, using number of citations in the six-year period immediately following publication as a proxy. Laband finds that more than 90 percent of all articles appearing in the forty top journals are cited fewer than twenty times over the ensuing six years, whereas only 0.3 percent are cited more than 100 times.

A modest attempt to uncover some determinants of article popularity follows. Laband utilizes a simple ordinary least squares regression to demonstrate that author reputation, article length, and journal quality are all significantly positively correlated with article popularity. However, the relevance of these findings must be seriously qualified since article quality—which is unlikely to be independent of these explanatory variables—cannot be objectively measured or controlled.[8] If it were possible to measure such things, it might be revealed, for example, that the profession's leaders produce significantly better work than ordinary practitioners. This would mean that the greater exposure that their work receives is warranted. Given this possibility, trends exhibited in the data cannot be assumed to reflect a determinant sociological bias in the selection process. The same holds with respect to the journal-quality variable, since it is likely that top journals can attract submissions from top authors.

Laband's paper is nonetheless useful in that it provides quantitative support to the perceived view that only a very small percentage of all research is significant in the development of economics. In Laband's words, "The evidence suggests that a select few economists may exert a dominant influence on advances in economic theory. Of even greater importance is the *possibility* that what is said is of less importance than who says it" (Laband 1986, p. 179; emphasis added). Thus, Laband is alluding to non-objective elements operating within the literature selection process. More specifically, he is suggesting a role for sociological influences in a discipline whose members often endorse positivist methods. Evidence that may help us assess the validity of this assertion is considered later in the chapter.

### Positive Appraisal During the Post-Publication Period

Evidence such as that presented by Laband substantiates the widely held notion that post-publication appraisal is highly selective. But what is the basis of this selectivity? What is it about those few top articles—such as those written by Sargent and Wallace (1975) or Sargent (1976)—and books—such as those by Friedman (1953) or Marshall (1890)—that generates such widespread debate which, in turn, stimulates further scholarship? Many economists would argue that, ideally, research—and, hence, the ideas, theories, and methodological prescriptions contained therein—should be judged based on the testability of its implications or on the relative strength of confirmation. In absence of a clear empirical verdict, proponents of this view might argue that additional, generally accepted criteria exist, which serve to guide the development of theory. Thus, empirical evidence combined with other standards make the selection process relatively objective.

In the last chapter, this methodological ideal was shown to be inconsistent with the practices that generate published literature in economics. However, we are now dealing with a different form of appraisal and selection. Thus we first ask, what forms of objective, or at least clearly applicable criteria do economists have at their disposal during the post-publication stage of theory choice?

The survey of referees in Chapter 4 indicates that failure to conform to disciplinary norms and basic standards of science—which objectively exist—adversely affects an author's probability of publication. These types of criteria continue to affect appraisal of a work *after* it has been approved by publishers. In either setting, research that is revealed to have utilized, say, faulty econometric techniques or incorrect calculations is susceptible to criticism. Exposure of mistakes, and sub-standard method in general, reduces the credibility of a work and damages its scientific stature. While judgments of this sort may not be objective in a purely philosophical sense, they are, on a practical level, based on relatively tangible criteria.

However, the evaluative potential of these clearly delimitable criteria diminishes with time. As the referee survey indicates, research that fails to measure up to established standards is likely to be rejected at the journal stage of selection. And if a work that displays a clear "lack of scholarship" does manage to slip past an editor's desk, its deficiencies will typically be exposed shortly thereafter. By the time the post-publication stage of theory choice is reached, the competition has been largely reduced to one between those works that display solid craftsmanship, acceptable technique, and topical value (all of which are determined by prevailing norms).

As the pool of literature is reduced, then, these easily discernible criteria become largely irrelevant to the appraisal process. In this sense, determination of a work's significance becomes more difficult in the long run. For example a practitioner, upon receiving his copy of the most recent issue of the *AER,* is unlikely to encounter numerous mathematical errors, grammar mistakes, or illegitimate statistical techniques. Research that displays such shortcomings has, for the most part, already been discarded. Hence, his estimation of each entry's contribution cannot typically be based on such criteria. Instead, he pursues those articles that he is interested in. Popular articles are those that manage to capture the discipline's aggregate interest.

But what makes an article interesting? This, of course, is a difficult question to answer. If the referee survey above is indicative, elegance, policy relevance, novelty, creativity, and prior reader knowledge are just a few factors that might whet the profession's collective appetite for an article; however, none of these factors is objectively measurable. As the clearly defined criteria become less relevant through time, we might suppose that these other factors become increasingly important. In this respect, determination of a work's significance becomes more subjective through time.

### Timing and Proximity of Empirical Evidence

On the other hand, some aspects of the positivist explanation may approximate scientific procedure better as the post-publication life of a theory or idea unfolds. In the last three chapters, considerable attention has been devoted to explaining why decisive empirical analysis is difficult to come by in social science; this entire line of reasoning need not be repeated here. However, one must not overlook the fact that, after publication, continued empirical observation can, in some cases, produce *additional* evidence concerning a work's validity. While, strictly speaking, verification (or refutation) of theories does not occur in economics, *persuasive* empirical evidence can nonetheless accumulate.[9] In this sense, the post-publication appraisal process can potentially take on a more objective appearance than its prepublication counterpart.

Certainly, many instances in the history of economic thought can be found where theoretical work has inspired an empirical counterpart. All of the so-called economic laws have, at some point, been tested against data. Recently, the search for correlations between economic variables has become especially ubiquitous. This apparent emphasis on testing hypotheses seems to validate claims that economics is the most scientific of the social sciences. Even before the popularization of econometrics and the proliferation of computers made empirical work commonplace, economists displayed a bent for quantitative methods. For example, publication of *The General Theory* inspired efforts to estimate consumption functions, multipliers, labor supply curves, and liquidity preferences. Long before Keynes, William Petty emphasized quantitative methods, employing whatever data he could find[10] :"Petty's method was to postulate functional relationships between economic variables ... and then make deductions therefrom with all the gay abandon of a modern econometrician" (Routh 1989, p. 35). In the meantime testing has become, without question, a standard part of economic method. What *is* open to question is the assessment of exactly what epistemological function this testing plays.

Empirical considerations, it may be argued, contribute to the general regard with which a particular theory (or explanatory device) is held. For example, the Phillip's Curve relationship was better supported by data from the 1950s and 1960s than it was by data from the 1970s, and in the wake of the more recent period, the proposition came under increasing fire. The same can be argued for certain hypothesized relationships posited in *The General Theory*. Originally, during the post-war period, the Keynesian system seemed to mesh with the factual realities of Western economies better than the classical model, and it won the support of the profession. When the economic climate shifted in the 1970s, enthusiasm abated and unity gave way to fragmentation. In each of these cases, changes reflected in the data precipitated a re-evaluation of firmly established beliefs.

While there may be elements of truth to such pleasing accounts, one must be careful not to conclude too quickly that economics is an empirically driven science. Before making this judgment, the proximity of empirical work to theory choice decisions must be considered. The mere presence of testing does not ensure that economists truly aspire to positivist tenets of science. Critical historical studies reveal a dearth of positivist or falsification-ist evidence contributing to the rise and fall of economic ideas. In particular, as an explanation of why theories are *initially* accepted or rejected, the empirical argument fails.

### The Secondary Nature of Testing—The Keynesian Example

In the history of economics, testing has occurred, for the most part, after theories have already gained widespread endorsement. For instance, empirical criteria appear to have played scarcely any role in the creation or subse-quent favorable appraisal of Keynes's ideas.[11] While Keynes was undoubt-edly inspired by empirical anomalies that plagued the classical orthodoxy, his macroeconomic theory was, like theirs, an exercise in pure deduction. This should be evident to anyone who has read *The General Theory*. It certainly appears to have been to William Beveridge:

> Mr. Keynes starts, not from any facts, but from the definition of a concept. . . .
> He proceeds to a fresh series of concepts and of their definitions. . . . Mr.
> Keynes does not return to the facts for verification. . . . It is the duty of the
> propounder of every new theory . . . to indicate where verification of this
> theory is to be sought in facts. . . . This is the demand that would be made of
> the propounder of any new theory in every natural science. It is not the
> demand that has been made of Mr. Keynes by his fellow-economists. (Bever-
> idge 1937, p. 464)

Beveridge concluded that economics is not held to the same standards as natural science because "it is a science in which verification of generaliza-tions by reference to facts is neglected as irrelevant" (ibid., p. 465).

Keynes's theory was appealing to economists for other reasons. A criti-cal and insightful account of this instance of theory choice can be found in Harry Johnson's *On Economics and Society*,[12] which seeks to identify the elements that contributed to the "rapid acceptance and propagation among professional economists" of Keynesian macroeconomics (Johnson 1975, p. 94). Benefiting from first-hand observation and "the blinding light of hindsight," Johnson identifies, in a somewhat Kuhnian spirit, characteristics of the social setting that facilitated the new theory's rapid acceptance. Furthermore, he argues that Keynes's method of presenting ideas and, specifically, the "characteristics of the new theory itself" accelerated, if not accounted for, the success of Keynes's challenge to the orthodoxy. Careful deployment of literary devices and an assortment of rhetorical techniques made the new theory palpable and appealing to other professional economists. In establishing his case, Johnson advances the idea that certain "theory types" are more likely than others to be chosen by economists to represent their collective beliefs. His carefully documented eyewitness account supports D. McCloskey's claim that "for better or worse the Keynesian revolution in economics would not have happened under the modernist legislation recommended for science" (McCloskey 1983, p. 489).

Johnson specifies a number of factors that he believes propelled *The General Theory* to a position of prominence.[13] These factors indicate the existence of a diverse methodology operating in economics. Specifically, by revealing how sociological, rhetorical, and even psychological features figured in the Keynesian revolution, he substantiates claims that more than "purely scientific considerations" motivate and influence the focus of academic study. If Johnson's interpretation is credible, then events surrounding the usurping of the classical system are inconsistent with positivist, Popperian, or Lakatosian characterizations of the scientific process. The "modernist" approach, which synthesizes aspects from these accounts, simply fails to explain what happened. Johnson's interpretation, on the other hand, produces a reasonable explanation behind why economists collectively chose to incorporate parts of *The General Theory* into the orthodoxy. Johnson establishes credibility in his interpretation by acknowledging—not ignoring—the subjective components of theory choice practices.

### The Problem of Conflicting Data—The Phillips Curve

Like Johnson, Nancy Wulwick argues, by way of example, that non-traditional factors affect the "process which governs the acceptance or rejection of theories." Her 1987 article indicates that the explicitly empirical Phillips Curve was adopted by the profession for largely "extra-scientific," or at least extra-empirical, reasons.

As is well known, testing of the price (or wage) inflation–unemployment relationship has historically produced conflicting results. Phillips hypothesized an inverse relationship between the two variables, suggesting an exploitable tradeoff for policy-makers. In contrast, Arthur Brown—a contemporary of Phillips—conducted similar tests and concluded that the relationship between wage inflation and unemployment had been highly variable throughout the period in question. Both researchers had access to the same data and they each studied common time periods. However, the two came to disparate conclusions concerning the stability of employment–inflation tradeoffs. During the years following the initial conjectures, additional empirical work has failed to produce a consensus on exactly what the practical significance of Phillips's research is to policy-makers.

Wulwick argues that a priori theoretical perspective pertaining to the source of inflation was an important determinant in the verdicts arrived at by researchers on each side of the debate. Phillips, like most monetarists at the time, subscribed to a demand-pull explanation while Brown, like the majority of Keynesians, adhered to a cost-push explanation. Regardless of the dispute's origins, empirical work "failed to verify the Phillips relationship in respect to either the long run or the short run. . . . Economists nevertheless did not drop the Phillips Curve as positivist methodology would predict"; instead, "the economics community rapidly institutionalized the long-run hyperbola" (Wulwick 1987, p. 841). Wulwick produces credible evidence to indicate that inconclusive testing was secondary to political and even rhetorical considerations in this instance of theory choice. The significance of this type of evidence will become clear, if it is not already, in the sections that follow.

### *Historical Context and Changing Structural Relationships*

Case studies such as these expose another clue indicating why, in economics, empirical evidence is rarely definitive: Causal relationships between economic variables are not stable. In each instance above, the profession's appraisal of an idea underwent serious revision as the economic landscape changed. The relevance of the Phillips relationship came into question during the stagflationary climate that marked the 1970s.[14] Similarly, the value of Keynesian theory in addressing prevailing economic problems is highly time and place dependent. The demand-dominated analysis is arguably appropriate for studying the United States, circa 1936, or perhaps Haiti today and yet may be highly limited as an approximation of current conditions in the United States or in a future Haiti.

This type of criticism, levied against aspects of the orthodoxy that are treated as universal, has been well developed by economists from the German historical, Marxist, and institutionalist schools. Furthermore, Austrian economists, especially Ludwig von Mises (1978) and Friedrich von Hayek (1978), assert that changing economic conditions limit the role of hypothesis testing to revealing trends in "the economic history of the recent past" (von Mises 1978, p. 74). Others, while acknowledging some practical uses for econometrics, have specified these empirical limitations. Gerald Garb argues that "certain economic phenomena are best characterized as non-recurring or infrequently occurring events," and Wassily Leontief points out that "economic change constantly affects the form and parameters of the structural equations assumed in economic models" (Tarascio and Caldwell 1979, p. 989). Tarascio summarizes: "The absence of universal laws means that even highly confirmed theories which have worked well in the past need not be applicable in the future, that 'laws' may work well in some cases, but fail in others" (ibid.).

For certain types of work, this exogenous, relativist dimension inherent in the subject matter of social science creates special long-run limitations. Theories (or, more likely, representative models) that seek to direct policy, and which contain observable variables may, over a period of time, be especially susceptible to declines in popularity. Any theory that maintains a link to the actual economy tends to lose (or gain) relevance as circumstances change. This partially explains why more "practical" theory, such as Keynesian macroeconomics, appears obsolete at times while highly abstract theory, such as Walrasian general equilibrium—which contains very few directly testable implications—appears more immune to anomalous external conditions. This lack of direct applicability gives highly abstract work a sort of timelessness that economists seem to value in long-run appraisal. So long as its method remains attractive by a discipline's internal criteria, such as elegance and mathematical tractability, a theory can exist peacefully in a variety of economic climates. Nonetheless, work of this sort must be appraised on some critical basis other than predictive adequacy. This line of reasoning will be developed in a section below, where the relationship between the structural characteristics of a theory and its longevity are discussed.

### Bias in the Post-Publication Theory Choice Process

By this point it should be clear that the positive–normative distinction made by economists (most conspicuously in introductory texts) is misleadingly simplistic and largely trivial. In the actual practice of science, value judgments are required during both the research creation and appraisal processes. Economists, even those who are diligent about maintaining their neutrality, arrive at different views concerning the workings of the economy. The manner in which a practitioner compiles knowledge of his field—what he chooses to read, the research path that he pursues, and so on—depends on his own interpretation of significance, which is ultimately subjective. Even the construction and interpretation of empirical evidence relies, at various stages, on non-objective factors. As Gunnar Myrdal pointed out more than a half century ago, data does not assemble itself; choosing a source, estimating accuracy, and interpreting test results are all contingent upon the researchers' discretion.[15] More importantly, since direct testing of theories is rarely possible in economics, practitioners must inevitably rely on a wide variety of alternative techniques to persuade colleagues of the merits of their work.

Among economists, we observe that the prominent role of value judgments has facilitated the development of contrasting beliefs concerning which methods and models are the most useful and accurate. It is essentially this characteristic of the discipline that divides macroeconomists into different schools. Conflicting perspectives have affected, at least indirectly, the way in which individuals practice their science.[16] Ideological factors, based on political or more general worldviews also dictate, to varying degrees, which group a practitioner associates with and, in turn, which methodological approach he advocates. Indeed, such factors influence the research topics to which the practitioner will be attracted in the first place. Similarly, sociological features underlying professional environments constrain the range of legitimate practice. In any human environment, academic communities included, where activity cannot be fully regulated by a system of pure logic, the potential exists for bias.

In the previous chapter, sources of bias were given considerable attention. There, it was noted that reputable journals take measures to safeguard against what might be termed "unscientific behavior" during the literature review process. If we take the topical scope and methodological norms prevailing at journals as given, it is not unreasonable to believe that, in general, submitting authors get a fair shake. However, a group's topical interests and methodological norms often originate from collective epistemological beliefs that contain political, ideological, and sociological components; this creates divisions across the academic spectrum that are not easily accounted for in positivist methodology.

As noted earlier, these divisions carry implications for research appraisal at the prepublication level. While some journals naturally maintain a broader perspective than others, each will typically avoid publishing research that falls outside of their established niche. This means that, to optimize the probability that his research is published, an individual must submit his article to a journal where it will appear consistent with prevailing discussions. The referee survey indicates that practitioners are indeed cognizant about choosing journals where similar work is found. Researchers do not knowingly subject themselves to biases that they can avoid. For example, an economist is unlikely to submit a paper with clear post-Keynesian political undertones to a journal where new classical methodology dominates, and vice versa. Thus, it is reasonable to suspect that "good work" is generally published independent of its underlying policy implications because participants in the academic process become aware of the properties of the system and submit their work to appropriate outlets.[17]

Nonetheless, sociological divisions based on political leanings, honest epistemological differences, and even geographical location do exist. As is usually the case in contexts characterized by personal interaction, biases toward one's own kind of work and against that of others do develop. Some undesirable effects resulting from these biases can be minimized during the carefully monitored journal stage of appraisal, but after publication, author and institution identity become fully visible. At this point, individuals and groups must argue the merits of their positions in the open, and unfortunately, idea production is not an industry that can accurately be approximated by a model of perfect competition. Authors and institutions compete for the recognition that makes practicing their craft rewarding. Likewise, journals vie for attention in order to elevate prestige, generate subscriptions, and maintain financial support. However, within academic disciplines, the production unit may be a giant or a dwarf. If a practitioner belongs to a smaller or less influential group, he will receive less attention than others, all other things equal. The academic world is an imperfectly competitive market, and the implications of this reality warrant further scrutiny.

### The Social Structure of the Academic Community

Much of the discussion concerning the sources and consequences of professional bias from the last chapter is also relevant here. However, after publication, the context of appraisal does change in significant ways. Thus, in specifically addressing the nature of bias in the post-publication period of theory choice, several additional comments are in order.

Academic communities, like other social organizations, are divided—both horizontally and vertically—into smaller groups. In economics, the horizontal grouping of practitioners into "schools" and sub-fields has evolved from political and epistemological alignments, and also in response to practical considerations. Within these groups, members are cast vertically into a hierarchy, based on achievement and recognition. This social structure, which is neither unusual nor necessarily avoidable, can create biases that affect the reception and promotion of work.

*Horizontal Division*

Over the past several decades, increasing depth and detail in the scope of study has precipitated the designation of many sub-disciplines in economics and a division of labor among practitioners. The profession is horizontally segregated into econometricians, micro-theorists, economic historians, and so on because no individual could possibly master (or be interested in) all fields. This trend is largely unavoidable and is certainly not undesirable in all respects.[18] However, given the absence of a clearly drawn system for establishing validity, the potential also arises for segmentation along epistemological, social, and political lines. This means that various factions may grow to emphasize different appraisal criteria in the practice of their discipline. One group might prioritize precision, mathematical rigor, and elegance in model-building while another might emphasize policy relevance, applicability, or realism of assumptions. In this context, disputes among economists arise because no one group can establish superiority in any objective, or even agreed-upon, sense.

Intellectual schools have traditionally united practitioners with like policy views and methodological perspectives. As Arjo Klamer (1984) so effectively demonstrates, competing groups that are divided by ideology are, at times, unable to overcome their differences and communicate effectively. In such an environment, partnerships and biases are generated. Solidarity is nurtured during graduate training, as academic departments frequently develop a particular bent that instills or reinforces biases against alternative approaches.

Additionally, the close proximity of politics to economic analysis elevates the role of ideology as a source of bias. Critics of the orthodoxy, most notably Marxists, have charged that economic theory has historically consisted of little more than political desideratum. For example, one of the centerpieces of Western economic thought—perfect competition—not only observes some aspects of the economy but also implicitly advocates a model for the *optimal* economy; in a sense it says what ought to be. Political maneuvering on behalf of various factions operates at many levels of professional discourse. Johnson observed, firsthand, the conspicuous presence of ideological motivation in the practice of economics at Cambridge during the 1950s:

> Cambridge people in my judgment were perverting economics in order to defend intellectual and emotional positions taken in the 1930s. In particular, for them Keynesian economics was not a theoretical advance to build on for scientific

progress and improved social policy. It was only a tool for furthering left-wing politics at the level of intellectual debate. (Johnson 1975, p. 124)

Similarly, a political dimension has, by reputable account, subtly colored economists' appraisals of the Phillips Curve. Wulwick's article traces the rise of this heuristically attractive expository device and reports the mixed evidence that has accrued since Phillips first put forth his empirical observation. Wulwick reasons that, given the absence of clear corroboration or verification, this instance of "theory" choice in economics must ultimately have been reduced to individual value judgments formulated on the basis of other factors.

Wulwick argues that political ideology permeated the profession's thinking during the reception and interpretation of Phillips's analysis. Specifically, the policy perspectives held by competing groups appear to have affected test outcomes and interpretations of data. Even in camps that recognized at least a short-run inflation–unemployment trade-off, appraisal of the Phillips relationship was far from uniform. Wulwick points out that "post-Keynesians strenuously opposed the Phillips models," largely because their "social philosophy excluded unemployment as the answer to inflation." Meanwhile, monetarists and "right-wing" Keynesians such as Frank Paish advocated tight monetary policies to combat the creeping inflation of the 1950s—measures which might theoretically create adverse affects on employment and income (Wulwick 1987, p. 852). In short, policy preferences affected both empirical work and overall assessment of the value of the Phillips Curve. Wulwick concludes that this episode defies explanation via conventional methodology because it demonstrates that, even in an environment where empirical proof was highly inconclusive, economists "tenaciously adhered" to rival positions. The basic grounds for this rivalry, and hence a major stimulus to research, was rooted in "external beliefs about the economic role of government" (ibid., p. 854). If Wulwick's version of events is accurate, then political bias is not, in all cases, an irrelevant facet of economic method as modernist accounts would have us believe.

*Vertical Division*

The economics profession is, in addition to being grouped into schools and sub-disciplines, also stratified vertically, with leaders at one end and ordinary practitioners at the other. The "ranking" of the profession's members is partly explicit, in that different titles (full, associate, or assistant professor) are awarded at various levels of achievement. There is also an unofficial, but acknowledged, hierarchy of institutions, which is possibly more important. Where a practitioner fits into this hierarchy potentially affects the impact that he can exert within his horizontally designated group. Other factors held constant, a paper or book written by a full professor at MIT is likely to attract more initial attention than one written by an instructor at a low-ranking institution (Laband's study is suggestive of this). The professor at MIT has—as prerequisite—already been recognized for accomplishments, which establishes his credibility a priori.

High-profile individuals benefit from direct access to resources, such as superior financial and staff support, which are essential in the production of quality work. Also, leaders operate within an environment where disciples (usually graduate students or junior faculty) are available to promote their work and generate additional exposure through a supportive secondary literature.[19] Tarascio (1986) points out that, given this natural order, the beliefs of high-profile individuals are of great importance to the development of any discipline. New practitioners, if they are to succeed, must be "tuned in" to the profession and attach themselves to a "premier literature." Thus, decisions regarding topical and methodological significance made at the top are crucial to the development of economics because of their impact on work carried out by researchers operating on other tiers of the hierarchy. Tarascio writes:

> The direction a discipline takes, (and) its success or failure to live up to expectations, depends how open or closed it is regarding ascendancy to leadership, how much tolerance towards diversity exists, and to what extent it can accommodate change and obsolescence of ideas. (1986, p. 7)

Independent of whether or not the current system is optimal (or justifiable), the social structure operating in science does impose a bias against individuals operating in secondary departments, and "upward mobility for faculty at a secondary institution to premier institutions is difficult." In other words, accessibility to positions of leadership is highly limited, if not closed, and this, according to Tarascio, has created something of a crisis in economics, as the same ideas tend to be rehashed and sources of criticism and, hence, change go undernourished:

> The development of economics as a science has been characterized by the professionalization of the discipline—standardization of professional training, adherence to professional norms prevailing at premier institutions. This standardization is reflected in the professional journals which, with few exceptions, tend to be quite similar in content. All this has an important bearing on the ability of the profession to respond to change and to cast off obsolete

theories and pursue new avenues of inquiry outside the standard framework of economics. (Ibid., p. 9)

Any number of instances can be drawn upon to illustrate the impact that this operative hierarchy imparts upon the theory selection process. The rise of new classical macroeconomics (or, more specifically, rational expectations) offers a case in point. To understand why the program was accepted by a substantial sub-population of economists, the nature of its propositions as well as the characteristics prevailing in the profession's social structure must be identified. Since rational expectations is essentially an assumption, a tool for modeling expectations within other theoretic structures, it could not have been accepted on grounds that legitimize *theory*. The accuracy or validity of an assumption depends on the circumstances in which it is being applied. Rational expectations does create a simplifying assumption, one that is more consistent with the core of microeconomics (which stipulates that individual agents optimize and use all available information). It is not, however, an empirically testable proposition; it is not even intended to be. Rather, the principal contributors to the development of new classical economics, such as Robert Lucas and Thomas Sargent, created a technique whereby expectations could be explicitly modeled. Until then, expectations had been treated exogenously (because treating them "realistically," as opposed to rationally, is forbiddingly complex). Whether or not this technique offers a reasonable approximation of aggregate behavior is, ultimately, a matter of opinion.

Thus, according to Rodney Maddock (1991), pioneers of the rational expectations method had to market their product aggressively, acquire funding, attract brainpower, and recruit followers. It helped that they had graduate students at high-status institutions such as Chicago and Minnesota who were captive of the program and who would admire, learn, and pass on the new techniques to advance their own professional careers (ibid., p. 353–54).[20] Realistically, this scenario—whereby a practitioner can create momentum for a research program—is only relevant for individuals operating from a position of authority.

New ideas and theories, if not produced by leaders in the field, must gain proponents from the top. Wulwick points out that the Phillips relationship acquired the endorsements of Samuelson and Solow at the 1959 American Economic Association convention, as they "gave the curve an eponymic title, like many a physical law" (Wulwick 1987, p. 841). In fact, it was Samuelson and Solow (1960) who specified an inverse relationship between the *price* level and unemployment.[21] Recall that Phillips had concentrated his efforts on the *wage* inflation–unemployment tradeoff.

Other transitional periods also reflect the nature of this relationship between the profession's hierarchy and idea reception. For instance, methodologists have questioned whether Keynes could have convinced economists of the value of his work had he not been operating from a position of preeminence, respect, and authority. Johnson's perspective as a Cambridge insider (where he was a visiting student and, during the 1940s, a faculty member) allowed him to witness, from close proximity, how sociological undercurrents facilitated the propagation of Keynes's ideas. While probably not the most important factor in the rise of Keynesian economics, Johnson points out that Keynes was lucky to have had a receptive audience available to him. It afforded him the opportunity to employ his universally recognized polemic talents to attract admirers, both students and faculty, who were eager to sort out and spread the new faith.

Johnson also articulates an awareness of more general social features that affected the practice of economics during the periods dominated by the Keynesian revolution and monetarist counter-revolution:

> A second factor in the transformation of Keynesianism into an orthodoxy has been that people who made their academic reputations and earned their present status on the basis of an early and enthusiastic conversion to Keynesianism in the late 1930s and early 1940s have continued to trade on their foresight, to the academic detriment of their juniors, who have never had the same chance to jump onto the front—and not the rear—of an academic bandwagon. This factor has been far more effective in paving the way for a monetarist counter-revolution in the United States, where institutional competition prevents centralized control of professional advancement, than in the United Kingdom, where Oxbridge continues to dominate the academic scene. (Johnson 1975, pp. 97–98)

These observations tie in naturally with Tarascio's leader–follower argument. In England, the orthodoxy tended to be very narrowly drawn around Keynesian macroeconomics because leadership was so concentrated. In the United States, where there are a large number of quality institutions, the number of leaders is greater and bastions of "radical orthodoxy," such as the monetarists at Chicago, can exist and create problems for members of the standard orthodoxy (in this case, Keynesians who dominated the elite East Coast universities). These dynamics in the development and appraisal of ideas are interesting and cannot be ignored if a full understanding of doctrinal development is to be achieved.

Examples such as these illustrate one of the central themes advanced here: It is important that sociological factors (such as institutional arrangements, power relationships, hierarchical structure, and the potential for bias between competing groups) be considered when constructing accounts of theory choice in social science. The modern scientific community is not necessarily unfair or in need of correction; its characteristics simply need to be acknowledged and understood to be fully utilized. It is careful consideration of these influences, in addition to the traditional determinants of scientific development, that makes the accounts outlined above complete and accurate. Simply put, Johnson's version of the Keynesian revolution and monetarist counter-revolution is superior to a positivist account because, under the latter, there is little to discuss. Within a positivist or Lakatosian framework, we cannot even reasonably discuss the effect of, say, institutional arrangements on the development and reception of research. In economics, sociological and political influences on theory choice cannot be deleted (or relegated to footnotes) because they figure too conspicuously in the discipline's historical development.

## Method of Presentation and the Reception of Theories

In economics, as in other fields of study, ideas can only attract support and endorsement if they are presented in a comprehensible form. Additionally, a work is made more or less attractive depending on the effectiveness with which its author conveys these ideas to his readers. The referees surveyed in the previous chapter indicate that research is enhanced when it is presented both rigorously and artistically; this can be accomplished by, among other things, observing disciplinary standards of scholarship, utilizing state-of-the-art techniques, or simply writing well. This line of reasoning, which emphasizes the importance of presentation, is also valid when considering post-publication theory choice—although it must be qualified. Within the modern journal literature, many fundamentally sound, attractively packaged, technically appealing articles appear. However, very few of these articles go on to influence economic thought in the long run; rarely does one change the way we think about economic problems.

What is it, then, that distinguishes the rare influential work from the rest? To address this question, let us begin with a simple observation. The overwhelming majority of research today is conducted with no intention of changing theory or generating theory choices. Rather, much work is motivated, and sometimes even contracted, to accomplish other more limited tasks. For example, the type of work that appears in many of the "applied" journals does not generally figure into more long-term theory development. A study that, say, seeks to estimate the costs and benefits associated with implementing a new national health care system is unlikely to exert any long-term influence on economic thinking, even though it may be quite useful in some other respects. Applied work—aimed at solving specific real-world problems—must necessarily employ a narrow, case-oriented approach. Given that the economic environment is constantly changing, the end-product can rarely be generalized to a wide range of problems. Hence, applied research is typically better suited for influencing current political decisions than it is for affecting economic theory. In contrast, work that remains influential over a long period of time and achieves doctrinal status is inevitably less issue and less empirically oriented; theory which has survived generations of economists and the transformation of economic institutions is inherently abstract. This elevates the role that other evaluative criteria, such as elegance, mathematical tractability, and internal consistency, must play in theory assessment, and may partially explain why economics, as taught in core theory courses, is commonly criticized for not offering the "practical" solutions that a policy science "should" offer.

There is another reason why the characteristics of a theory are especially important during the post-publication appraisal process. As time elapses, the personality traits and reputation of a theory's originator, which may affect contemporary research appraisal, become increasingly remote.[22] Therefore, certain aspects of theory choice, such as sociological or political bias, may have less impact on the continued assessment of long-established concepts such as the law of demand, marginal analysis, or the model of perfect competition. Many components of the modern orthodoxy now stand independent of the theorists who created them. More recent work, on the other hand, may still carry ideological baggage reflecting an author's personal and subjectively developed preferences. For instance, during professional debate, one commonly hears questions such as, "What is Becker's or Friedman's ideological perspective?" Or even, "What was Keynes's political agenda?" In the long run, the characteristics and nature of the theory itself, rather than the theorist, become relatively more important.[23] This is potentially a relevant point in constructing an explanation of what promotes work in economics. In this spirit, we look tentatively at "successful" theory in order to develop an understanding of what distinguishes it from the rest. In the process, specific aspects of the post-publication theory choice process are illustrated.

### An Interpretation of the Macro-Revolution

Historical evidence lends credibility to our thesis that literature appraisal is, generally speaking, a multidimensional process, even in the case of major works. Stylistic and strategic aspects of research presentation—or rhetoric criteria—appear to have added an intangible element to past theory choice decisions. Johnson (1975), in the context of the Keynesian revolution, argues that this criteria type has contributed to the success of new theory (as opposed to "normal research") in economics. Three aspects of Johnson's argument are outlined below; none is purely scientific in the traditional epistemological sense.

1. As a prerequisite for success, new theory must attack central propositions of the orthodoxy that appear inadequate or anomalous.[24] The attack, however, must offer an *academically acceptable* alternative. The problematic central proposition mandated under the classical system is that the economy unwaveringly tends toward full employment. Keynes created an academically acceptable alternative and exposed the limitations of Say's Law by combining "Kahn's concept of the multiplier and his own invention of the propensity to consume" (Johnson 1975, p. 95).

Further, the political implications underlying *The General Theory* were more ideologically palatable than those contained in the more radical socialist alternatives of the day. Keynes's system did not, by conventional interpretation, question the superiority of the basic market-oriented economy. In fact, he appealed for continuity: "To ensure the preservation of a reduced inequality of income and wealth produced by private enterprise (requires) merely a gradual but prolonged continuance of what we have seen recently in Great Britain, and will need no revolution" (Keynes 1936, p. 376). Keynes's policy prescription for mending the economic ills of the day appealed to common sense and did not require painful measures such as those mandated by Marxist remedies.

2. Another ingredient contributing to a new work's academic acceptability is found in its ability to appear novel while incorporating as much existing doctrine as possible.[25] Although Keynes's eminent position within the profession afforded him greater latitude than most, maintaining links with the orthodoxy was still important because it ensured that ambitious practitioners, who were looked to for support, were not intimidated into a purely defensive stance. The amount of effort required on their part to complete the transition toward the new material could be judged as reasonable. Johnson and other Keynes scholars have painstakingly established that *The General Theory* retained familiar definitions, recognizable symbols, and—most importantly—established concepts, such as the marginal productivity-based theory of labor demand. Keynes had been, in his own words, "a faithful pupil of the classical school," and the Marshallian tradition, which formed the basis of his training, maintains a strong presence in the Keynesian system. Thus, even though *The General Theory* contains an unmistakably confrontational component, Keynes skillfully managed to preserve some sense of continuity and, in this sense, displayed what rhetoric scholars term the "conciliatory persona."

3. Finally, according to Johnson, new theory must attain an appropriate level of difficulty. It must be challenging enough so that the older generation finds it not worth their time to invest the effort required to understand it. (They also face the prospect of abandoning a much greater intellectual investment in the orthodoxy than their younger counterparts.) Consequently, "the senior academic colleagues" are unable to mount a unified and viable counter-attack to support their methods and theoretic perspective. Instead, they "waste their efforts on peripheral issues, and so offer themselves as easy marks for criticism and dismissal by their younger and hungrier colleagues" (Johnson 1975, p. 95).

Simultaneously, however, confrontational theory must not appear *too* difficult. The young generation of practitioners must be able, through ambitious study, to understand enough of the new material to form an influential group of proponents. Keynes himself gives us the best indication of why his new system initially appeared imposing but, after its reinterpretation into textbook versions, boiled down to relatively simple principles: "The ideas which are here expressed so laboriously are extremely simple and should be obvious. The difficulty lies, not in the new ideas, but in escaping the old ones, which ramify, for those brought up as most of us have been, into every corner of our minds" (Keynes 1936, p. viii).

Additionally there was, in this case, a methodological component to this "degree of difficulty" criterion, which divided the profession. Keynes's approach offered a viable and accessible alternative to the malady-ridden orthodoxy in part because younger economists had gained a facility in mathematics and statistics that the older generation had not commonly attained; "*The General Theory* found a middle ground in an aggregated general-equilibrium system which was not too difficult or complicated to work with—and which offered a high degree of apparent empirical relevance to those who took the trouble to understand it." This apparent empirical relevance was not, however, "formulated as statistical propositions until the early 1950s, well after the bulk of younger economists had become persuaded they were true" (McCloskey 1983, p. 489).

Keynes's proficiency in literary technique further enhanced his tactical approach. Despite its sometimes awkward structure, *The General Theory* displays at its origin a brilliant coordination of language. Keynes used his expository skills to direct his ideas toward the appropriate audience. His concern with presentation surfaces in the opening paragraph of the first chapter:

> I have called this book *The General Theory of Employment, Interest and Money,* placing the emphasis on the prefix general. The object of such a title

is to contrast the character of my arguments and conclusions with those of the classical theory of the subject, upon which I was brought up and which dominates . . . economic thought. (1936, p. 2)

Also, as pointed out above, Keynes's use of the term "general" was intended to draw an analogy to developments in physics, where Einstein's theoretic work had invalidated certain reductionist constructs of the Newtonian system that were also present in classical economic theory.

When viewed in composite, literature describing the ascent of Keynesian macroeconomics supports the thesis that such processes are multidimensional by nature. In balance, however, we must bear in mind that not all aspects of the theory choice episode involving Keynesian macroeconomics are representative of everyday research in economics; the validity of generalization drawn from this case must be qualified. Specifically, we are considering the role of factors that contribute to the acceptance of not ordinary work, but work that produces *new theory*. Johnson's critical analysis pertains to extraordinary circumstances—a context quite distinct from that which was discussed as prepublication journal appraisal. Nonetheless, Johnson is persuasive in recounting a case of theory choice that does not fit well into a positivist methodology. This, in itself, is enough to show that the scientific process, at least in economics, does not entail a recurring and highly predictable pattern.

### *Mirowski's Case Study of Neoclassical Economics*

Phillip Mirowski's *More Heat than Light* uncovers other rhetorical aspects that are relevant to theory choice—although this was not his primary intent. The central thesis contained in *More Heat than Light* consists of essentially three components. First, Mirowski shows, very convincingly, that neoclassical pioneers such as Walras and Jevons, trained in engineering and natural sciences, lifted their analytic apparatus from "proto-energetics" to create a field theory of value based on utility (that is, a field of preferences by a consumer establishes utility levels, individual demand, and hence a basis for value). Here, Mirowski contributes to our understanding of theory *creation*.

*More Heat than Light* persuasively advances a second case—that when the methods of energy physics are extended to neoclassical utility theory, they lose much of their coherence. Mirowski demonstrates that, to maintain the mathematical tractability of the conservation principle (which is central in proto-energetics), economic theory must, in its application, make invalid assumptions (for example, total utility plus total expenditure must be constant, despite being measured in different units). In short, the physics metaphor adopted in marginal utility theory was done so "in a slipshod manner" because the economic system does not share the same properties as physical systems that make the mathematical structure relevant (Mirowski 1989, p. 108).

Mirowski's first two conjectures shed new light on the history of marginal analysis.[26] However, he goes further—and with less success. His third major assertion is that the improper adoption of this metaphor wholly invalidates modern neoclassical economics. In essence, the entire Marshallian synthesis is on shaky ground because inconsistent concepts of value underlie supply and demand. To believe in the total extent of Mirowski's claim here, one would first have to believe that the energy metaphor does indeed dominate modern economic theory. Mirowski's claims can be dampened by pointing to other influences, and indeed adoption of other metaphors, in the history of economic theory.[27] The evolution of neoclassical theory has involved some thoughtful, if ad hoc, amendments that have pared down the role of the energy metaphor. At any rate, the persuasiveness of this third of Mirowski's conjecture is only indirectly related here.

*More Heat than Light* proves most useful to our thesis where it uncovers rhetorical devices employed by nineteenth-century marginal utility theorists. In particular, Mirowski details the most extensive use of metaphor in economics literature. The adoption by economists of physics concepts corroborates D. McCloskey's point that literary use of metaphors is not always "ornamental" but often substantive. The actual content and methods associated with the theoretical framework of neoclassical economics has been influenced, if not dictated, by its flawed energy metaphor. Mirowski, in fact, argues that insistence on maintaining the model inspired from the energy metaphor has kept economists from investigating other potentially more relevant physics theories such as modern relativity and quantum mechanics.

Mirowski posits that the "brazen" transformation of energy theory to utility theory by early marginal theorists was motivated, in part, from a desire to bring scientific respectability and legitimization to economics.[28] It would be difficult to estimate how important such considerations were to Walras, Jevons, or Fisher; this would entail a study into psychological aspects of the *context of discovery* (or, in this case, *of method emulation*). Regardless of motivation, however, the end-product of this movement reveals an assimilation of mathematical techniques that brought economics closer in appearance to physics, deemed then and now as the quintessential science. It created, for economics, the image of being the most scientific of the social sciences.

The form in which "revolutionary" marginal theory materialized[29]—with its use of metaphor, elegant mathematical structure, and abstraction—impacted its reception. Adoption of methods common to physics did *eventually* contribute to the increased scientific respectability afforded to economics. The modern standard of expressing theoretical relations in economics is based on the mathematical frameworks (both marginal and general equilibrium) developed by Walras. It should be noted, however, that Walras's mathematical representations were resisted early on and the marginal revolution did not proceed with unprecedented speed. George Stigler (1973) argues that non-academic economists concerned primarily with business-related matters had no particular interest in the new and highly abstract theory. It flourished in environments where economists operated from a university setting.[30]

It is interesting that, at the time when marginal theory was *chosen* as the theory of value over competing substance theories of value, it was done so for extra-positivist reasons. The mathematics gave the impression of real science, but the new theory did not advance economics according to Popperian, positivist, or Lakatosian criteria. Marginal utility theory did not posit economic relationships in falsifiable terms. It did not increase potential for empirical confirmation, and it did not represent a theoretical or empirical problem shift as defined by Lakatos. The marginal revolution did not occur for empirical reasons.[31]

What did make the new theory appealing in the long run was its elegant, if inappropriate, adoption of mathematical techniques developed in physics. It enabled economists to follow the law structure of physics and increase their scientific personae. Assumptions that underlie marginal utility theory (such as the Slutsky conditions) were specified, not as a means of increasing the accuracy with which the theory represents reality, but to restore the mathematical tractability and hence elegance of energy theory. Furthermore, the level of abstraction that characterizes marginal utility theory—its distant proximity to observable variables—has facilitated its longevity. Lack of empirical content and, hence, immunity from direct testing has enabled marginal analysis to exist even as economic circumstances have changed.

Cast in the beneficial light of hindsight, historical overview does not compellingly support the contention that economists of the marginalist school won over the profession because their work satisfied a modernist list of criteria. Instead, evidence again suggests that the validity of research is established via a highly variable and multidimensional process.

*Other Examples*

Additional case studies can be drawn upon to illustrate other rhetorical components of the theory choice process. Wulwick's account of the rise of the Phillips Curve offers another clear explanation of how presentation can contribute to the success of a piece of research. As Mirowski and others have observed, economists have historically aspired to the physical science ideal and, as such, value "simple, constant, quantifiable observational laws in the form of Euclidean functions" (Wulwick 1987, p. 841).[32] Wulwick argues that the case of the Phillips Curve exemplifies much of this spirit, as it was "hailed by economists as reflecting 'natural laws' "; the hypothesized inflation–unemployment tradeoff, it was thought, might be "immutable" (ibid.). Furthermore, Phillips's choice of a rectangular hyperbola "suited his polemical aim." In addition to its eye-catching functional form, it was considered a "versatile heuristic device," because the product of its coordinates is constant (as with certain indifference curves), which is a "useful expository property" (ibid., p. 842). The empirical device appealed to the scientific persona that economists have nurtured through time.[33]

The rationale behind the acceptance of even some of the most basic constructs of economic theory are inexplicable from a positivist perspective. McCloskey chooses the law of demand to illustrate that a wide range of critical factors serve to validate even economists' most concrete and "scientific" beliefs. First, he considers the empirical aspect of the law: "Some economists have tried recently to subject the law to a few empirical tests. After a good deal of throat-clearing they have found it to be true for clear-headed rats and false for confused humans" (McCloskey 1985, p. 58). McCloskey's treatment here is a bit simplistic in that he fails to distinguish between theory testing and representative model testing. Empirical results are difficult to interpret and have not led to significantly diminished confidence in the law of demand in part because the specified theoretical relationship between price and quantity demanded cannot be clearly isolated and directly tested. Substantively, however, his point that even the most basic components of economic theory, such as the law of demand, fail to satisfy modernist criteria is intact. McCloskey's view is that this failure is not problematic: "Even though the modernist argument yields mixed results" (ibid.), economists do not and should not be overly concerned because there are additional, non-modernist, reasons why the proposition contained in the law is convincing.

Among the criteria that potentially contribute to favorable appraisal, McCloskey lists introspective thought experiment, cases in point, and analogy, and he provides examples of each: Through introspection, an economist asks himself what he would do if the price of gasoline doubles. The 1973–74 oil embargo serves as a case in point; the decrease in the consumption of gasoline associated with price increases serves to illustrate the law of demand but is, in itself, statistically insignificant. Employing analogy, the economist may reason that, "if the law applies to gasoline . . . then it is easier to believe that it applies to housing; and if to housing, then medical care; and then to political power; and then to love. Analogy is essential to science, but it is of course the quintessential literary device" (ibid., p. 60).

McCloskey adds, "The lore of the academy persuades too. The argument from authority is not decisive, of course, but must be given weight. Scholarship could not advance if all questions were reopened every ten years." Also, explicit literary devices such as symmetry and definition are valuable techniques available to the writer. If, for example, we believe in the law of supply, might it then be attractive to pursue a law of demand. If we *define* money income as fixed, then a higher price of gasoline means that, if we consume the same amount, other goods cannot be consumed at the previous rate (ibid.).

McCloskey's point, then, is to show that economists are convinced for a multitude of reasons that the price–quantity-demanded relationship specified in the law of demand is useful. Further, the range of persuasive techniques engaged in by a theory's advocates may grow even broader and less modernist in hue, in the case where a more esoteric theory, such as marginal productivity theory of the firm, is involved. For our purpose, it should seem no great leap of faith to believe that members of the profession, when initially appraising the merit of new ideas, have been influenced by some of the variables to which McCloskey calls our attention.

## Summary

In this chapter, the point that methodological pluralism exists, although somewhat covertly, has been reinforced. Specifically, instances of theory choice display highly variable characteristics from one case to the next. Also, the discipline's approach to research appraisal necessarily changes at different stages of literature development. For example, during publication the decision-making process is explicitly controlled by journal personnel. Referees and editors indicate that they are able to eliminate a number of candidates from consideration on the basis of invariant criteria. Work that contains obvious mathematical or modeling errors or that fails to comply with accepted standards prevailing in the discipline can typically be rejected outright. Even in cases where supportive empirical evidence is absent (which is most of the time), clearly established norms can regulate certain elements of the appraisal process. Although determination of a work's quality and significance ultimately entails value judgments by the reviewer, institutional regularities help to systematically guide article selection. In this sense, the evaluative system in place at individual journals is likely to yield somewhat predictable results.

In contrast, no one person or group can predict, with certainty, future trends in the discipline's general theory development. This is, no doubt, partly attributable to the fact that the economy itself evolves irregularly. There are other reasons as well, however. Over time, an ever-increasing proportion of deficient work is eliminated, and hence, the relevance of more tangible disciplinary criteria diminishes. Because so much research is technically correct, assessment of the relative merits of previously published work must be based on other, less definite factors. At some point, perhaps after ten or twenty years, this filtering process leaves only those works that are regarded as classics.

Other types of "positive" evidence would appear to enter the appraisal process more conspicuously in the long run, however. In *principle,* empirical evidence can, over time, accumulate and either reaffirm or corrode confidence in a theory. Alternatively, new data can increase or decrease the validity of a theory in the collective judgment of the scientific community. In this way, theory (or model, or research program, or idea) choice becomes less subjective as the field of visible literature narrows.

In *practice,* however, empirically based theory appraisal has not maintained a clearly discernible presence in economic method. While data-generated evidence can be persuasive, it has not often contributed to the initial acceptance or rejection of hypotheses. Historically, the verdict has generally been returned long before any sort of systematic empirical work is carried out. For example, economists did not wait patiently for the model of perfect competition to be carefully tested against alternative explanations before incorporating it as a principle of economics. When testing occurs post facto, it does not increase the clarity with which theory choices can be made; it can only stimulate reconsideration. In most cases, other factors propel the decision to accept or reject new work.

Furthermore, because economic circumstances change, functional relationships must frequently be cast as generalizations rather than as laws. Validity at one time, such as at the time of publication, does not ensure universal applicability. In this sense, context limitations actually make the long-run appraisal of theories *more* complicated. This added relativist dimension of social science means that, even if a theory could be shown to be true for a particular situation, it need not be true in the future. Logically speaking, one must concede that theory choices are ultimately based on criteria that are, to some degree, interpretive. The critical historical accounts cited throughout this chapter reveal this to be the case, at the very least, part of the time.

This chapter also makes the case that subjective elements of scientific method can become skewed by socially and politically rooted biases. Vertical and horizontal segregation of practitioners dictates the distribution of resources, which, in turn, may affect both the creation and appraisal of research. Ideological differences between schools exacerbate (and can even create) these horizontal divisions, and are especially conspicuous in sub-fields such as macroeconomics that are closely tied to policy issues. The vertical hierarchy, which ranks the profession's members according to ex-perience and accomplishment (as judged by peers), effectively assigns a priori levels of credibility to emerging literature. Influential groups, which include practitioners working in high-profile topical areas or operating from prestigious institutions, enjoy superior funding, staff support, and access to journal resources. This increases the probability, perhaps justifiably, that the work of leaders will be favorably appraised.

Economic doctrine has been shaped by a wide range of perspectives that, throughout its evolution, have affected the underlying philosophy of theory choice. Because of the inherent presence of political sentiment in economic thinking, it is simple to exhume examples that illustrate non-positivist elements of theory choice. The influence of bias appears most acutely during struggles between ideologically opposed sub-groups within the profession. The division between classical liberal economists (who advocate laissez-faire) and modern liberals (who view the economy as inherently unstable and who advocate government intervention as a remedy for unemployment) is most conspicuous. Modeling the impact of policy effectiveness, for example, has certainly been affected by this philosophical polarization. New classical economists choose to portray a world in which expectations are formed rationally, and where no exploitable tradeoff between unemployment and inflation exists. Keynesian interventionists, on the other hand, are inclined to attack the problem in such a way as to demonstrate policy effectiveness. In this context, where issues con-cerning proper scope and method are not founded on "positive" scientific criteria, disputes cannot be objectively settled.

This chapter also draws on case studies that indicate that certain theory characteristics enhance a work's life expectancy. Abstract, conceptually simple, and empirically ambiguous theory dominates the major areas of economic inquiry. Untestable propositions, such as the basic maximizing postulates in consumer theory, seem immune to anomaly; in contrast, most applied work eventually slips into obscurity. In one respect, this differenti-ates the publication process from long-term appraisal. In the former envi-ronment, complex modeling and highly technical work is often rewarded. At the journal level, authors direct their articles toward a relatively narrow audience, and their approach can therefore be more specialized. Nonethe-less, theory that, at its inception, does not fit the long-run success pattern must inevitably be pared down and standardized before it is embraced by the mainstream.[34] This trend is conducive for maintaining methodological stability within the discipline, but it renders the orthodoxy somewhat unreceptive to change.

In summary, a number of distinct features inherent in economic science complicate the theory choice process. When estimating the value of work, whether it is a narrowly directed article or an entire theoretic apparatus, judgments are based, at least partially, on traditional empirical criteria, such as apparent corroborating evidence, and non-empirical criteria, such as internal consistency. The point developed here is that the evaluative process must be completed on the basis of additional criteria. Factors that elevate the role of subjectivity in economic method include the following:

1. Because the critical process operates at numerous stages of literature development (most notably during, then after publication), the essence of appraisal and selection cannot be captured by a singular, homogeneous description.

2. The existence of different literature types (such as syntheses, extensions, and challenges) produces distinct contexts in which professional evaluation of ideas is required. An article intended to challenge aspects of the orthodoxy will be held to different standards than one that effectively corroborates existing ideas.

3. Inability to directly test economic hypotheses elevates the roles of other forms of persuasion—forms which ultimately appeal to the subjective judgment of the reader. Furthermore, empirical work tends to follow—rather than precede—theory choice in economics.

4. The fact that economic conditions are in constant flux reduces the feasibility of creating universally valid models and theories. Hypotheses contained in a work may appear valid at one point and invalid at another.

5. Segregation of the academic community along both horizontally and vertically designated lines creates potential biases in appraisal. For instance, political ideology—which maintains an especially visible presence in economics—may skew an individual's or group's critical approach.

6. The manner in which research is presented, including its literary characteristics, affects appraisal both at the publication and post-publication stages. Furthermore, the criteria that appear important to referees and editors do not appear especially consistent with those that facilitate long-run theory success.

In light of these methodological considerations, it should come as no surprise that the most revealing and accurate studies into the history of economic thought are those that expand their scope and investigate the complex web of subjective factors that underlie development of the science. Positivist accounts, in contrast, reveal little about the actual determinants of literature success in economics.

## Notes

1. This chapter, because it addresses a far-ranging topic, is bounded by certain limitations; thus, the treatment here must admittedly be selective. A full understanding of the topic will only be possible after more studies into how theories have actually been chosen in economics are conducted from a highly critical (as opposed to an idealized, positivist, or near-positivist) perspective.

2. The invention of computers, itself, represents an internal stimulus in that it has revolutionized the discipline's "tool box" of techniques. Even though computer proliferation is only indirectly related to the actual subject matter of economics, it has changed the nature of that which economists do.

3. As was pointed out in the last chapter, editorial selection, strictly speaking, is merely a component of (and should not be equated with) theory choice. During journal production, choices must certainly be made concerning which research submissions to publish. However, these choices rarely carry direct implications about the relative merits of *competing* ideas or theories. Instead, most journal work displays a confirmatory bias and, in the end, serves merely to justify existing analytic frameworks. Given that the discipline currently invests most of its resources into the production of this type of literature, avenues capable of producing true theory choices go unexplored.

4. Nonetheless, it is during these transitional phases that the discipline's practitioners must directly confront actual theory choices.

5. It is interesting that, throughout the history of economics, a significant amount of theory that was intended to challenge and indeed overturn the orthodoxy was, eventually, simply incorporated into it. Probably the best example of this trend is the development of imperfect competition models in microeconomics, initiated by Edward Chamberlin and Joan Robinson.

6. This is why two history of thought books, each superbly argued, can reach contrary conclusions. Guy Routh (1975) argues that economic theory has historically failed to respond to actual economic conditions, while John Kenneth Galbraith (1987) argues essentially the opposite position.

7. We already know that rejection rates are high at the publication stage (rejection rates do not exactly reflect the percentage of research that is eventually published, however, since articles can be resubmitted to other journals).

8. This is analogous to evidence indicating that article acceptance rates increase with the rank of authors' base institutions. Again, one cannot objectively calculate whether or not the work of high-status authors is in fact proportionately better than the work of others. Obviously, in both these cases, correlation does not imply causation.

9. Strength of confirmation is relevant in practical theory choice decisions. Falsification is, however, nearly absent from economic practice. As noted elsewhere there is, in economics (like many other sciences), a distinct confirmatory bias that motivates testing.

10. Mortality records, which were quite comprehensive in London as far back as 1592, proved to be an especially convenient and useful source.

11. Citing individual cases certainly does not *prove* which criteria (objective versus subjective, or internal versus external) are the most important in the development of

economics. However, examination of enough instances of theory choice should convince all but the most stubborn positivists that subjective elements are central to literature assessment. The examples cited here serve merely to illustrate these interpretive aspects of post-publication appraisal.

12. Specifically, see the chapter called, "The Keynesian Revolution and the Monetarist Counterrevolution."

13. Johnson's observations pertaining to the importance of specific non-objective appraisal criteria will be incorporated, where relevant, throughout the remainder of the chapter.

14. Tarascio and Caldwell point out another clear example of this phenomenon: "Thomas Malthus's 'law' of population, if stated in a testable form, did not adequately describe the Western European demographic experience of the nineteenth and twentieth centuries. Malthusian doctrines were revived in the 1960s because of their apparent relevance for certain less developed countries" (1979, p. 1001n).

15. The Phillips Curve example illustrates this point clearly enough.

16. The mere presence of subjectivity in scientific inquiry need not, in theory, lead to biased (or systematically skewed) results. However, any time value judgments are called for, the potential arises for political or social ideology to become a factor. In contrast, the opportunity for bias to influence appraisal cannot arise within a system that is based solely on an objective set of rules, such as those specified in hypothetical positivism. See Homa Katouzian (1980) for a clear discussion, in the context of idea presentation, on the distinction between subjectivity and ideology.

17. This, of course, assumes that the author's methods fall into the acceptable range for at least one group. This observation would not necessarily apply for the case in which a completely alternative approach is involved.

18. See Chapter 4 for a discussion on the advantages and disadvantages associated with increased specialization.

19. Tarascio (1986) makes this distinction between the "premier literature," produced by leaders, and the supportive literature, which is secondary in nature, contributed by lesser-known researchers.

20. Maddock also points out that a Lakatosian interpretation omits this important element from the story.

21. The authors compiled data from the twenty-five-year period following the Depression to demonstrate the stable relationship similar to that hypothesized by Phillips.

22. For example, Thorstein Veblen's eccentric behavior rendered it difficult for him to secure a reputable academic position. Today, we are far-enough removed from the situation that such factors are not important; Veblen's written work can be assessed independent of the professional status that he achieved during his own time.

23. Historians of thought still ask these questions about theorists from the distant past, but the topic is of little concern to everyday practitioners. In general, if a work remains reputable over a long period, focus on ideological underpinnings tends to diminish.

24. It follows that, in an environment where everyone is satisfied with current theory, alternative approaches are unlikely to arouse much interest.

25. There is no doubt that Keynes viewed his new theory as a challenge to the orthodoxy, similar to the one he observed to have occurred in physics. James Galbraith and William Darity (1994) point out that Keynes's title was, in all likelihood, "cribbed, and quite consciously so," from Einstein's revolutionary 1915 paper, *The General Theory of Relativity.* In their view, "The parallelism that Keynes intended, between his revolution and Einstein's runs very deep" (p. 12). Passages from *The General Theory,* which serve to develop the analogy between economics and physics further, demonstrate that use of this tactic was a component of Keynes's rhetorical approach.

26. This is not to say that the relationship between economics and physics was

completely ignored prior to Mirowski. Both Irving Fisher and Vilfredo Pareto acknowledged and examined similarities between economics and social phenomenon on the one hand, and mechanics and mechanical phenomena on the other.

27. Consider, for example, the importance of Lockian concepts such as natural rights and individualism, which entered economic doctrine through Adam Smith and remain today.

28. Hal Varian (1991, p. 595) offers a more tempered assessment: "It is hardly surprising that some economists, educated in the mathematics of the nineteenth century [and] familiar with classical mechanics [and] energy conservation law . . . might try to utilize the mathematical techniques developed in physics to clarify concepts in their own science."

29. I qualify the term "revolutionary" once again because there was no overthrow of the orthodoxy. The emphasis of inquiry was simply altered.

30. See the book's introduction for a more comprehensive account.

31. It is ironic that Karl Popper was convinced by economists that their discipline was "scientific" in its practices. Katouzian, in fact, finds it "truly astonishing." He suggests that some economists, in demonstrating their mathematical theory representations, misled Popper: "A substantial portion of mathematical economic theory is not even directed to the explanation and solution of problems which exist in reality; let alone having a factual and empirical content. . . . The only explanation of this otherwise mysterious view of Popper's on orthodox economics is that he must have been misinformed by economists themselves" (Katouzian 1980, p. 90).

32. Note that, unlike marginal utility theory, the Phillips Curve relationship can be stacked against empirical evidence. Thus, even though data have a tendency to be compiled with a confirmatory bias, the evidence produced during the 1970s overwhelmingly called into question the "universality" of the Phillips Curve. This illustrates the point that close proximity to real-world variables may stunt a proposition's longevity, especially in the context of changing conditions.

33. Of course, Wulwick is unable to quantify the extent to which the reception of the Phillips Curve was affected by the specification of its functional form. It is only possible to argue that certain properties are likely to be appealing to economists.

34. *The General Theory* offers a perfect example. Before the profession identified the basic principles as orthodoxy, difficult and even contradictory messages had to be streamlined into a simplified form (i.e., "Keynesian-cross" and IS-LM models).

# CHAPTER 6

# Summary, Assessment, and Directions

Two basic themes that are essential to methodological inquiry emerge from the chapters above. First, existing philosophy of science frameworks can only be usefully applied to economics in a limited capacity. The types of questions that engage philosophers of science are relevant to economists, but theories and concepts have been inappropriately extended, especially to investigations into the real practices of science. To put it another way, non-discipline–specific philosophical questions—such as, what distinguishes good science from bad, or is it feasible to logically prove or disprove statements—are important and interesting but, in the case of economics, are too abstract to produce much insight into actual method. The second and more difficult task motivating this book is to begin filling the gaps in our understanding that adherence to traditional methodology has left. By examining appraisal and selection processes more rigorously, a more comprehensive account emerges.

## Theme 1: Limitations of Generalized Methodology

Philosophy of science is an intriguing subject, one that has produced a diverse and insightful body of literature. Scientists in any field who wish to understand or contribute to methodological debates must first gain a fundamental knowledge of this literature. However, in assessing their own discipline's unique methods, economists must be cautious about adopting these non-social-science–specific, and frequently prescriptive, methodologies. Appropriate application requires a critical approach, which, regretfully, has not uniformly been the practice.

This book, specifically Chapters 1 through 3, argues that neither positivism nor the more recent philosophy of science literature compellingly explains the evolution of economic theory; interpretations that adhere to these frameworks often fail to adequately characterize, or simply ignore, important components of the process. This shortcoming does not imply that positivist, Popperian, Lakatosian, or Kuhnian scholarship is inferior. Rather, it is a matter of scope and emphasis. These philosophers (or philosophical schools) have expressed little or no intention to explain how economics works.[1] The fault lies more with those who were, perhaps, overly eager to extend insights derived from these major intellectual traditions to the economics case. Indeed, a primary objective of this study is to identify misappropriations of philosophy of science concepts and to sort through some of the resultant confusion that has plagued methodological debate among economists.

The analysis in Chapter 1 begins with an assessment of the underlying validity of positivism. Chapter 2 outlines how variants of positivism became especially influential in the development of economists' methodological perspectives. The discussion exposes the central problem with positivism (when employed as a tool for approximating historical reality): It does not facilitate critical appraisal of actual methods and, in the process, produces idealized accounts.

Philosophy of science, as articulated by the Vienna Circle, emphasizes the importance of developing objective demarcation criteria—namely, verifiability—and is essentially prescriptive in focus. For positivism to be *descriptively* accurate, science would have to display a history where theory choices had been dictated by empirical confirmation. It is argued that such an account has limited relevance to the economics case, where the acceptance or rejection of theories has rarely hinged upon the outcomes of crucial tests. Even a casual inspection of the discipline's history reveals that empirical research has tended to play a secondary role and that establishing the significance of work typically involves a far wider range of factors.

A simplified version of positivism is embodied in what philosopher Alan Chalmers calls, the "widely held common-sense view of science." This stylized view maintains that facts can be exposed by observation and experiment and that the validity of theories can be rigorously ascertained in an objective fashion. Normative preferences, personal opinion, and speculation need not be called upon in the practice of science. In short, science is reliable because it is founded on objective methods and proven facts.

Judging from descriptions of method in their textbooks and articles, many economists tacitly accept this view. Applied to the economics case, this common-sense view of science implies a dynamic mechanism that can be represented by the following schemata:

Figure 1. **Simplistic View of Economic Science**

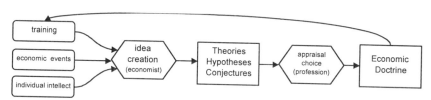

Figure 1 depicts, first, the idea creation stage of the scientific process. During this stage, the economist calls upon his own intellect, which is shaped by—among other things—professional training in the scientific method, which conditions him to perform activities in a manner that is detached from subjective considerations. The investigator observes subject matter and conducts tests to answer questions about the economic environment, which arise during evolution of the science. By way of this objective process, theories, hypotheses, and conjectures are produced and, in turn, proved or disproved over time. Significant theories that are proven to be true are then incorporated into economic doctrine. As the recognized body of literature evolves, professional training adapts to keep up with the ever-improving explanations generated by this process.

It was shown in Chapter 1 that, during this century, such characterizations of science have come under increasing attack in the philosophy of science. More robust explanations of science, such as Karl Popper's or Imre Lakatos's, serve to expose inadequacies with this simplistic conception. Popper clarified logical as well as practical problems associated with "proving" theories, hypotheses, and conjectures based on verificationist criteria. Lakatos, in modifying Popper's approach, calls attention to similar problems with falsificationism. When viewed as a whole, twentieth-century philosophy of science has generated a rich literature indicating the complexity of empirical appraisal (which, in Figure 1, links theories, hypotheses, and conjectures to doctrinal development). The common-sense view that theories can simply be judged true or false by appeal to facts has been largely dispelled.

As was the case with positivism, Popper's falsificationist methodology has been hugely influential in science generally. The point here is not to undermine the value of Popper's contribution; the value of his scholarship is indisputable. Rather, the objective has been to demonstrate that unbridled application of falsificationism to the history of economic thought leads to misleading conclusions. The primary reason is that, even today, most economic theories cannot be unambiguously tested. Variables are unobservable; initial conditions shift; and data are only sporadically reliable. As a philosophical ideal or a means of inquiry into the logic of discovery, Popper (or positivism for that matter) is relevant; as a tool for studying how theories are selected in economics, it is limited.

Even the more refined Lakatosian methodology does not, at its core, deviate substantially from this traditional depiction of science. With Lakatos, the type of empirical appraisal—distinguishing between degenerating and progressive "research programs"—is slightly different, but the process described by Figure 1 remains essentially intact. A myriad of problems arise when the Lakatosian apparatus is used to produce a description of economic method. First, it is dubious to presume that economists think in terms of attaching themselves to empirically and theoretically progressive programs. Furthermore, even if they wanted to, it would be difficult due to the lack of identifiable and directly testable relationships inherent in economic behavior. Within the methodology of scientific research programs, nearly all of economics would have to be considered a "fledgling program," which means its "degree of progressivity" cannot yet be judged. Hence, there are no remaining theory choice criteria. But, of course, economists do appraise and select theories. Unfortunately, the Lakatosian framework offers few insights into this process whereby work is initially accepted or rejected.

The unifying principle that ties positivism, falsificationism, and the methodology of scientific research programs is that certain characteristics, imposed to demarcate scientific theory from non-scientific statements, should provide a basis for theory choice. Although these views are irreconcilable on many points, they all reach the conclusion that appraisal and hence choice in science should have an empirical grounding.[2] Methodology prescribed under these now orthodox philosophies lends insight into the economics case only to the extent that research has been legitimized or made more appealing by stipulating testable relationships. However, the history of economic thought reveals that which is vaguely realized but infrequently discussed: Many factors contribute to the favorable (or unfavorable) appraisal of research and to the ascendance (or fall) of theories; evolution of the discipline's literature has not normally been paced by falsificationist or verificationist methods.

As a result, efforts that seek to characterize the evolution of economic theory based solely on empirical criteria are woefully incomplete. Contributors to the Mark Blaug and Neil de Marchi volume, for example, were simply unable to adequately explain theory appraisal when constrained by the Lakatosian apparatus. Work that imposes philosophy of science constructs as a proxy for economic method often fails to identify that logical positivists, Popper, and Lakatos were primarily interested in establishing methodological rules, not in accurately analyzing the practices of science.[3] Consequently, interpretations of economic method continue to distort the role that empiricism plays in both the historical development and appraisal of research, and practicing economists still pay lip service to a vision that evolved from physical (not social) science and bears little resemblance to actual method.

During the 1960s, an alternative perspective—centered around a different set of questions—became available. Thomas Kuhn's *Structure of Scientific Revolutions* initiated the movement to examine sociological aspects of science as a means to understand its workings. One of Kuhn's objectives was to accurately portray scientific practice; he emerged as the most notable post-positivist philosopher to assert that science contains significant subjective and non-rational elements.[4] However, Kuhn's scope is broad, and consistent with his message, one must investigate an individual scientific community to understand its methodological intricacies. For instance, in the case of economics, Kuhn's description of "normal science" appears somewhat realistic while his account of scientific revolutions does not. Thus, while Kuhn's philosophy may be too general to produce detailed insights into the history of economic thought (an application for which it was not explicitly intended), it encourages broader interpretation of scientific method.

**Theme 2: Toward a More Complete Account**

It is, then, the shortcomings of these general philosophical interpretations—created for the natural sciences—which motivates this discipline-specific foray into economic methodology. Evidence compiled in Chapters 4 and 5 necessitates restructuring the dynamic mechanism summarized in Figure 1. Figure 2 illustrates a schemata that allows for a more accurate depiction of method in economics:

As in Figure 1, Figure 2 represents economists producing research. However, the presumption that all work is oriented toward testing or developing theories, hypotheses, and conjectures is omitted. Instead, research is produced with publication, and its accompanying recognition and rewards, in mind; instances where a new theory or hypothesis is advanced are the exception. This alternative account acknowledges traditional influences on idea creation, such as individual intellect and observation of the economic environment. However, both acceptable method and content are constrained by disciplinary standards that are generated, to a substantial degree, by professional training and the dominant publishing system.[5] Textbook in-

Figure 2. **Multistage Representation of Economic Science**

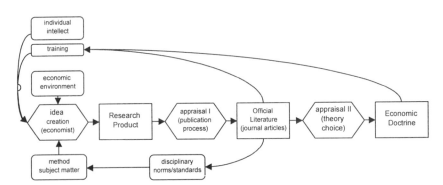

struction dominates training and mandates that beginning students learn the accepted body of material in a standardized manner. This process generates an abundance of competent practitioners but redirects intellectual capital away from searches for alternative approaches to economic problems.

Norms and standards prevailing within publication institutions place methodological and topical constraints on practitioners. The view here counters assertions that research production is motivated solely by some pure ideal to advance scientific knowledge by empirical proof or disproof. In reality, an economist must conform to discipline-sanctioned activity and maintain a concern with the judgments of his peers if he is to gain recognition or influence.

Following research creation, an article or book is evaluated and, depending on the outcome of this process, may be incorporated into the discipline's permanent literature and, in rare instances, even influence the development of economic theory. This multi-stage scientific process, represented in Figure 2, explicitly decomposes appraisal and choice into two phases. It is important to recognize that publication decisions, based on appraisal I, and longer-run theory choices, based on appraisal II, are linked sequentially but are essentially unique. The task of journal editors and referees is to judge the quality and estimate interest in research submissions; this type of appraisal (I) represents the first stage in the literature screening process.

After literature is legitimized by journal publication, members of the profession implicitly assign a status rating to new ideas by acknowledging, then following up, articles that interest them. Work that attracts attention affects the course of research by inspiring a supportive, or critical, secondary literature. The outcome of appraisal II has a direct impact on how new branches of inquiry will develop. Yet a third type of appraisal, that which is performed from a philosophy or history of science perspective, occurs much later and is peripheral to the interests of most practitioners. Failure to clearly identify these distinct contexts of appraisal has led to ambiguous and unproductive methodological discussion.

### Appraisal I

A central point in Chapter 4 is that, because few articles advance or test theories in a traditional positivist sense, appraisal I necessarily becomes the by-product of a highly interpretive process. The survey of referees identifies at least thirty criteria that are invoked in decisions to reject or accept submissions. Thus, from one referee to another, the mechanism whereby a work's significance is determined is highly variable. This subjectivity is reflected by the fact that, among referees, quality judgments demonstrate high variance, producing an impression of randomness.

Clarity of exposition, degree of empirical rigor, topical relevance, and personal interests are just a few of the most commonly cited appraisal criteria; the relative importance of each depends on which referee is asked. Quantifying article characteristics exposes evidence that authors employ a variety of institutionally acceptable techniques to persuade colleagues of their work's validity. Currently, econometric evidence (even if quite inconclusive) is highly valued, as it is seen to lend an element of scientific legitimacy to work. As reflected in the surveyed referees' comments, work that is most valued by journals shows mastery of existing technique, then extends it in a way that is considered innovative. This is not a simple process of proving or disproving conjecture, but an art form. Recognizing the dichotomy between novelty and conformity is a key facet of this art. Most successful research offers a new twist, but is tied to established programs and employs sanctioned techniques to which referees can relate. Economists expect top journals to somehow advance the existing knowledge; however, an author's probability of publication is not enhanced by asking entirely new questions or employing unprecedented approaches.

The absence of clearly defined procedures elevates the role of interpretive criteria, and precludes appraisal from being carried out in a formula-like manner. A discipline's standards (even if narrowly defined to a single journal's practices) cannot always be uniformly applied. For example, there have been many instances when articles were rejected at one point then, later, went on to be published. Gary Becker, Milton Friedman, Franco Modigliani, Robert Lucas, and James Tobin are just a few of the many notable economists who have had articles rejected that eventually came to be regarded as classics.[6] Also, work can be ignored initially, then revived as disciplinary standards change. Joshua Gans and George Shepherd point out that Lucas's highly technical 1972 paper, "Expectations and the Neutrality of Money," which "introduced rational expectations concepts into monetary theory and macroeconomics" was rejected by the *American Economic Review* based, in part, on referee remarks that it was exceedingly formal and too mathematical (Gans and Shepherd 1994, p. 172).[7]

Inconsistency during the publication stage of theory choice can result from changing conceptions of significance, but can also emerge as the by-product of inherent biases cultivated within the profession.[8] Recently, more attention has been given to problems associated with biased, inconsistent, or simply careless journal practices. Literature cited in Chapter 4 provides preliminary insights into how group or individual biases can enter the picture. Political predilection appears to distort appraisal most conspicuously in policy-related fields such as macroeconomics. For example, the division between Chicago and Keynesian macroeconomists was clearly evident during the 1950s and 1960s. Today, similar rifts between new classical and new-Keynesian economists inhibit effective communication and add a "non-rationalist" element to the proceedings. An inability to clearly prove conceptual superiority keeps the sub-discipline from achieving the level of unity that exists in the physical sciences, or even in other areas of economics.

At times, these biases have affected submission patterns and acceptance rates. In economics, journal specialization does generate a means for dividing labor sensibly, but can also be motivated by conflicts along ideological lines.[9] Referee comments suggest that researchers go out of their way to obtain information about editorial propensities in order to avoid submitting articles to journals where their views would be considered heterodox. Evidence also indicates that non-scientific considerations, such as author identity, can significantly affect publication decisions (in ways that are still not entirely clear).[10] An author's credentials, rank of base institution, or political clout within the science community potentially affect his ability to succeed in the competition for scarce journal space.

Finally, it was argued that reliance on the journal system for literature production carries certain ramifications for the development of economics. Because publication translates into recognition and rewards, practitioners conduct their research in a manner that is consistent with prevailing standards so that they maximize their probability of success. Observing article characteristics and referee propensities, it is clear that journals are typically geared toward thoroughly investigating existing questions using accepted frameworks. However, the tendency of journals to promote depth of inquiry is not costless. Literature trends indicate that the intellectual aim of expanding the scope of research has been neglected. Historically, journals have not provided an outlet for non-orthodox economics. Prominent journals operate within the mainstream, promoting continuity within economics while, perhaps, stunting highly original or controversial research. Thus, as the discipline becomes increasingly reliant on a journal-based system, we should recognize that conduits for generating entirely new theory may go unnurtured.

## Appraisal II

As Figure 2 indicates, literature appraisal does not end with the placement of research into the pages of a journal or book. New ideas, hypotheses, and theories undergo further scrutinization after they have attained the sort of legitimization that publication signifies. Post-publication appraisal and selection take place in a context that is entirely distinct from the one in which publication decisions are executed. Additionally, this second set of disciplinary choices (the by-product of appraisal II) is motivated by different objectives than publication decisions. Appraisal conducted by journal editors and referees is comparatively formal and highly specialized. In contrast, the forces that propel theory to doctrine are more nebulous and less clearly structured. While additional case studies might further illuminate the situation, the historical record—as it now stands—suggests that the process whereby new work is elevated to doctrinal status is far from homogenous. Contrary to the simplistic impression conveyed under positivism, the existence of sociological, ideological, and psychological factors in the practice of science makes cataloguing the determinants of theory choice extremely complex.

Nonetheless, some general observations concerning long-term theory appraisal and selection are advanced in Chapter 5. First, post-publication and prepublication processes are unique because appraisal II takes a different form than appraisal I. For instance, we may note who, in each case, makes influential choices. Publication decisions are executed by journal personnel whose objective is to share research that is valid, is relevant, and (perhaps most importantly) will be of interest to its readers. Appraisal II, on the other hand, is not a task that is assigned to any specific individual or group. Members of the profession attach themselves to various research projects and, as consensus arises as to which of these projects are most important, the science proceeds.

In both contexts, the discipline's elite assert the greatest influence. However, more factors lie outside the control of individual practitioners during the second phase of appraisal. During the publication stage, editors and referees are empowered, to varying degrees, with direct control over the content of upcoming journal issues. In contrast, the course of action that the entire discipline takes—how new economists align themselves, how practitioners react to changes in the economic environment, what topics become hot, and so on—is the by-product of an aggregate momentum.[11]

Also, the tools available for assessing the validity, interest, and applicability of research change from one stage of the process to another. It has been pointed out, for example, that clearly recognized criteria become less important as the period of appraisal is extended. Work that contains technical errors, internal contradictions, or is inconsistent with disciplinary standards is typically eliminated early on, most likely by referees or editors. This implies that, during post-publication appraisal, a relatively simple mechanism for ranking research quality is lost. Highly interpretive criteria (which are already important during the publication stage) necessarily assume an even larger role, which, in itself, makes long-run theory choice more difficult to formalize.

On the other hand, empirical evidence can continue to accumulate after publication and may, with time, "objectify" quality judgments. Hindsight can either strengthen or weaken an hypothesis; post facto observation may corroborate a position (as was arguably the case with the Phillips Curve in the 1950s and 1960s) or it may erode confidence (as in the 1970s). Additionally, a long-term perspective is required to expose aspects of a theory that become inconsistent with external conditions, such as actual market activities, or internal factors, such as a discipline's intellectual or sociological norms. Judgments concerning an idea's validity evolve as circumstances change.

One cannot, however, justifiably assert blind confidence in the potential for empirical evidence to settle disputes in economics. Substantial disagreement persists even in—perhaps especially in—sub-fields that have witnessed the most rapid incorporation of sophisticated econometric and statistical techniques. Empirical work has failed to unify theory. Furthermore, as has been argued throughout, testing generally occurs long after theories have been accepted or rejected, if at all. This no doubt relates to the inherent difficulty of measuring variables and identifying stable causal relationships associated with human behavior.

Finally, certain theory types display resilience while others are susceptible to anomaly. Specifically, the level of abstraction maintained in an analytic framework seems to be positively correlated with its longevity. Narrowly focused, applied work may hold keen interest for a particular audience or to the readers of a certain journal; such work may also contain information that has significant practical value. However, much of this task-oriented research becomes obsolete as circumstances change and, consequently, has minimal long-term influence. Work that contains directly visible empirical implications is, over a period of time, more likely to experience a decline in popularity than purely theoretical work, which functions detached from the damning evidence created by observation of actual economic phenomena. Because only the most general work can be reduced to economic principles, it is no coincidence that classroom material often appears to students to be far removed from real-world issues. Abstraction becomes a necessity if maintaining a stable core of subject matter is desired.

These general observations aside, appraisal II is no doubt highly variable from one case to the next: The rapid acceptance of Keynesian macroeconomics bears little resemblance to the rise of marginal analysis, which, in turn, is distinct from the flourishing of comparatively recent formalist movements. Recognition of this methodological diversity is, in itself, significant as it contradicts most philosophy of science accounts, which seek to impose a timeless basis of appraisal and promote a universal concept of procedure. In reality, a wide range of non-positivist factors have, historically, affected theory choices. Structure of the scientific community, the nature of theory itself, as well as changing economic conditions are (in addition to traditional rationalist criteria) capable of influencing the discipline's path of development. For instance, sociological bias, arising from vertical and horizontal divisions within the profession, can create barriers for practitioners operating at lesser known institutions or working on non-mainstream issues. Political alignment, which is especially conspicuous in macro-sub-fields, can create rivalries, personal stock in intellectual traditions, and animosity between groups which—by introducing an ideological element—colors appraisal in a distinctly non-positivist fashion. Similarly, a theory's proximity to policy questions or even its literary characteristics can influence its reception. Throughout the chapters above, cases are cited that illustrate how such factors affect economists' practices. However, the appraisal and selection process displays little constancy of form; a particular factor may be important in one instance and less conspicuous or even absent from the next. A better understanding can only be gained by acknowledging, then investigating the subjective aspects of theory choice.

## Conclusions

What, then, can be gained by pursuing an understanding of actual scientific practice? Or, conversely, what is lost by limiting methodological study to a framework confined by idealized philosophy of science? First, economists in general can benefit from the exercise in intellectual honesty. Methods can most readily be improved by critically confronting, not avoiding, uncomfortable issues (such as ideological bias at journals, or the role of subjectivity in theory selection).[12] In studying society's economic behavior, inherent difficulties do exist; assessing science based on a mythical interpretation is unlikely to generate solutions for dealing with these difficulties. Accurate (as opposed to preapproved, self-pleasing) portrayal is more likely to uncover unproductive or destructive elements in a discipline's methods. Ignoring the murky side of science will not make it go away. Finally, propagating accounts that exaggerate the purely rational elements of economic science retards our understanding and, hence, potentially inhibits full utilization of methods that are actually available.

From a history of thought perspective, the exercise creates a more thorough checklist of angles to consider when recounting past theory development. It has been demonstrated that full understanding of the creation, acceptance, and proliferation of economic ideas is not forthcoming when the inquirer adheres to adopted philosophy of science frameworks. Of course, this realization that there is more to economic method than textbook statements imply is not new; hopefully, however, this study has produced insights into other, less frequently discussed aspects of theory appraisal and selection.

For methodologists, perhaps some ambiguous aspects of recent debate have been clarified. At the very least, a few specific sources of confusion have been identified (for instance, the inappropriate, and awkward, application of prescriptive philosophy for other purposes, or non-specification of the many contexts of appraisal). The central task here, however, has been to identify and examine the important but heretofore non-rigorously treated theory choice issue. Traditionally, study into the procedures and aims of economics has taken an abstract, prescriptive approach. Methodologists have managed to sidestep critical analysis into how a discipline confronts choice—how it appraises research and, in turn, selects from competing ideas and theories. The goal here has been to produce a direct inquiry into actual method. In the process, every effort has been made to avoid the temptation to replace one simplistic approach (such as positivism) with another.[13] Open-minded historical study must enrich—not restrict—our capability to examine the broad range of activity that contributes to scientific enterprise. This, of course, does not mean that methodology must *condone* all practices that it studies. In fact, establishing links between a discipline's shortcomings and flawed methodological practices, which should be an objective of methodologists, is *only* made possible by traveling beyond an idealized philosophy of science.

### Notes

1. In some cases, they have not been interested in descriptive accuracy at all; their work is focused on purely prescriptive, logic-oriented issues.

2. This is a subjective viewpoint. It cannot be falsified or verified; it is basically a matter of opinion. However, the statement that this is how science actually proceeds can be checked against the facts.

3. This is less true for Lakatos's later writings, however, in which he sought to "rationally reconstruct" history.

4. Some critics argue that historical accounts of "successful science" implicitly maintain a prescriptive tone—that is, descriptive history and prescriptive philosophy are inextricably linked. While this observation may be valid, there is also a clear difference in the scholarly objectives of Kuhn and Lakatos.

5. See Arjo Klamer and David Colander (1990) to get a feel for how graduate training creates a "very real socialization process" (p. 27). In interviews, students reveal that their attitudes about economic issues are shaped by traditions and currents dominating at their institution. Chicago students and Harvard or MIT students develop different philosophical approaches. For instance, each group assigns different levels of validity to the neoclassical framework and to the positive–normative distinction; they also disagree about the usefulness of fiscal policy and the causes of inflation.

6. Joshua Gans and George Shepherd's 1994 article, "How Are the Mighty Fallen: Rejected Classic Articles by Leading Economists," offers a compelling account of inconsistencies and arbitrariness in journal publishing practices. In the process, clear evidence of the non-positivist nature of research appraisal is generated.

7. This reinforces the point made in Chapter 4 that work that fails to conform to *current* methodological standards is typically not highly regarded by editors and referees. Before the 1970s, highly mathematical techniques had still not yet permeated the orthodoxy. Gans and Shepherd write, "editors regularly rejected articles because they contained technical mathematics . . ." Early papers by Jan Tinbergen, Milton Friedman, Harold Hotelling, Gerard Debreu, and Robert Lucas were all rejected for "excessive mathematics." The authors point out that, as late as the 1950s, many journals were not even equipped to print mathematical notation (p. 177).

8. It is well known, for instance, that John Maynard Keynes was extremely opinionated about what types of articles should appear in the *Economic Journal,* which he edited for many years.

9. The cold war between the *Quarterly Journal of Economics* and *Journal of Political Economics* during the 1950s provides a clear case of how ideology can shape journal policies. Refer back to Chapter 4 for details.

10. A "final list" of successful research determinants can never be constructed, as appraisal criteria are in constant flux. However, with work by Rebecca Blank (1991), Daniel Hammermesh (1994), Joshua Gans and George Shepherd (1994), as well as this book, hopefully a clearer picture is emerging.

11. Such factors make post-publication theory choice extremely difficult to characterize. This is why material in Chapter 4 can be presented more systematically and comprehensively than material in Chapter 5. Many questions regarding the forces that propel work to prominence have, admittedly, been left unanswered and require additional attention.

12. Note that such an admission does not necessarily imply that economists' methods are purely arbitrary or generally faulty. Nor does it mean that economic inquiry is carried out in an unintelligent or uncritical manner. Rather, it is simply important to recognize that certain constraints impose special problems for social scientists.

13. This is a common complaint with the message underlying recent rhetoric studies. D. McCloskey ends up trying to eliminate philosophy of science from his methodology and, in the process, upends potentially complementary explanations.

# Referee Survey

1. Approximately how many articles have you refereed for economics journals during the past two years?

2. If one exists, what is your most common criticism of articles that you recommend not be published?

3. Top journals seek "significant advances in economic theory" (*QJE* editorial policy). What, in your view, are the most important criteria when determining the significance of an article?

    1.

    2.

    3.

4. In appraising the value of an article, do you find it helpful, harmful, or irrelevant to know the author's identity?

5. When *you* submit an article for publication, what are the three most important considerations in choosing the appropriate journal?

   1.

   2.

   3.

# BIBLIOGRAPHY

Ayer, Sir Alfred, ed. 1959. *Logical Positivism*. Glencoe, IL: The Free Press.

Backhouse, Roger E. 1991. "Comment on Morgan." In *Appraising Economic Theories: Studies in the Methodology of Research Programs,* ed. Neil de Marchi and Mark Blaug, pp. 266–69. Aldershot, U.K.: Edward Elgar.

Bacon, Francis. [1621] 1960. *Novum Organum.* New York: Bobbs-Merrill.

Barnes, Barry. 1982. *T. S. Kuhn and Social Science.* New York: Columbia University Press.

Beed, Clive. 1991. "Philosophy of Science and Contemporary Economics: An Overview." *Journal of Post-Keynesian Economics* 13, no. 4 (summer): 459–94.

Bentham, Jeremy. 1948. *An Introduction to the Principles of Morals and Legislation.* New York: Hafner Publishing.

Berkson, William. 1976. "Lakatos One and Lakatos Two: An Appreciation." In *Essays in Memory of Imre Lakatos,* ed. Robert S. Cohen, Paul K. Feyerabend, and Marx W. Wartofsky, pp. 39–54. Boston, Dordrecht: D. Reidel.

Beveridge, William. 1937. "The Place of the Social Sciences in Human Knowledge." *Politica* (September): 460–82.

Black, R. D. Collison, Alfred W. Coats, and Craufurd D. W. Goodwin, eds. 1973. *The Marginal Revolution in Economics.* Durham, NC: Duke University Press.

Blank, Rebecca M. 1991. "The Effects of Double-Blind versus Single-Blind Reviewing: Experimental Evidence from the American Economic Review." *American Economic Review* 81, no. 5 (December): 1041–67.

Blaug, Mark. 1973. "Was There a Marginal Revolution?" In *The Marginal Revolution,* ed. Black, Coats, and Goodwin, pp. 3–14.

———. 1976. "Kuhn versus Lakatos or Paradigms versus Research Programmes in the History of Economics." In *Method and Appraisal in Economics,* ed. Spiro Latsis, pp. 149–80. Cambridge: Cambridge University Press.

———. 1980. *The Methodology of Economics.* Cambridge: Cambridge University Press.

———. 1985. *Economic Theory in Retrospect.* Cambridge: Cambridge University Press.

Bronfenbrenner, Martin. 1966. "Trends, Cycles and Fads in Economic Writing." *American Economic Review* 56: 538–52.

———. 1971. "The 'Structure of Revolutions' in Economic Thought." *History of Political Economy* 3: 136–51.

Caldwell, Bruce. 1982. *Beyond Positivism.* London: George Allen and Unwin.

Ceci, Stephen J., and Douglas P. Peters. 1982. "Peer Review Practices of Psychological Journals: The Fate of Published Articles, Submitted Again." *Behavioral and Brain Sciences* 5 (June): 187–252.

Chalmers, Alan. 1982. *What Is This Thing Called Science?* 2d ed. St. Lucia, Queensland: University of Queensland Press.

Clapham, John. 1922. "Of Empty Economic Boxes." *Economic Journal* 32: 305–14.

Clark, John Bates. 1922. *Essentials of Economic Theory.* New York: Macmillan.

Clark, Norman, and Calestous Juma. 1987. *Long-Run Economics.* London: Pinter.

Cleary, Frank R., and Daniel J. Edwards. 1960. "The Origins of Contributors to the American Economic Review." *American Economic Review* (Communications) 50: 1011–14.

Coats, Alfred W. 1967. "Sociological Aspects of British Economic Thought (1880–1930)." *Journal of Political Economy* 75: 706–29.

———. 1969. "Is There a 'Structure of Scientific Revolutions' in Economics?" *KYKLOS* 22: 289–96.

———. 1976. "Economics and Psychology: The Death and Resurrection of a Research Programme." In *Method and Appraisal in Economics,* ed. Latsis, pp. 43–64.

Cohen, Bernard. 1985. *Revolutions in Science.* Cambridge, MA: Harvard University Press.

Cohen, Robert S., Paul K. Feyerabend, and Marx W. Wartofsky, eds. 1976. *Essays in Memory of Imre Lakatos.* Boston, Dordrecht: D. Reidel.

Collins, Harry M. 1991. "History and Sociology of Science and History and Methodology of Economics." In *Appraising Economic Theories,* ed. de Marchi and Blaug, pp. 492–98.

Crane, Diane. 1967. "The Gatekeepers of Science: Some Factors Affecting the Selection of Articles for Scientific Journals." *American Sociologist* 2 (November): 195–201.

Darity, William A. Jr., ed. 1984. *Labor Economics—Addresses, Essays, Lectures.* Hingham, MA: Kluwer-Nijhoff.

Deaton, Angus, Roger Guesnerie, Lars Peter Hansen, and David Kreps. 1987. "Econometrica Operating Procedures." *Econometrica* 55 (January): 204–6.

De Grazin, Alfred. 1963. "The Scientific Reception System and Dr. Velikovsky." *American Behavioral Scientist* 7: 38–56.

De Marchi, Neil, and Mark Blaug, eds. 1991. *Appraising Economic Theories: Studies in the Methodology of Research Programs.* Aldershot, U.K.: Edward Elgar.

DeVroey, Michel. 1975. "The Transition from Classical to Neoclassical Economics: A Scientific Revolution." *Journal of Economic Issues* 9: 415–39.

Diesing, Paul. 1991. *How Does Social Science Work? Reflections on Practice.* Pittsburgh: University of Pittsburgh Press.

Dorfman, Joseph. 1934. *Thorstein Veblen and His America.* New York: Viking Press.

Duhem, Pierre. 1954. *La Théorie Physique.* Princeton: Princeton University Press.

Eagly, Robert V., ed. 1968. *Events, Ideology and Economic Theory.* Detroit: Wayne State University Press.

Fels, Rendigs. 1994. "Research Strategies in Economics Journals." In *Research in the History of Economic Thought and Methodology,* ed. Warren J. Samuels and Jeff Biddle, vol. 12, pp. 45–63. Greenwich, CT, and London: JAI Press.

Fetter, Frank W. 1958. "The Economic Articles in the Quarterly Review and Their Authors, 1809–1852." *Journal of Political Economy* 66 (February): 47–64.

Feyerabend, Paul K. 1975. *Against Method.* London: New Left Books/Verso.

———. 1970. "Consolations for the Specialist." In *Criticism and the Growth of Knowledge,* ed. Imre Lakatos and Alan Musgrave, pp. 197–230. Cambridge: Cambridge University Press.

Fisher, Irving. [1892] 1925. "Mathematical Investigations in the Theory of Value and Prices." Ph.D. dissertation, Yale University, reprinted in *Transactions of the Connecticut Academy of Arts and Sciences,* vol. 9. New Haven: Yale University Press.

Flew, Anthony, ed. 1984. *A Dictionary of Philosophy.* New York: St. Martin's Press, 1984.

Friedman, Milton. 1953. *Essays in Positive Economics.* Chicago: University of Chicago Press.

Galbraith, James, and William Darity. 1994. *Macroeconomics.* Boston: Houghton Mifflin.

Galbraith, John Kenneth. 1987. *Economics in Perspective.* Boston: Houghton Mifflin.

Gans, Joshua S., and George B. Shepherd. 1994. "How Are the Mighty Fallen: Rejected Classic Articles by Leading Economists." *Journal of Economic Perspectives* 8, no. 1 (winter): 165–79.

Ghiselin, Michael T. 1984. *The Triumph of the Darwinian Method.* Chicago: University of Chicago Press.

Gilbert, Christopher L. 1991. "Do Economists Test Theories?—Demand Analysis as Tests of Theories in Economic Methodology." In *Appraising Economic Theories,* ed. de Marchi and Blaug, pp. 137–68.

Gordon, Donald. 1965. "The Role of History of Economic Thought in the Understanding of Modern Economic Theory." *American Economic Review* 55 (May): 119–27.

Gordon, Michael. 1979. "Peer Review in Physics." *Physics Bulletin* 30 (March): 112–13.

Gowdy, John M. 1978. "Evolutionary Theory and Economic Theory: Some Methodological Issues." *Review of Social Economy* 2: 316–23.

Gruchy, Allen G. 1972. *Contemporary Economic Thought.* Clifton, NJ: Augustus M. Kelly.

———. 1987. *The Reconstruction of Economics.* Westport, CT: Greenwood Press.

Hammermesh, Daniel S. 1994. "Facts and Myths about Refereeing." *Journal of Economic Perspectives* 8, no. 1 (winter): 153–63.

Harre, Rom. 1972. *The Philosophy of Science.* London: Oxford University Press.

Hayek, Friedrich von A. 1978. *New Studies in Philosophy, Politics, Economics and the History of Ideas.* Chicago: University of Chicago Press.

Hempel, Carl, and Paul Oppenheim. [1948] 1953. "Studies in the Logic of Explanation." In *Readings in the Philosohy of Science,* ed. Herbert Feigl and May Brodbeck, pp. 319–52. New York: Meredith Corporation.

Hicks, Sir John. 1976. " 'Revolutions' in Economics." In *Method and Appraisal in Economics,* ed. Spiro Latsis, pp. 207–18.

Hoover, Kevin D. 1991. "Scientific Research Program or Tribe? A Joint Appraisal of Lakatos and the New Classical Macroeconomics." In *Appraising Economic Theories,* ed. de Marchi and Blaug, pp. 364–94.

Hutchison, Terence W. 1953. *A Review of Economic Doctrines, 1870–1929.* Oxford: Clarendon Press.

———. 1976."On the History and Philosophy of Science and Economics." In *Method and Appraisal in Economics,* ed. Spiro Latsis, pp. 181–206.

———. 1978. *On Revolutions and Progress in Economic Knowledge.* Cambridge: Cambridge University Press.

Jevons, William Stanley. 1886. *Letters and Journal.* Ed. Harriet A. Jevons. London: Macmillan.

———. [1879] 1970. *The Theory of Political Economy.* Harmondsworth, U.K.: Penguin Books.

Johnson, Harry G. 1975. *On Economics and Society.* Chicago: University of Chicago Press.

Katouzian, Homa. 1980. *Ideology and Method in Economics.* New York: New York University Press.

Kearl, J.R., Clayne L. Pope, Gordon C. Whiting, and Larry T. Wimmer. 1979. "What Economists Think. A Confusion of Economists?" *American Economic Review* (Papers and Proceedings) 69 (May): 28–37.

Keynes, John Maynard. 1936. *The General Theory of Employment, Interest and Money.* London: Macmillan.

Kim, Jinbang. 1991. "Testing in Modern Economics: the Case of Job Search Theory." In *Appraising Economic Theories,* ed. de Marchi and Blaug, pp. 105–31.

Klamer, Arjo. 1984. *Conversations with Economists: New Classical Economists and Opponents Speak Out on the Current Controversy in Macroeconomics.* Totowa, NJ: Rowman & Allanheld.

Klamer, Arjo, and David Colander. 1990. *The Making of an Economist.* Boulder, CO: Westview Press.

Klein, Burton H. 1977. *Dynamic Economics.* Cambridge: Harvard University Press.

Knight, Frank H. 1956. *On the History and Method of Economics: Selected Essays.* Chicago: University of Chicago Press.

Koertge, Noretta. 1976. "Rational Reconstructions." In *Essays in Memory of Imre Lakatos,* ed. Cohen, Feyerabend, and Wartofsky, pp. 359–70.

Krupp, Steven R., ed. 1966. *The Structure of Economic Science, Essays in Methodology.* Englewood Cliffs: Prentice Hall.

Kuhn, Thomas S. 1970a. *The Structure of Scientific Revolutions,* 2d ed. Chicago: University of Chicago Press.

———. 1970b. "Reflections on My Critics." In *Criticism and the Growth of Knowledge,* ed. Lakatos and Musgrave, pp. 231–78.

Laband, David N. 1986. "Article Popularity." *Economic Inquiry* 24: 173–80.

Lakatos, Imre. 1963. "Proofs and Refutations." *British Journal for the Philosophy of Science* 14: 1–117.

———. 1978. *The Methodology of Scientific Research Programmes.* Cambridge: Cambridge University Press.

Lakatos, Imre, and Alan Musgrave, eds. 1970. *Criticism and the Growth of Knowledge.* Cambridge: Cambridge University Press.

Latsis, Spiro. 1972. "Situational Determinism in Economics." *The British Journal for the Philosophy of Science* 2: 207–45.

———. 1976. "A Research Programme in Economics." In *Method and Appraisal in Economics,* ed. Spiro Latsis, pp. 1–42.

Latsis, Spiro, ed. 1976. *Method and Appraisal in Economics.* Cambridge: Cambridge University Press.

Leamer, Edward. 1983. "Let's Take the Con Out of Econometrics." *American Economic Review* 73: 31–43.

Leijonhufvud, Axel. 1976. "Schools, 'Revolutions' and Research Programmes in Economic Theory." In *Method and Appraisal in Economics,* ed. Latsis, pp. 65–108.

Lipsey, Richard, P. Langley, and D. Mahoney. 1986. *Positive Economics for Australian Students,* 2d ed. London: Weidenfeld and Nicolson.

Maddock, Rodney. 1991. "The Development of New Classical Macroeconomics: Lessons for Lakatos." In *Appraising Economic Theories,* ed. de Marchi and Blaug, pp. 335–59.

Mahoney, Michael J. 1977. "Publication Prejudices: An Experimental Study of Confirmatory Bias in the Peer Review System." *Cognitive Therapy and Research* 1 (June): 161–75.

Marshall, Alfred. 1961. *Principles of Economics,* 9th ed. New York: Macmillan (1st ed. 1890).

———. 1925. "Mechanical and Biological Analogies in Economics." In *Memorials of Alfred Marshall,* ed. Arthur Cecil Pigou, pp. 312–18. London: Macmillan.

Masterman, Margaret. 1970. "The Nature of a Paradigm." In *Criticism and the Growth of Knowledge,* ed. Lakatos and Musgrave, pp. 59–89.

Mayr, Ernst. 1982. *The Growth of Biological Thought: Diversity, Evolution, and Inheritance.* Cambridge, MA: Belknap Press.

McCloskey, D. 1983. "The Rhetoric of Economics." *Journal of Economic Literature* (June): 481–517.

————. 1985. *The Rhetoric of Economics.* Madison: University of Wisconsin Press.

Mill, John Stuart. 1884. *A System of Logic.* London: Longmans, Green.

Miller, A. Carolyn, and Victoria J. Punsalan. 1988. *Refereed and Nonrefereed Economic Journals: A Guide to Publishing Opportunities.* New York: Greenwood Press.

Mirowski, Phillip. 1987. "The Philosophical Basis of Institutional Economics." *Journal of Economic Issues* 3: 1001–38.

————. 1989. *More Heat than Light: Economics as Social Physics, Physics as Nature's Economics.* Cambridge: Cambridge University Press.

————. 1991. "Comment on Weintraub." In *Appraising Economic Theories,* ed. de Marchi and Blaug, pp. 291–93.

Mokrzycki, Edmund. 1983. *Philosophy of Science and Sociology: From Methodological Doctrine to Research Practice.* London: Routledge and Kegan Paul.

Myrdal, Gunnar. 1954. *The Political Element in the Development of Economic Theory.* New York: Simon and Schuster.

O'Sullivan, Patrick J. 1987. *Economic Methodology and Freedom to Choose.* London: Allen and Unwin.

Pareto, Vilfredo. [1896–97] 1964. *Cours d'économie politique.* 2 vols. Lausanne, Switzerland: Rouge. Reprinted as vol. 1 of *Oeuvres complètes,* ed. Giovanni Busino. Geneva: Librarie Droz.

Patinkin, D. 1972. "Keynesian Monetary Theory and the Cambridge School." *Banca Nazionale del Lavoro Quarterly Review* (June): 142–59.

Pigou, Arthur Cecil, ed. 1925. *Memorials of Alfred Marshall.* London: Macmillan.

Polanyi, Michael. 1946. *Science, Faith and Society.* Oxford: Oxford University Press.

Popper, Karl. 1959. *The Logic of Scientific Discovery.* New York: Harper Torch-books.

————. 1968. *Conjectures and Refutations: The Growth of Scientific Knowledge.* New York: Harper and Row.

————. 1970. "Normal Science and its Dangers." In *Criticism and the Growth of Knowledge,* ed. Lakatos and Musgrave, pp. 51–58.

Prelli, Lawrence J. 1989. *A Rhetoric of Science: Inventing Scientific Discourse.* Columbia, SC: University of South Carolina Press.

Reisman, David. 1953. *Thorstein Veblen: A Critical Interpretation.* New York: Doubleday.

Robbins, Lionel. 1946. *An Essay on the Nature and Significance of Economic Science.* London: Macmillan.

Robinson, James Harvey. 1923. *The Humanization of Knowledge.* New York: G. H. Doran.

Rosenberg, Alexander. 1986. "Lakatosian Consolations for Economists." *Economics and Philosophy* 2: 127–39.

Routh, Guy. 1989. *The Origin of Economic Ideas.* Dobbs Ferry, NY: Sheridan House.

Samuels, Warren, and Jeff Biddle, eds. 1994. *Research in the History of Economic Thought and Methodology,* vol. 12. Greenwich, CT, and London: JAI Press.

Samuelson, Paul. 1947. *Foundations of Economic Analysis.* Cambridge: Harvard University Press.

————. 1980. *Economics,* 11th ed. New York: McGraw-Hill.

Samuelson, Paul, and Robert Solow. 1960. "Problem of Achieving and Maintaining a Stable Price Level: Analytical Aspects of Anti-Inflation Policy." *American Economic Review* (May): 177–201.

Sargent, Thomas J. 1976. "The Observational Equivalence of Natural and Unnatural Rate Theories of Macroeconomics." *Journal of Political Economy* 84: 631–40.

Sargent, Thomas J., and N. Wallace. 1975. "Rational Expectations, the Optimal Monetary Instrument, and the Optimal Money Rule." *Journal of Political Economy* 83 (June): 241–54.

Schumpeter, Joseph A. 1981. *The History of Economic Analysis.* Reprint. New York: Oxford University Press.

Scriven, Michael. 1959. "Explanation and Prediction in Evolutionary Theory." *Science* 130, 3374 (August): 477–82.

Smith, Adam. [1904] 1976. *The Wealth of Nations.* Ed. Edwin Cannan. London: Methuen and Company; Chicago: University of Chicago Press.

Solow, Robert M. 1990. "Discussion." *American Economic Review* (Papers and Proceedings) 80: 448–50.

Spengler, Joseph J. 1968. "Exogenous and Endogenous Influences in the Formation of Post-1870 Economic Thought: A Sociology of Knowledge." In *Events, Ideology and Economic Theory,* ed. Robert V. Eagly, pp. 159–187. Detroit: Wayne State University Press.

Spiegel, Henry William. 1983. *The Growth of Economic Thought,* 2d ed. Durham, NC: Duke University Press.

Stanfield, J. Ronald. 1974. "Kuhnian Scientific Revolutions and the Keynesian Revolution." *Journal of Economic Issues* 8 (March): 97–109.

Steedman, Ian. 1991. "Negative and Positive Contributions: Appraising Sraffa and Lakatos." In *Appraising Economic Theories,* ed. de Marchi and Blaug, pp. 435–50.

Stigler, George J. 1973. "The Adoption of Marginal Utility Analysis." In *The Marginal Revolution,* ed. Black, Coats, and Goodwin, pp. 305–20.

Tarascio, Vincent. 1971. "Value Judgements and Economic Science." *Journal of Economic Issues* 5 (March): 98–102.

———. 1977. "Intellectual History and the Social Sciences: The Problem of Methodological Pluralism." *Social Science Quarterly:* 37–54.

———. 1986. "The Crisis in Economic Theory: A Sociological Perspective," *Research in the History of Economic Thought and Methodology,* vol. 4, pp. 283–95.

Tarascio, Vincent, and Bruce Caldwell. 1979. "Theory Choice in Economics: Philosophy and Practice." *Journal of Economic Issues* 4: 983–1006.

Toulmin, Stephen E. 1970. "Does the Distinction Between Normal and Revolutionary Science Hold Water?" In *Criticism and the Growth of Knowledge,* ed. Lakatos and Musgrave, pp. 25–38.

———. 1972. *Human Understanding.* Oxford: Clarendon Press.

———. 1976. "History, Praxis and the 'Third World.' Ambiguities in Lakatos' Theory of Methodology." In *Essays in Memory of Imre Lakatos,* ed. Cohen, Feyerabend, and Wartofsky, pp. 655–76.

Varian, Hal R. 1991. "Review of *More Heat then Light: Economics as Social Physics, Physics as Nature's Economics,* by Philip Mirowski." *Journal of Economic Literature* 29: 595–96.

Veblen, Thorstein. 1948. *The Portable Veblen.* Ed. Max Lerner. New York: Viking Press.

Vercelli, Alessandro. 1991. "Comment on Maddock." In *Appraising Economic Theories,* ed. de Marchi and Blaug, pp. 360–63.

Von Mises, L. 1978. *The Ultimate Foundation of Economic Science,* 2d ed. Kansas City: Sheed, Andrews, and McMeel.

Ward, Benjamin. 1972. *What's Wrong with Economics.* New York: Basic Books.

Wartofsky, M.W. 1976. "The Relation Between Philosophy of Science and History of Science." In *Essays in Memory of Imre Lakatos,* ed. Cohen, Feyerabend, and Wartofsky, pp. 717–38.

Weintraub, E. Roy. 1985. *General Equilibrium Analysis: Studies in Appraisal.* Cambridge: Cambridge University Press.

————. 1991. "Stabilizing Dynamics." In *Appraising Economic Theories,* ed. de Marchi and Blaug, pp. 273–90.

Whewell, William. 1837. *History of Inductive Sciences fron the Earliest to the Present Times.* London: J.W. Parker.

————. [1858] 1967. *The Philosophy of Inductive Science.* New York: D. Appleton and Company; New York: Johnson Reprint Corporation.

Whitley, Richard. 1991. "The Organisation and Role of Journals in Economics and Other Scientific Fields." *Economic Notes* 20 (1):6–32.

Williams, Rhonda M. 1984. "The Methodological Practice of Modern Labor Economics: A Critique." In *Labor Economics—Addresses, Essays, Lectures,* ed. William A. Darity Jr., 23–52. Hingham, MA: Kluwer-Nijhoff.

Worrall, John. 1976. "Imre Lakatos (1922–1974): Philosopher of Mathematics and Philosopher of Science." In *Essays in Memory of Imre Lakatos,* ed. Cohen, Feyerabend, and Wartofsky, pp. 1–8.

Wulwick, Nancy J. 1987. "The Phillips Curve: Which? Whose? To Do What?" *Southern Economic Journal* 53 (April): 834–57.

Yotopoulos, Dan A. 1961. "Institutional Affiliation of the Contributors to Three Professional Journals." *American Economic Review* 51: 665–70.

Zuckerman, Harriet, and Robert K. Merton. 1971. "Patterns of Evaluation in Science: Institutionalisation, Structure and Functions of the Referee System." *Minerva* 9 (January): 66–100.

# INDEX

Academic communities. *See* Scientific communities
Academic publications. *See* Publication process
Academics, economics in, 7–8, 104
Acceptance of papers. *See* Publication process, acceptance/rejection rates
*American Anthropologist,* article rejection rates for, 94
American Economic Association convention (1959), 148
*American Economics Review (AER)*
  acceptance rates of women authors, 113
  and article rejection, 95
*American Journal of Physical Anthropology,* article rejection rates for, 94
Anti-positivism, 42, 48, 50
  *See also* Positivism
Applied research, 150–51
Appraisal
  of actual theory vs. theory choice, 84–85
  of economics discipline, 58, 60, 62–65
  favorable, 76
  post-facto, 67
  publication. *See* Publication process
  types of, 61–62, 121, 170–71

Appraisal *(continued)*
  *See also under individual theory or type*
*Appraising Economic Theories: Studies in the Methodology of Research Programs* (de Marchi and Blaug), 70, 71, 72, 78, 168–69
Aristotle, 13–14
Arrow, Kenneth, 81
Articles. *See* Publication process
Audience
  of economic journals, 91, 102
  tailoring to, 123
Authors
  gender and article acceptance rates, 113, 114
  identity in referee process, 98–99, 114, 124, 127*n.29*
  reputation, 113, 136
Ayer, Alfred, 17, 47–48

Backhouse, Roger, 80–81
Bacon, Francis, 13, 14
Barnes, Barry, 56
Bayesian-type decision matrix, 85
Becker, Gary, 131, 172
Bedford College Conference (1965), 32
Beed, Clive, 41–42, 48, 49–50
Bentham, Jeremy, 7
Beveridge, William, 139
Bias
  author identity and referee, 98–99, 114, 124, 127*n.29*

189

**Christopher D. Mackie** received his Ph.D. in economics from the University of North Carolina, where he studied history of economic thought and methodology under Dr. Vincent Tarascio. He has taught economic theory and economic history at North Carolina State University and at Tulane University. Currently, Dr. Mackie is a senior economist specializing in labor and personnel economics at SAG Corporation near Washington, D.C. The author is also a top amateur soccer player in the Washington area.